Politics

3rd Edition

by Ann DeLaney

for
dummies®
A Wiley Brand

Politics For Dummies®, 3rd Edition

Published by: **John Wiley & Sons, Inc.**, 111 River Street, Hoboken, NJ 07030-5774, www.wiley.com

Copyright © 2020 by John Wiley & Sons, Inc., Hoboken, New Jersey

Published simultaneously in Canada

For general information on our other products and services, please contact our Customer Care Department within the U.S. at 877-762-2974, outside the U.S. at 317-572-3993, or fax 317-572-4002. For technical support, please visit https://hub.wiley.com/community/support/dummies.

Wiley publishes in a variety of print and electronic formats and by print-on-demand. Some material included with standard print versions of this book may not be included in e-books or in print-on-demand. If this book refers to media such as a CD or DVD that is not included in the version you purchased, you may download this material at http://booksupport.wiley.com. For more information about Wiley products, visit www.wiley.com.

Library of Congress Control Number: 2019954498

ISBN: 978-1-119-65295-3; 978-1-119-65299-1 (ebk); 978-1-119-65300-4 (ebk)

Manufactured in the United States of America

SKY10023980_011221

Contents at a Glance

Table of Contents

Introduction

Welcome to *Politics For Dummies,* 3rd Edition.

Like many older women who grew up in a traditional two-parent family with a mother who never worked outside the home, I was taught that a lady was mentioned in the newspaper when she was born, when she married, and when she died — and certainly at no other time. Politics wasn't a topic that was discussed in our home at the dinner table. I think my parents voted, but I couldn't tell you how, and I know they never went to a fundraiser for a candidate or volunteered for a campaign.

When I became active in politics and began appearing in the press and on television with some regularity, my mother wondered where she and my father had gone wrong. What I had discovered, to my parents' dismay, was that politics wasn't all that complicated and actually could be fun. It could also be tough, even dirty and nasty at times, but winning and being part of something bigger than yourself bring a tremendous sense of satisfaction and control, even if your only involvement is to vote for the candidate of your choice. You're exercising your rights, and the candidates have to consider your views. You are in control!

What Is Politics?

What exactly is politics? That depends on who's doing the defining. Some people use the word *politics* as an expletive. Suppose you've just seen a particularly vicious negative political advertisement on TV, where one candidate challenged the honesty, patriotism, or parentage of the opposing candidate. You would not be alone if you dismissed the ad by saying, "That's just politics."

Many of us use the phrase "That's just politics" to express our displeasure with everything we see wrong with the US political system. We get disgusted with special legislation that gives certain types of people tax benefits. We dislike seeing officials get favorable treatment from regulatory agencies for constituents or contributors.

Many of us are offended by Congress's generosity to itself (pensions, free lunches, and golf trips from lobbyists). We disapprove of members of Congress saying one thing and voting for another (such as supporting term limits but not retroactively). And we tend to condemn these activities with our disgust: "That's just politics!"

It may be "just politics," but after you learn the ropes, you can have an impact on politics. You can find out how candidates stand on issues of importance to you. You can make elected officials listen to your concerns and those of your neighbors. You can make a difference!

Politics is more than just what is wrong with our system. Politics *is* our system. It orders our lives. It determines who wins and who loses when governments make decisions. It determines whether the future will be brighter or bleaker for our children.

Here's just a sample of the many things that politics determines:

>> Who serves in office and for how long

>> The policies our governments enact

>> Who wins and who loses when groups compete for resources or favorable legislation

>> Who pays taxes, how much, and what kind

>> Whether a landfill opens near your neighborhood despite your concerns about having potentially toxic waste close to where your children play

>> What your children are taught in school, what tests they take, and what scores they must achieve to graduate

>> How much you pay to send your children to a state-supported college and whether student loans are available to help you pay the cost

>> When your garbage is collected and what items are accepted

From the sublime to the ridiculous, politics is everywhere!

Regardless of how you define it, politics is the glue keeping our entire society together and determining the relationships of all the members of that society. You can't avoid politics. You can refuse to participate in the process by not registering or voting, but the process will still affect you and your family every day of your lives, in ways you know and in ways you can't imagine.

You can't avoid it, no matter how far you try to bury your head in the sand. So, you may as well find out enough about politics to understand what's really happening. As soon as you understand politics, you can act to improve your position in those decisions that have an impact on you, your family, and your neighborhood. Who knows, with *Politics For Dummies,* 3rd Edition, at your side, you may decide to run for president of the United States or at least for school board or county or city council. Anyway, you can make politics work for you.

Why You Need This Book

Americans have been taught to think that politics is something that decent people don't know anything about and certainly don't participate in. The combination of late-night talk shows and jokes at the expense of politicians has convinced most people that politics is dirty, sleazy, and incomprehensible to normal people.

Most people will never run for office. They'll never work in a political campaign or directly give money to a political party or to a candidate. A substantial number of people in the United States, more than one-half of eligible voters, will either never register to vote or won't vote regularly. Most adults know little or nothing about politics, but they're not to blame. The process by which people serve in elected office, and what they do when they get there, remains a mystery to most. What-ever meager attempts are made to teach civics in schools are limited to how a bill becomes a law and the like. Schools make little if any effort to prepare students to understand politics.

This book can help you understand what's going on, how people are trying to influence or manipulate you, and what you can do about it. Whether you like it or not, politics affects your life, for better or worse, in many different ways. Wouldn't you like to have a voice in these decisions that have a direct effect on your life? You have opinions on these issues. Those opinions should be considered before such decisions are made. Because you can't avoid politics, you may as well understand it and make it work for you.

The key to understanding politics is to realize that it isn't all that complicated. Selling a candidate isn't really much different from selling a product, any product — even deodorant! The words the media uses on the nightly news and never bothers to define — such as *caucuses, primaries, pollsters,* and *political action committees* — are just jargon.

This book tells you what really happens, starting from when you register to vote. It helps you sift through the many conflicting messages you see and hear in the media and from the campaigns. Then you can vote for the candidate who is right for you — the one you can trust with important decisions that affect your life.

I hope that this book will peel away the layers of misperception and distrust so that, after you understand politics, you can also understand how politics can work for you. Who knows? As soon as you understand what's going on, you may decide that politics can be fun, even as a spectator sport!

How to Use This Book

This book is meant to be a reference that you can take off the shelf whenever you have questions about what's happening politically. You can read it through from cover to cover, if you like, and if your social life is at an unusual lull. *Politics For Dummies,* 3rd Edition, is designed to answer your questions by easy reference to the table of contents, the index, the icons, and the sidebars. As your questions arise, you can find exactly what you want to know without having to read the entire book.

This book answers the questions most frequently asked by intelligent people who have avoided the perils of politics to date. If you have little or no knowledge of politics, don't be embarrassed. You're like most people, and this book can help you understand and make politics work for you. If you have some knowledge and want to increase it, this book is the vehicle to do so.

How This Book Is Organized

Each chapter attempts to answer a frequently asked question about politics. The chapters are organized into parts, each of which covers an area of politics. Here's a summary of what you will find in each part.

Part 1: Politics and You

This part is all you need for intelligent cocktail party conversation to demonstrate that you're in the know and taking the first step in any kind of political activity.

Part 2: Making Your Voice Heard

In Part 2, I tell you how to communicate with the big shots as well as how to start changing the world as we know it by becoming a political player. Here, you can find out how to start getting yourself involved in politics. The last chapter opens up the world of politics on the Internet. Politics is one of the top three topics on the Internet, so whatever your political beliefs, there's a website out there for you.

Part 3: Politics Is a Team Sport

Part 3 discusses why the United States has only two major parties and all sorts of minor parties and independent candidates. It tells you some of the differences between Democrats and Republicans, how to become a member of a political party, and what happens when you do. Are you part of a special interest? This chapter tells you what special interest groups are, how to join one, and how to make them work for you.

Part 4: It's All Marketing

In Part 4, you find out how a campaign introduces and sells the candidates, and you see how to separate the truth from the advertising run by the campaigns. All this should help you choose which candidate you want to vote for.

Part 5: Let the Campaigns Begin!

This part talks about campaigns at the local, state, and national levels. Find out where the money goes and where the special interests are. The parties also want to know what you think about everything under the sun, so I include a chapter telling you about all those polls that the parties — and the media — like so much. Then I talk about the issues that candidates and parties don't want to discuss in public because you might not like what they have to say. This part also explores the dark side of politics — the whys and wherefores behind negative campaigning and the reforms needed for politics to clean up its act.

Part 6: Presidential Politics

Part 6 covers the presidential campaigns: from the Iowa caucuses to the national party conventions to the electoral college. Turn here to find out what actually goes into electing a president.

Part 7: The Part of Tens

Part 7 is the famous *For Dummies* part that's all lists. Here, I've included the ten things you need to teach your kids or yourself about politics, the ten commandments of politics, and, of course, the ten most common political mistakes, just so that you can see whether the latest candidate might have figured out a new way to screw up.

Icons Used in This Book

The little round pictures in the margins of this book point out information, warnings of thin ice, things you should remember, and ways you can become active in politics. Here's a list of the icons and a brief description of what each one does:

POLITICAL STUFF

This icon highlights the interesting, technical parts in the book that are good to know but that you can skip over. These are case studies, historical anecdotes, and all kinds of political trivia for the would-be political buff.

SPEAKING UP

This icon flags ways you can find your own voice in politics and make politicians listen to what you have to say.

POLITICAL MYTH

This icon sheds light on stories about politics that are part of the common wisdom but may not be true. Look here to find out what the reality is.

TIP

This icon marks political words of wisdom that can help you navigate the system.

WARNING

This icon alerts you to things to avoid and common mistakes people make.

REMEMBER

This icon is a friendly reminder of information discussed elsewhere in the book or stuff you definitely want to keep in mind.

Where to Go from Here

You can either read this book straight through or skip from chapter to chapter. If you need to brush up on some of the political basics, turn the page. If becoming an active player in politics is what you're looking for, go straight to Part 2. Use this book to find out about politics and to become a player in your community, state, or the country itself.

REMEMBER

In addition to the pages you're reading right now, this book comes with a free access-anywhere Cheat Sheet that offers a number of politics-related pearls of wisdom. To get this Cheat Sheet, visit www.dummies.com and type **politics for dummies cheat sheet** in the Search box.

1

Politics and You

Chapter **1**

It's Politics, Baby!

Politics is that unique situation in which you choose people to run parts of your life — by choosing the people who run your government. The US government has all kinds of elected politicians, from the nation's president down to the animal-control officer in your locale. In most cases, you can choose any candidate you think will do the best job.

Elected Politicians — a Quick Look

Elected officials come in three levels: federal, state, and local. You have a role in determining who gets elected to all three. You can think of these officials as tiers of a wedding cake: As you move down the cake, each layer grows larger and larger, and holds more and more politicians. Check out Figure 1-1. The president and the vice president stand atop the cake of politicians, but it's up to you to decide whether their "marriage" with the voters continues or they get dumped at the next election.

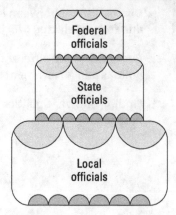

FIGURE 1-1:
The levels of the
US political
system are like
the tiers of a
wedding cake.

Federal officials

The federal government consists of three branches: judicial, legislative, and executive. Here's how they break down:

>> The *judicial branch* consists of all federal courts, from trial courts all the way to the US Supreme Court. Federal judges are nominated by the president and confirmed by the Senate. You don't have a direct vote in the selection of federal judges, but you do have a sort of indirect vote because you elect the president who makes the selection, and you elect senators who confirm it. Also, both the president and the senators consider public opinion when making their choices.

The judicial branch interprets federal laws when lawsuits are filed in federal courts. It also decides whether state and national laws conform to the federal Constitution. Decisions of the trial courts can be appealed to the Circuit Courts of Appeals and, ultimately, to the Supreme Court.

>> You elect the members of the *legislative branch,* called Congress. Congress drafts bills, which, if passed and signed by the president, become laws. Congress is able to enact laws on power given to the federal government by the Constitution and the amendments to the Constitution. All other powers are reserved to the states.

>> You also elect the heads of the *executive branch:* the president and the vice president. The executive branch plays a role in making laws by the use of the president's *veto* of legislation. The president may block legislation by vetoing it, or at least force Congress to change proposed legislation by threatening to veto it.

The executive branch also carries out the laws that Congress enacts and the courts clarify. The president then chooses the other top members of the executive branch of government: the Cabinet. Cabinet secretaries run the various departments of the executive branch, such as Treasury, Justice, State, Labor, and Homeland Security. Cabinet secretaries are appointed by the president and confirmed by the Senate. The top few levels of each department are occupied by political appointees and must also be confirmed by the Senate. All the rest of the tens of thousands of federal employees in these departments are civil service employees. The civil service employees can keep their jobs no matter who the president is, but those political appointees can keep their jobs only as long as the president who appointed them is still in office or until the president who appointed them wants them to leave. They serve at the pleasure of the president.

How we elect federal officials — the president, the vice president, senators, and representatives — is shaped by the US Constitution, which has been changed several times to encourage more participation by voters. For example, until the 17th Amendment to the US Constitution in 1913, voters didn't directly elect their US senators — voters elected their state legislatures, and the state legislatures elected the US senators. The 19th Amendment to the Constitution, adopted in 1920, gave women over the age of 21 the right to vote. The 26th Amendment, adopted in 1971, gave citizens 18 and older the right to vote.

The president and the vice president

The United States elects a president and a vice president every four years. They're elected together to prevent having the president from one party and the vice president from another — a rather awkward arrangement that actually did happen early in our country's history, when it was standard practice for the candidate who received the most votes to become president, with the candidate who came in second, from the other party, becoming vice president. It didn't damage the republic, but it created enough fuss to suggest that it was not a good idea.

The president signs or vetoes legislation which passes both houses of congress. If the president vetoes legislation, a two thirds vote in the House and the Senate is required to override the veto and enable the legislation to become law.

You don't elect the president and vice president directly, but your votes do determine who holds both offices. See Chapter 23 for more information about this process.

Representatives

Each state elects members of Congress, called *representatives*, who serve in the House. The number of House seats is limited to 435, so the average member now represents almost three-quarters of a million people. The census, taken every ten years, determines how many of those 435 representatives each state receives.

States with growing populations gain congressional seats after the census. States that have fallen behind in population usually lose seats, although the Constitution guarantees them at least one.

After the census results are tallied, each state draws its own congressional districts (although federal courts sometimes force changes afterward). Usually, state legislatures take responsibility for this task, but sometimes states set up other means for determining their election maps, such as independent commissions. The exact boundaries of congressional districts can be the subject of much political fighting, turf warfare, and teeth gnashing, as powerful politicians try to sweet-talk the mapmakers into drawing districts that will promote their own personal and political ambitions.

Members of Congress are elected every two years, in even-numbered, *general election years* (2018, 2020, 2022, and so forth).

Senators

Each state, regardless of its population, also elects two senators to serve 6-year terms. Every two years, one-third of the US Senate is elected, so your state may or may not have a Senate contest in a given *general election, or even-numbered, year.* Because they are responsible to entire states, senators usually represent a much larger number of people than members of the House do, but the number of people each Senator represents can vary widely. For example, the senators from Alaska represent about three-quarters of a million people, whereas the senators from California represent almost 40 million people.

Some state and local elections can occur in odd numbered years!

State officials

Just like the federal government, each state government is divided into three branches: judicial, legislative, and executive. The functions of these three branches are largely the same as they are within the three branches of the federal government:

>> **Judicial:** Judges in state courts interpret state laws. Some states elect their trial court and appellate court judges; some don't. Some states permit citizens to vote to retain or remove judges but don't permit partisan elections for judicial positions. Whether you can play a role in the selection of judges depends on your state law.

>> **Legislative:** State legislatures enact laws that apply to their state. In each state, voters are grouped into legislative districts for the state legislature or general assembly. Most state legislatures include two chambers: an upper

house (usually called the *Senate*) and a lower house (usually called the *House of Representatives*). Terms of service vary from two to four years.

The ever-efficient and tidy state of Nebraska has only one house in its legislature, consisting of 49 members with no party affiliations. The 49 are called senators and are elected for 4-year terms. (For more information about parties and affiliations, see Chapters 6 and 7.)

>> **Executive:** The role of the executive branch of a state is to administer the laws. Just like the president, governors also have the power to veto a bill or piece of legislation. However, not all governors' vetoes must have a two-thirds vote of the state legislatures to override. Some governors can have their vetoes overridden by a simple majority of votes in the legislature. Because it took a majority of votes to pass the bill in the first place, it's not that difficult to pass the legislation again. Governors in states with majority override of vetoes don't have as strong a weapon in dealing with their state legislatures as the president does in dealing with Congress.

The voters of each state elect their state governor. Both the date that the election takes place and the length of the governor's term depend on state law. Most states have 4-year terms for their governors and elect them in general-election years. Vermont and New Hampshire have 2-year terms. A few states, like New Jersey, elect their governors in odd-numbered years. Virginia has no term limit on its governorship, but a governor may not serve consecutive terms.

Most states elect a governor and a lieutenant governor on the same ticket, and many states limit the number of terms a governor can serve to two or even one.

Local officials

Counties, cities, and towns also have elections to choose officials for their legislative and executive branches. Some judicial offices may be elected at the local level, but these courts handle small-claims issues or local ordinances for minor matters. State law largely governs criminal and civil matters.

Mayors, city council members, county commissioners, and the like are elected at the local level. How, when, and for how long these officials are chosen depends on state law. Some states elect local officials in odd-numbered years; others, in even-numbered years. Some officials have term limits; some don't. Some elections are partisan, and some aren't. Your state or county election board or clerk's office can tell you how these elections work in your community. Many local governments also maintain web pages that contain election information.

Politics versus Government

Politics and government don't differ much, but the rhetoric changes somewhat. A government official may discuss issues in policy-motivated terms. Republican officials, for example, may talk about getting government off the backs of small-business people and about adopting tax policies to encourage initiative. Those Republican officials won't say that Democratic opponents are Robin Hoods robbing the rich to give to the poor, even if that's what they think. On the other hand, Democratic officials may question the fairness of tax breaks for corporations and bemoan the plight of the working man or woman. The Democratic officials probably won't say that the Republican tax proposals are corporate welfare, even if that's what *they're* thinking. The terms, particularly the labels, differ from those used in explicitly political appeals, but the sides are basically the same.

Politics has spin doctors

In the heat of a political campaign, the campaign manager, the press person, or the Democratic or Republican Party official is the public spokesperson. This person advances and defends ideas proposed by one side of the campaign, and the corresponding person on the opposite side responds. The forum shifts from politics to government as soon as the election is over. Now the person trying to launch the elected official's ideas into the media in the correct way is the press secretary for the elected official. That press secretary is a government employee and must not be seen as political while voters are paying their salary.

The campaign or party spokesperson is responsible for controlling the *spin* of a story — in other words, trying to get the media to portray a story in a way that's favorable to the party official's campaign. The spin, or the way the media approaches a story, determines whether a story helps or hurts a campaign. The person charged with dealing with reporters and getting the message of the campaign into print or on television is referred to as the campaign's "spin doctor." Sometimes, the need to work with the media in understanding the candidate is obvious, as reflected in the following political joke:

> *General Washington was crossing the Delaware during the Revolutionary War when his hat blew off and into the water. The general got out of the boat, walked across the water, retrieved the hat, and walked to the other side. The headline in the next day's newspaper read, "General Washington Can't Swim!"*

Obviously, this joke is extreme, but it does illustrate a point: Media portrayal can turn a perfectly positive story into a negative one and vice versa. Spin doctors play a vital role in campaigns because they make sure that the desired image and message of the candidate are portrayed. Every good campaign has at least one, and the campaign attempts to make the spin doctor the only contact person for the media.

The government has spokespeople

In government, as opposed to politics, the person who does the talking (the *spokesperson*) is the elected official himself or the press secretary. The official and the press secretary take turns working the media to attract coverage and to make that coverage as favorable to the official as possible, but they try to avoid partisan rhetoric.

Sometimes in public policy debates over legislation, private groups outside of government weigh in to persuade the public to support or oppose the legislation. These private groups are ideologically close to one of the major parties but are separate entities. In recent years, the tactic of using nonpartisan groups rather than political parties to debate a proposal has become quite common because the statements made by these outside groups tend to have more credibility with the media and the public than do either party's official statements. (Whether they deserve such credibility is another story.)

The use of such outside groups has accelerated in the wake of the US Supreme Court decision in the case *Citizens United vs. FEC*. As a result of that decision, these outside groups aren't limited in the amounts they can raise or spend and they do not always have to report who is contributing to their campaigns. They can use high-sounding names to sponsor advertisements supporting or attacking proposals or candidates without disclosing which people or what special interest is behind them. The same political calculation — where are the votes, and where is the money — is done for almost every governmental decision. In that way, politics and government are the same. (See Chapter 2 for more on the money-versus-vote analysis.)

Politicians can wrap packages with pretty ribbons and call decisions by favored names, but the decisions made in the name of government remain political decisions. That's because the heart of any decision about how the government chooses among competing interests vying for scarce resources is political. Every decision a government makes benefits some groups and takes away from others. For example, if a government decides to cut taxes on middle-income people, it will have to raise taxes on the rich or the poor to make up for the money it isn't receiving in income tax from middle-income people — or else it can explode the *deficit*, which is the amount of money the government has spent over and above what it has taken in. If governments spend more on roads, people with cars and trucks will benefit, but those who rely on railroads will see more of their tax money going to support a resource they don't use. There will never be enough money to do everything everyone wants to do, so choices have to be made. Those choices about how to allocate resources and about who benefits and who doesn't are decisions that are political in nature.

After all, democracy is about allowing the will of the majority to prevail while protecting the constitutional rights of the minority.

Voters look with disfavor on elected officials who don't vote the way the voters want. You shouldn't be surprised when disgruntled voters *vote out* those politicians who disagree with them by not reelecting them to office. It takes an exceptional officeholder or circumstance to risk thwarting the will of a majority of voters on an issue of importance.

Officeholders don't remain in office for longer than one term if they fail to keep those risks in mind. Some other candidate will come forward and accuse the officeholder of failing to listen to the voters. The campaign rhetoric will call for a new officeholder who will listen to what the voters want.

THE MAJORITY RULES, BUT THE CONSTITUTION CONTROLS

REMEMBER

The Constitution restricts some of the effects of majority rule. If a right is protected by the US Constitution, the majority cannot pass laws or adopt policies restricting that right. The courts would declare such actions unconstitutional. The law or policy would be invalid and unenforceable. For example, the vast majority of citizens in this country disagree with the principles of the Ku Klux Klan. They are deeply disturbed by the hatred that the group preaches.

Suppose that I'm a spokesperson for that vast majority. I question whether Klan members have any place in American society. I recognize that the Klan is a very small segment of our population, and I don't believe that it should be able to disrupt our cities. We citizens shouldn't be required to pay for police protection when the group marches and spreads its venom. We would prefer not to hear it or see it march again. A majority of American citizens would like to see Klan rallies banned. A majority of them would favor outlawing the group itself.

Despite how most of us feel, the will of the majority cannot determine the treatment accorded the Klan. The Constitution says that the Klan has rights, whether anyone else likes it or not. The First Amendment to the Constitution states that Congress "shall make no law abridging the freedom of speech . . . or the right of the people peaceably to assemble." The Klan is free to march and speak, regardless of how violently the rest of us react to its message. The Constitution protects the rights of minorities no matter how unpopular they are. In fact, the more unpopular they are, the more they need the protections afforded by the Constitution.

When our Constitution protects a right or an action, government can't interfere with that right or action. Even if most voters want their elected officials to interfere, our system won't let that happen.

What Do You Want from Your Elected Officials?

What do you want from your elected officials? The answer is pretty simple: You want your elected officials to be responsive to you. You may want them to lead, but first you want them to listen to what you have to say. On most issues, you know what you want and what is best for you. You want respect and attention to your point of view. Few issues are so complicated that you need the official's expertise and experience to decide for you what you want. On those few issues, you may be willing to allow elected officials to choose the best means for achieving your goals, but you still will judge them according to whether those goals are met.

When Representative Joe Schmoe does something that you, Jane Voter, oppose, he'd better have a very good reason for his action. And the reason had better not be that a well-heeled contributor asked him to do it! You have a right to ask Representative Joe what his reasons were for doing what he did. The explanation may convince you that what he did was the right thing, or it may only convince you that he did what *he* thought was the right thing. You don't have to agree with Joe's decisions 100 percent of the time to vote for his reelection. But you do need to tell him what you want and ask him to explain why you can't have it, if the answer is no.

Elected officials who don't listen to voters risk their political careers, even when the elected official follows a course of conduct that later proves to be the right one. The political risk involved with being out of touch with voters helps to explain why pollsters have become so important in modern politics. Elected officials spend a great deal of time and money finding out what you and other voters think about an issue. (Flip to Chapters 5 and 15 for more on voter feedback.)

REMEMBER

You *can* force an elected official to do what you think is right, even if they (or their campaign finance director) don't want it done. You simply have to organize enough people like you to send a clear message. Having the energy and organization on the right side of an issue are enough if you know what you're doing. You *can* make the political system work for you. You *can* have clout. Check out Chapter 5 for tips on how to organize to use your political clout.

DO POLITICIANS EVER BECOME STATESMEN?

What is a *statesman*, anyway? Harry Truman said, "A statesman is a politician that has been dead 10 or 15 years." A less-barbed definition might say that a statesman is someone who acts to do what is right regardless of the political risk involved. A statesman puts the public good ahead of partisan politics.

A statesman makes decisions based on what is right, not on what is popular. This person does what they think is right, even if it isn't what the voters want. Occasionally, an honorable politician will risk their career to take an unpopular position on an issue, but the instance is rare.

One excellent example of statesmanship — of putting principle ahead of political self-interest — occurred in 1964, when the Civil Rights Act was passed. Through seniority, Southern conservative Democrats controlled the powerful Rules Committee of the US House of Representatives and, thumbing their noses at the House Democratic leadership and President Johnson, prevented civil rights legislation from reaching the House floor for a vote.

To break the logjam, the House leadership moved to expand the membership of the Rules Committee so that civil rights supporters could be appointed to create a majority in favor of the legislation. When the resolution to expand the Rules Committee was put to a vote, everyone knew the vote would be close. A key vote in support was cast by a first-term Democrat from rural Louisiana, Gillis W. Long. The Rules Committee expansion passed, Congress approved it, and the Civil Rights Act became law. When Representative Long ran for reelection in 1964, he was painted as a liberal and was defeated.

But this story has a happy ending: When the representative who defeated Long retired in 1972, the voters of the district returned Long to Congress, where he served until his death in 1985.

And when Representative Long returned to Capitol Hill in 1973, to which key committee did the House leadership appoint him? That's right — the Rules Committee.

Sometimes, a politician who is sufficiently well respected by their constituents can take an unpopular position on a volatile issue and survive the next election. Indeed, sometimes that politician can convince the voters of the rightness of their position rather than simply convince the voters to support them despite it.

More often, a politician who swims against the tide to do the "right thing" on a tough issue finds that the cost of having a clear conscience may be their elected position. If the politician was correct on a matter that someday makes the history books, future voters may label that politician a statesman. However, the politician unfortunately will be known as a statesman only after they are employed in another field.

Chapter **2**

The Money-versus-Vote Analysis

Both money and votes play starring roles in politics, whether the politics is local, state, or national. You need to know what factors determine the stances that politicians take on any and every issue so that you can figure out how each politician's stance affects you.

The Factors behind Any Political Stance

Most issues and campaigns have at least two sides: one side supporting a candidate or an issue and the other side opposing it. But even if a campaign for election or legislation has more than two sides, a politician's analysis is the same. And it doesn't matter whether the issues are local, state, or national — the analysis works the same way at every level.

When legislators and candidates analyze an issue, they take into account what's at stake for them in terms of votes and money. They find out which side of a campaign for election or legislation

>> Is more popular with a large number of motivated voters

>> Has the support of special interest groups that have money to contribute

REMEMBER

You should know how your elected officials are likely to behave given the money-versus-vote analysis. That knowledge helps explain their conduct. It also explains why they sometimes don't behave as you want them to. You may be on the losing end of the money-versus-vote analysis. The other side may be better organized or more willing to spend money on campaigns or issues. These advantages guarantee them more attention from the elected official. You need to know this system so that you can compensate. (You may also become an advocate of campaign finance reform — check out Chapter 19 if you're interested.)

Weighing public opinion

Be aware that politicians analyze an issue to find out which stance will gain or lose them the most votes. Far from voting out of gut feeling or conscience, these questions are the first ones that a politician asks:

>> Where are the votes?

>> Who cares about this particular issue?

>> Which side is better organized?

>> Which side can turn out more voters or demonstrators in support of its position?

>> Which side feels more strongly about this issue?

>> Is one side or the other more likely to cast votes in the next election based on this issue alone?

>> What are the risks to the official or the candidate in supporting one position or the other?

No matter whether these are local, state, or national campaigns or issues, the analysis is the same for all. Officials who desire reelection and candidates who want to win must have a majority of the voters supporting them. The composition of that majority may change many times during an official's term or the duration of a campaign, but having a majority is essential to any victory.

Officials and candidates are reluctant to take any action or position that could alienate large segments of the voting public, for obvious reasons. After that segment is alienated, wooing it back is difficult. Officials and candidates may take unpopular actions or articulate unpopular positions when doing so is unavoidable, but usually *only* then. Sometimes, officials or candidates can get caught between the proverbial rock and a hard place: An issue can be so polarizing that politicians will alienate a significant segment of the voting population no matter which way they go.

Failing to act or to take a position has the potential to alienate everyone, so officials and candidates must go one way or the other.

At other times, the issues aren't quite so volatile. In those cases, absent an overarching and strongly held philosophy, the candidate or official performs a money-versus-vote analysis. Which position will cost more votes in the next election? Which position will gain more money in the next election?

Counting the money

After looking at how a stance will affect votes, the next question a politician must ask in assessing a political issue is this: Where's the money on this issue? Who will respond to my opposition by giving money to candidates who run against me? Who cares enough about this issue that my support will help attract substantial sums of money from them?

I'm not suggesting that many elected officials or candidates benefit personally from this money. Some do, but they usually wind up under indictment. Despite what you may hear, however, the majority of elected officials are honest people. (They're too scared to be anything else!)

Money plays a significant role in politics because elections cost so much. It isn't surprising that, when contemplating an issue or the wants of an important contributor, a politician may consider more than what is popular or even best.

Imagine this situation: The US military is proposing to revamp its entire computer system, and several businesses are competing for the contract. The PAC of one senator who is urging the military to hire a particular business has received several million dollars from that business. Now, it may be the case that the senator truly believes that the business which has been so generous to him is the best one for the contract, or it may be that he wants to stay on the good side of the business and continue receiving contributions. It is for the senator's constituents to decide.

CANDIDATES AND TOUCHY ISSUES: GUN CONTROL

POLITICAL STUFF

Periodically, a debate arises on the national scene over gun control — usually, after another mass shooting.

Proposals are made for universal background checks, limits on the size of magazines, gun show background checks, and so on. Such proposals are opposed by many of those supporters of the Second Amendment to the Constitution and the National Rifle Association (NRA). Opposition to many of these proposals serves as a litmus test for support by or opposition from the NRA, which is a powerful political force in many states.

In a district or state where the NRA plays a significant role, supporting these proposals can cost a candidate sufficient votes to lose an election because many advocates for gun rights are single-issue voters — that is, they cast their votes on the basis of this issue alone. They may agree with a candidate's position on many other issues, but this is the issue that tips the balance as to which candidate will get their votes. When you analyze this issue to see what is really going on, you understand what your elected official is likely to do and why. If you're opposed to the likely course of action for your elected official, you can begin to exert pressure on the official to vote the other way.

Many issues like this one must be subjected to both prongs of the money-versus-vote analysis. See the earlier section "Weighing public opinion" to see how votes influence an issue, but you need to know (if you don't already) that money is at the heart of this debate, as it is for many policy issues.

Many gun owners are worried that any attempt to limit ownership of weapons is the first step on a slippery slope to outlawing all guns completely. Advocates for background checks, restriction on ownership of guns for people with mental illnesses, outlawing military-type weapons, and the like see these proposals as reasonable restrictions to protect public safety. Polls show that there are more voters in the camp favoring some regulation of firearms, but those regulations don't successfully make their way through Congress, because the antiregulation faction has the greater influence.

Though money and votes don't always determine an officeholder's position on an issue, they are factors that all successful politicians consider, whether or not they admit it. Candidates consider money and votes because they want to be reelected. No candidate likes to lose. As Abraham Lincoln said, when asked how he felt after losing an election: "I'm too big to cry, but it hurts too much to laugh." No candidate wants that to happen to them, and so they weigh the risks of taking on the special interests, and possibly standing in the political unemployment line.

Money Makes the World Go 'Round

For you to assess the impact of proposed legislation on *you*, you first need to understand who benefits from the legislation. Your best clue comes from examining who is leading the effort to get the legislation enacted.

TIP

When you know which groups are bankrolling campaigns to pass certain laws, you can understand *why* the legislation is being pushed and, therefore, what is really happening. *Then* you're in a position to determine whether it affects you.

POLITICAL STUFF

One example of the impact money can have on policy is the tax law enacted at the end of 2017. For a number of years, corporations had complained that the 35 percent corporate tax rate was higher than in any other country and needed to be lowered. Corporations had no success in getting the rate lowered — until Donald Trump's election. He had campaigned on lowering the rate from 35 percent to 15 percent. Republican donors told their elected officials that it had to be done before the 2018 elections. As Rep. Chris Collins (R–NY) stated: "My donors are basically saying, 'Get it done or don't ever call me again.'" From the time the tax bill was introduced on November 2, 2017, until the end of the year (a 60-day period), dozens of millionaires and billionaires gave a total of over $31 million to Republican members of Congress. The bill passed and lowered the corporate tax rate from 35 percent to 21 percent and abolished the corporate alternative minimum tax.

Fundraising

The money that politicians gain by supporting or opposing legislation goes into their campaign coffers — not into their own pockets. Raising money is a significant task for any campaign. Congressional campaign spending for 2018 was four times higher than levels in 1998. Spending totaled over $5.6 billion in the 2018 cycle.

The average House member represents more than 700,000 citizens, according to the 2010 census. In terms of fundraising, the most expensive special election for the House was in Georgia's 6th Congressional District in 2017 where the two candidates in the general election spent over 56 million dollars combined. That seat was up for election again in 2018!

Leverage and money

Incumbents raise money year-round. They also spend a substantial amount of time fundraising to come up with the amount of money needed for reelection.

Our elected representatives and senators spend time with people and groups that have money to give and reasons to give it — a political reality that likely gives us all pause and makes our wallets ache.

Basically, your elected official pays a great deal of attention to the wishes and opinions of big-money contributors. If the position that you want the elected official to take is at odds with one that a big-money contributor wants, you may lose the debate. The official may well give more consideration to the opinion of the contributor than to you. That fact is true even if the contributors (along with their bank accounts) don't live in your district or even in your state.

REMEMBER

That's the way it is now, but if concerned citizens like you educate themselves about politics and get involved, the system can be changed for the better. Reading this book and doing your analysis are your ways of finding out what is really going on and what to do about it. You won't be fooled by the pious rhetoric about the issue.

Senate money

Senate campaigns are in a whole different league from House of Representative campaigns. Senators are elected by a majority of the voters of each state, but only every six years. One-third of the Senate runs every two years. According to the Federal Election Commission, candidates running for the US Senate in 2018 raised a total of almost $580 million. That number includes the special elections in Alabama and Mississippi.

THE RIDICULOUS COST OF CAMPAIGNS

The most expensive Senate race in the 2018 cycle was in Florida, which cost over $200 million. This was the most expensive race ever. Comparisons of Senate races between election cycles are difficult because of the unique nature of the races. The numbers can be skewed because contests in large states such as New York, Texas, Florida, and California cost so much more than those in small states such as Delaware. For example, in the 2018 race for Delaware, both candidates spent a combined total of less than $5 million. That's still a substantial amount of money, but nothing like the more than $200 million spent in Florida.

Chapter 19 discusses campaign finance reform.

Hatred Is a Greater Motivator than Love

Given human nature, motivating voters to vote *against* a candidate is easier than getting them to vote *for* a candidate. An official or a candidate must consider whether a political action committee (PAC) or another group will spend money to attack instead of support. Also, will a PAC or group spend *enough* time and money to actually cost the official votes in the next election?

Evil versus good

Politicians are more successful in attracting the attention of voters by emphasizing the divisions that separate people rather than the ties that unify them behind a common cause. For people who are minimally involved in an issue or a campaign, the images that stick with them are those that arouse an emotional reaction. This principle is true in life as well as in politics. For instance, when you read or watch the news, you probably remember the story of a firefighter who died battling a blaze more readily than you remember the story about the opening of a new fire station.

When a candidate finds an issue to exploit or distort to make an opponent appear awful, evil, or even capable of tormenting puppies, voters' choices become clear. The sharper the contrast a candidate is able to create between themselves and their opponent, the easier the choice. (See Chapter 12 for more on how campaigns use comparative advertising.) A candidate who demonizes an opponent is more likely to attract attention and votes than a candidate who patiently explains the ten points that make them a slightly better candidate.

But who is the bad guy?

Many campaigns feature warm-and-fuzzy positive images of the candidate they're marketing and then carry out hard, negative attacks on the opposition. You pay attention to the hard, negative attacks because often those attacks provide concrete information about the victim of the attack that makes you dislike the candidate. This sort of information is easy to process. You don't have to weigh the fine points of the backgrounds of the two candidates — you can react against the awful or evil opponent, just like in championship wrestling.

The religious right and the anti-gun-control groups have used their financial resources effectively to do just that to candidates who have opposed them, as have environmental groups and public sector unions. Their attacks have demonized the candidates who dared to oppose these special interests and encouraged those voters who are sympathetic to the special interests to vote against the candidates. An official or a candidate must consider the effect of *indirect* money from these groups in the campaign as well as *direct* contributions to the opposition.

Your Stake in the Election

By completing the money-versus-vote analysis, you can determine what is really happening. You can determine who is on which side of an issue and why.

These are the next questions you need to ask yourself:

>> Does this issue matter to me at all?

>> Will the issue have any impact on me?

Is the legislation good for you?

Many elected officials propose legislation because they believe it will be good for the country or the economy. Just because they honestly believe a bill is good doesn't mean that they're right. Good-thinking, intelligent people can disagree about the nature of a problem as well as the solution to a problem. You need to make your own, independent decision on the wisdom of the legislation.

Occasionally, a public official sponsors a bill because a special-interest group supportive of the official wants it. But the discussion of the merits of the bill is always couched in terms of the good of the country or the state.

REMEMBER

Don't listen to rhetoric from a public official. It is the rare public official who will tell you that they're sponsoring a bill because a well-heeled contributor wants it and just deposited $10,000 in the campaign PAC as a show of good faith. The bill always has some lofty public purpose. You need to decide for yourself whether the bill is in your interest.

Because you can't count on the rhetoric of the official to tell you what's going on, how do you know if you have a dog in the fight?

Independent sources of information

In judging whether a bill is in your interest, look to independent sources. Analysis by government watchdog groups like Common Cause can help you understand what's going on. Taxpayer groups like the Tax Policy Institutor the Peter G. Peterson Foundation that analyze tax fairness and public interest groups that monitor the effects of tax changes on the deficit can be valuable sources of information on what is truly happening. The media solicits comments from these groups when they're reporting on the pros and cons of a proposal. However, you're also free to contact these groups directly if you want additional information.

TIP

Don't rely on any single source of information for your opinions. Each group of independents and journalists can have its own slant on an issue. Look at all the information available and decide for yourself.

SURPRISING BEDFELLOWS

Particular issues can create odd alliances, as reflected by the old expression "Politics makes strange bedfellows." As an example of the tough bedfellow choices that politics requires, suppose that you're an advocate for nonsmokers' rights. You've supported the restrictions imposed on smokers during airline flights and in public buildings. You're worried about the effects of secondary smoke on nonsmokers like yourself. You're more than willing to curtail the rights of smokers to protect yourself and your family from the dangers of exposure to secondary cigarette smoke and ugly ashtrays.

But you were raised on a family farm and believe that the existence of family farms should be protected, so you also support federal support payments for farmers, called *subsidies*. You think that the federal government should do all it can to protect family farms, by adopting policies to make farming profitable.

The Agriculture Committee of the US Senate wants to reduce or eliminate subsidies in order to cut the deficit. A strong supporter of agricultural subsidies for farmers is the tobacco industry, because many of the farmers grow tobacco. However, the tobacco industry is also, naturally, one of the biggest opponents of smoking restrictions and ashtray control.

Do you participate in a campaign financed by the tobacco industry to defeat the plan to reduce agricultural subsidies? Does your shared opposition to repealing subsidies make you an ally of the tobacco industry? Does the enemy of your enemy suddenly become your friend? It's food for thought! (And, for some, it's grounds for a cigarette.)

Who's on what side?

Another part of your assessment of whether an issue matters to you is to examine who is on either side of the issue and whether you're comfortable supporting one of those sides. For you to assess whether you're comfortable supporting one side of an issue, you should know as much as possible about who is contributing to that team. Many people are uneasy about aligning themselves on an issue with a group they wouldn't normally support.

After you listen to the arguments from both sides, you have a better idea of what is going on. You're now in a position to trust your gut instincts because you're aware of many of the pros and cons of the legislation. You will probably never know all the facts, but, at some point, you decide which side of an issue you find most persuasive and then decide whether to act.

Does the legislation touch your life?

TIP

To find out if and how legislation can affect you, take a close look at what a piece of legislation says it will do and what other people say it will do. Try these strategies:

>> Listen to what all sides in the debate are saying.

>> Read and watch news stories about the impact of the legislation.

>> Review any analysis by independent people or groups concerned with the legislation, such as that provided by *think tanks* (research institutions) or the Congressional Budget Office.

>> Determine the positions of groups you generally support — such as the chamber of commerce, senior citizens' groups, public interest groups, women's groups, environmental organizations, church organizations, or labor unions.

>> See where elected officials you trust and support stand on the issue.

>> Trust your instincts and decide for yourself.

2

Making Your Voice Heard

IN THIS PART . . .

Realizing that, if you don't vote, you don't count

Participating in campaigns — with talent, time or treasure

Letting the candidates know what you think

Communicating and participating through social media

Chapter **3**

Be a Part of the Solution — Vote!

As Adlai Stevenson, U.S. Ambassador to the United Nations, said of Eleanor Roosevelt upon her death: *She would rather light one candle than curse the darkness.*

The same philosophy holds true for our government. Your vote counts. You may have noticed through the years that our system of government isn't perfect — it has its warts and flaws — but it's still the best system in the world. Our country is the single most successful exercise in democracy in history. If it's not perfect, or even not as good as it could be, maybe that's because not enough good people like you are involved. Try answering the following questions:

» Do you tell yourself that you're so busy you can't spare the 15 minutes it takes to vote in every election?

» Do you tell yourself that your vote doesn't count anyway?

» If you're critical of politics and government, do you use that criticism as an excuse not to participate?

If you answered *yes* to any of these questions, that's a cop-out. You need to participate, and this book can help you become more involved. Your participation *can* make a difference. Politics is an opportunity where you can be in control. You can decide what level of involvement you want to have. You can decide how much you want to do. You're the only one who knows how much time and money you have. But you must do one thing in order to have this control: *You must vote.* If you don't vote, you have no right or leverage to complain about politics, politicians, or government.

Should You Register to Vote?

Many of us — more than 255 *million* citizens in this country — are eligible to vote but only about 140 million voted in the 2016 national election. Every citizen of the United States who is at least 18 years of age may register and vote.

Twenty-one states and the District of Columbia permit some form of same day registration. In all other states, you must register before Election Day in order to vote. Registration in those states stops in advance of an election — usually thirty days in advance!

REMEMBER

You must be registered to vote for any elective office in the United States, from president to township advisory board. You only have to register once, though, as long as you live at the same address and vote periodically.

Upsides and downsides of registering

Maybe you're not registered because you've convinced yourself that you should avoid politics. Check out this book's Introduction — avoiding politics is impossible. Political decisions will be made for you even if you elect not to participate. You still have to pay taxes even if you don't vote. Elected officials make decisions about which streets get paved, which sidewalks get repaired, and which schools close without regard to your opinions, if you don't vote. There's no hole deep enough for you to bury your head in to avoid politics completely. You can't run, and you can't hide — so you may as well participate.

Make a difference

If you do participate, you can make the system better. It may never be perfect, but improvement is possible. With the knowledge you gain by reading this book, you can make your elected officials respond to you. Your voice will be loud enough to be heard by everyone.

Voting is a valuable right that you, as an American, have. Many Americans take that right for granted . . . even the politicians. In the 2010 elections, a wave of voter reaction — a "throw 'em all out" attitude after years of inaction and deadlock by Congress — shook up both major political parties, changed the dominant party in Congress, and made the politicians brutally aware of the issues about which voters had been concerned for years, and which the politicians had bypassed.

That reaction reminded every politician not to take the voters for granted. The politicians heard the discontentment among voters, and they had to respond.

Become important

Voting isn't required in the United States, as it is in some other countries. The former Soviet Union used to brag about its 98 percent voter turnout on Election Day — but citizens faced stiff fines and punishment if they failed to turn out to support the government's approved candidate. By contrast, this country gives us so many compelling reasons to vote, it's a wonder the voting turnout here doesn't come close to approaching that of the countries that demand it.

REMEMBER

When you vote and participate, elected officials have to consider what you think. They may not always do what you want, but they have to listen to your opinions. When you vote, you become someone important.

Cynics are probably saying, "Yeah, but not as important as PACs (*political action committees*) and special interest groups with money." (See Chapter 8 for more on PACs and special interests.) Keep in mind, though, that a district (be it a small town or the entire country) has only so many voters. Although money is in potentially limitless supply for a candidate (it can be raised from many sources), it's illegal to buy votes, and you can't give someone else your proxy to vote for you — so the only way money can make a difference is if it's used to communicate a message that makes you want to support the candidate who's spending it. Your vote has the same weight as the vote of every other citizen. Rich or poor, young or old, male or female, Black or White, each vote is equally important.

Wield your political power

Each one of us has the same number of votes. You may not have an equal share of the world's financial resources, but the secret ballot gives us all an equal amount of voting power. Each registered voter has one and only one vote to cast — regardless of what you hear to the contrary about certain big-city or downstate rural districts, where the concept of "vote early and vote often" is allegedly in force, or where that age-old question "Is there voting after death? — is supposedly answered in the affirmative.

The vote of a person who has contributed $1 million to a candidate counts for no more than the vote of the person who has given nothing to a campaign. After all, winning elections is all about getting a majority of the votes cast. Votes are one-size-fits-all. Politicians need the votes of the "little people," because this country has more "little people" than rich and powerful ones.

Since John F. Kennedy was elected, the percentage of eligible voters participating in presidential elections has declined in almost every election. That statistic is true in local elections as well.

When we all vote, we are a powerful force that can move mountains, or at least politicians. When we don't, the small number of special interest voters have more clout because they are a bigger percentage of a smaller pie.

TIP

Figure 3-1 illustrates just how few people who are eligible to vote actually do. The outer circle represents the number of people in the United States who are eligible to vote. The next circle in the figure represents the number of people who registered to vote in the 2016 elections. The next circle represents the number of people who actually voted in the 2016 presidential election. (The number of people who actually voted is the *2016 voting population*.) The smallest circle is the group of people who voted in the primaries. Think how different things might be if everybody who could vote actually voted.

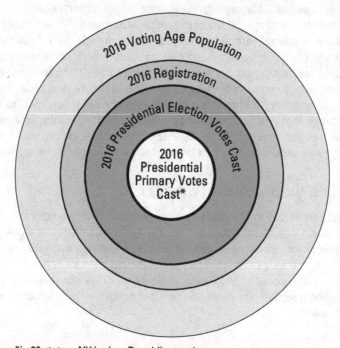

FIGURE 3-1:
What would election outcomes be if every eligible citizen voted?

2016 Voting Age Population
2016 Registration
2016 Presidential Election Votes Cast
2016 Presidential Primary Votes Cast*

*in 38 states- NY had no Republican primary

THE JURY DUTY MYTH

Some people don't register to vote because they may focus on the downside of registering: They fear that registering will cause them to be selected for jury duty

Some jurisdictions do rely on voter registration rolls to select their jury pools, but fewer than most people think. Many more jurisdictions use motor vehicle and tax records (statistics) to select jurors. People who haven't registered to vote regularly get called for jury duty. These days, you'd be better off not getting a driver's license if you're so eager to avoid serving on a jury.

What if registering to vote does get you selected for jury duty? Most of the time, you stand around at a courthouse for a day and then go home. Most people called for jury duty don't serve on juries. The few people who do end up on juries serve for a trial that lasts a day, or maybe three days. If the trial you're there for will last longer and you have a reason you cannot serve, you will be excused. Neither the prosecution nor the defense wants to seat jurors who are worried about events outside the courtroom. They want you to pay attention to the evidence and the arguments. If you have a deadline to meet at work or have no arrangements for child care, you probably will be excused.

The jury system works only when average citizens take seriously their duty to serve on juries. Everyone who is charged with a crime, no matter how important or unimportant that person is, is entitled to a trial by a jury. You have benefited greatly by living in this country. Isn't it time to take some responsibility for that citizenship?

Even if you don't believe that you have a civic responsibility to serve on a jury when your number comes up, not registering to vote doesn't give you the protection you think it does! Unless you're prepared to give up driving and risk not paying property taxes, you may as well register to vote. You really have no reason not to.

THE POLL TAX: A HURDLE OVERCOME

One of the more recent voting hurdles to bite the dust was the use of a poll tax in many Southern states. The *poll tax* was a fee charged to everyone who voted in an election. The tax was cumulative — that is, if you failed to vote in one election, you had to pay the fee for that election as well as the current fee when you tried to vote in the next election.

The poll tax discouraged poorer voters, particularly African Americans, from exercising their voting rights. The 24th Amendment to the Constitution outlawed poll taxes in federal elections. The Supreme Court outlawed them in state elections. Both White and Black voter participation increased sharply after the poll taxes were outlawed.

REMEMBER

After you register to vote, you can vote for the president, congressional representatives, and US senators when your state has a contest. You can also vote in your state and local elections. Registering takes only a few minutes — less time than it would take to call your mother-in-law and wish her a good day, and it no longer costs a thing. It's time well spent — after all, how often does someone enjoy calling their mother-in-law? You make the call because you want to stay on your mother-in-law's good side. Register to vote because you want the government to stay on *your* good side.

After you know all that you need to know about politics from reading this book, you can put that knowledge to good use by voting. Registering to vote doesn't *require* you to vote in any election; it's a *prerequisite* for voting in all elections. Register to vote now. You can always decide later not to vote. If you later decide to vote, and haven't registered, it may be too late.

Why Vote in Primaries?

I tell you more about primaries in Chapter 20, but you should know about them when you register to vote, because a primary is the first place you have an opportunity to vote and have an impact. However, most voters don't vote in primaries.

REMEMBER

Primaries are one of the methods by which parties select candidates to represent them in the general election. Parties use primaries to select their nominees for important offices, such as governor, senator, and member of Congress. In addition, most states use primaries to select their delegates to presidential nomination conventions. Primaries are also commonly used to select legislative candidates, mayors, sheriffs, prosecuting attorneys, and other local officeholders.

The nominees of political parties for some statewide offices that aren't as visible as governor and senator — such as secretary of state, lieutenant governor, superintendent of public instruction, and attorney general — may be selected by a statewide convention convened by the political parties. Some states, like New Jersey, permit the governor to appoint some or all of these officeholders.

Taking your chance to choose the candidate

SPEAKING UP

If you vote in a primary, you have a voice in choosing all of your party's candidates, including president and vice president. Not only do you have a voice — your voice is also loud. So few people vote in primaries that your vote carries much more weight in a primary than it does in a general election. Primary voters definitely have clout!

REMEMBER

If you don't have input into the selection of the nominees of the parties in a primary, your choices usually are limited in the general election to the two major-party nominees already chosen in primary elections. You may be stuck choosing the lesser of two evils! And keep in mind, if you're dissatisfied with the incumbent and feel that a new occupant is in order for that office, the primary gives you a second shot to send the incumbent into blissful retirement. Of course, you may vote for a third party or an independent or write in your own selection for an office, but those methods are rarely successful — and then usually only at the local level.

Besides, because so few people vote in the primaries, your vote can have a much more significant impact in a primary than in the general election. In fact, in 2018 only 57.6 million people in total voted in Republican and Democratic primaries. That number is only 28.5 percent of the estimated eligible voters. Proportionately, your individual vote is much more important in a primary than in a general election, so get out there and vote.

Declaring your party affiliation

Some states have *open primaries,* allowing voters to pick a party primary when they show up to vote. In other words, you may decide that you want a Republican ballot, a Democratic ballot, or another party's ballot.

This system allows you to vote in the Republican primary one election year, in the Democratic primary the next year, and so on. That way, you can have a say in who is on the ballot for the final election and still maintain your position of independence.

Other states have *closed primaries,* which restrict you to the primary for whatever political party you joined when last registering to vote. You're given an opportunity to vote for the candidates of that party, but only that party, in the primary election. Independents may be altogether excluded from party primaries in such states.

Regardless of which system your state uses, though, you can't vote for one of the Republican candidates for governor and one of the Democratic candidates for Congress during the same primary election. You must make a choice between the parties at some point before casting your votes. Of course, in the general election you are free to pick and choose candidates from either party. For example, you can vote for a Democratic nominee for governor at the same time you vote for the Republican nominee for senator, and so on. The only exception is in Louisiana, which doesn't use party primaries for state office. In that state, all candidates for an office, regardless of party affiliation, face off in a primary election. If a candidate gets 50 percent of the vote outright, they win. If no candidate reaches

50 percent, the two candidates with the highest number of votes run in the general election. (To find out more about parties, see Chapter 6; for tips on choosing a party, skip to Chapter 7.)

Do Elected Officials Care What You Think?

The answer is a resounding *yes,* but only if you're registered to vote! If you don't register, you declare yourself out of the game, and no one makes any effort to find out what you think or what you want. Officials don't contact you to solicit your ideas or concerns because you don't show up on their carefully compiled lists of registered voters. You must be registered if you want your opinions to count. Even if you don't vote, the fact that you're registered means that your support and opinions will still be solicited. If you don't register, you don't count and you don't matter. Period.

Elected officials make genuine efforts to know what you, as a registered voter, want them to do and not do. They hold town hall events to interact with average voters like yourself and to find out what's on your mind and what worries you most about your city, state, or country. Successful elected officials — who, along with their families and staffs, have a deep and abiding interest in whether they keep their jobs — know that the key to reelection is understanding what the voters want and, within reason, delivering it.

Your opinions are worth real money

Your elected officials pay good money to pick your brain (provided you're a registered voter). They hire special consultants to organize focus groups and professional pollsters to conduct surveys. The burning question is this: "What's on *your* mind?" . . . followed by, "How can I get what's on your mind into my mind so that you will keep me in mind come election day?"

Focus groups

Elected officials sometimes, particularly in an election cycle, pay large amounts of money to stage cozy little get-togethers, called focus groups. *Focus groups* are small, scientifically selected groups of voters in an official's district. These voters, selected at random from the list of registered voters, are paid a small fee to meet for several hours with a political consultant to discuss issues and impressions in much greater depth than polls allow.

Campaigns use focus groups to test "average" voters' reactions to campaign themes, plans of attack that the campaign is thinking of using on the opposition, and defenses that the campaign may use to fend off attacks from the opposition.

The small group doesn't even know who's paying for the session, which helps the consultant obtain their candid responses. These responses can help an official know whether the voters are paying attention to what they're saying on the stump and whether the right information is being communicated.

Because the focus group is such a small part of the electorate, usually no more than a dozen people, the campaign also conducts scientific polls on the information obtained in the focus group. But both of these expensive methods are used to discover what you think about the candidates and the issues. Elected officials and candidates spend all this time, money, and effort because they want to know what you want as well as what you think.

And you didn't think they cared.

Polling

Elected officials — particularly, occupants of higher offices (governor, senator, congressperson, and so on) — spend tens of thousands of dollars in every election year trying to find out what you think about the issues and about the officials themselves. Pollsters even ask how you personally feel about the candidate — for example: Are they honest? Do they care about people like you? Are they intelligent? Are they trustworthy?

Those same pollsters ask what you think about important policy issues. How do you feel that the state or country is doing? Are you better off now than two or four years ago? Are you (or is anyone in your family) afraid of losing a job? How do you feel about a particular tax increase proposal? Do you think education funding should be increased? Are you willing to increase sentences for violent crimes, even though the construction of more prisons will increase the tax burden? You get the idea.

POLITICAL MYTH

Contrary to popular belief, officeholders, if they're smart, really want to do what most of the voters want done. If an officeholder can determine what you want and deliver that to you, the officeholder keeps getting elected and perhaps moves on to a higher office. That's why elected officials and candidates pay huge amounts of money to campaign consultants: to find out what you, as a registered voter, want.

Officials spend time and money inventing new ways or refining old ways of interacting with the average voter in their districts. Pollsters are paid tens of thousands of dollars to select voters at random and question them. These voters are a cross-section of the electorate in the official's or candidate's district. The pollsters are paid because of their expertise in drafting questions and analyzing the results of the interviews. This expensive expertise is just another way to permit the officeholder or candidate to communicate with you.

THE MEDIA'S POLLSTERS

It isn't just the elected officials and candidates who are extremely curious about what exactly you want them to do about the issues and problems you care deeply about. The news media also spends huge amounts of money to satisfy its abundant curiosity on these points, with extensive polling at the state and national levels. Like the candidates, the media is way too impatient to wait until election night to get a handle on what you're thinking. The networks and major daily newspapers want to be able to stay on top of a campaign by trying to figure out the mood of the voters while they're still in the mood.

The media recognizes that the key to electoral success is identifying what a majority of the voters in a district, a state, or the country want or don't want.

REMEMBER

The pollsters may not do a perfect job of finding out what you think and interpreting your opinions for the elected official. Sometimes, the method of asking the questions influences the answers. Sometimes, accidentally, the sample that the pollster selected is biased in favor of one group of voters. Polling may not be a perfect way to determine what you and other registered voters think, but it's the preferred way. If you want to find out more about polling, flip to Chapter 15.

REMEMBER

Almost every poll screens contacted people to determine whether they're registered to vote and, if so, likely to vote. If your answer to either of these two questions is *no*, the interviewer writes you off as a nonperson and finds inventive ways to terminate the interview immediately. Spooky, isn't it? Politically, you don't exist. The elected official won't know what you think about important issues, and probably doesn't care. Either way, nobody will bother to ask.

Giving voters what they say they want

Once candidates or officeholders accurately determine what the voters want, they can fashion a way to deliver it. Sometimes, of course, voters want it all. People do have a tendency to ask their candidates to give them better roads, more prisons, extra dollars for education, and, while they're at it, lower taxes. Sometimes voters want one thing one year and forget about it the next. Yes, as voters, people often have whims. And those whims can change as quickly as the length of women's skirts.

REMEMBER

No matter how hard officials try, and no matter how good they are, they're not magicians. Inconsistent goals may not be possible, no matter how much the voters want them. (Scientists still haven't developed a tree that produces dollar bills.) So, without making the thoroughly unappreciated decision to raise taxes, an official may not be able to provide for all the increased services the voters want.

Elected officials face the challenge of determining which item is most important to a majority of voters, whether they can deliver it, and how they can explain the impossibility of delivering on all goals. If delivering on the most important goal isn't possible, officials still want to be in a position to demonstrate to voters that they're fighting to get what they want and will keep doing so if people keep supporting them with their votes in the next election.

For example, Governor Jill Shmoe may complain that too few of the dollars her state sends in taxes to Washington are returned by the federal government. She can meet with the state's representatives and senators to ask for help in moving more federal dollars back to the state. She may write letters to the president. She may complain about the federal government in speeches and press conferences.

SPEAKING UP

ANSWERING SURVEYS GIVES YOU A VOICE!

A statewide poll to determine voters' positions has a typical sample of 800 voters. (Statewide campaigns occasionally use samples as small as 400 to 600 voters.) Elected officials use the information gained from those 800 people to determine how to make a case for election and which ideas to champion.

National polls taken by newspapers and the TV networks rarely exceed 2,000 respondents. Usually, these entities tell us what the entire country is thinking by interviewing fewer than 1,100 people! Just like primary voters, interviewees for polls are important people.

Of course, selection for poll interviews or focus groups is completely random; you may never be called. You can't guarantee yourself a voice via polls and focus groups, but you can be heard via the primary elections that come along almost every year. If you follow the suggestions for getting involved that I give you in this chapter and in Chapter 4 of this book, the role you play may increase in importance. You may never be selected for a poll or a focus group even if you register. The only thing you can guarantee is that, if you don't register, you'll never be selected, and you don't matter.

If you don't register, you shouldn't be surprised that elected officials and candidates aren't spending any time thinking about you. You shouldn't even complain about that lack of consideration. After all, you've declared yourself to be out of politics, and they've simply taken you at your word. You can't ask for much more than that. Although we all try to do so, you probably shouldn't expect to have it both ways: You can't be too good to be involved in the greedy and self-centered world of the politician and expect that greedy and self-centered politician to turn handsprings to figure out what you want and then get it for you, no matter what the cost to them.

Nothing may result from all this effort, but at least Governor Jill Shmoe would've demonstrated that she's willing to fight for what her constituents feel is the state's fair share of federal money. She's responsive. She's trying. This governor would deserve reelection if you agreed with her goals.

On the other hand, you may disagree completely with what the polls say that "the people" want. You may think that Governor Shmoe is barking up the wrong tree completely. You may want to see someone else in office, promoting better ideas in a better way. But — and by now you know what's coming — you have no say if you're not registered to vote.

Chapter **4**

Contributing Your Time or Money

Are you looking for direct involvement in the game of politics, beyond simply exercising your constitutional right and civic duty to vote? If you've decided to take the plunge, this chapter tells you how to find the pool.

REMEMBER

You can get involved in politics on a number of levels. Which one is right for you depends on how much time and effort you're willing to commit, as well as how fat your wallet is and how willing you are to slenderize it on behalf of a candidate.

Donating Your Time

Campaigns need volunteers to drive candidates to events, monitor local newspapers and social media, make phone calls, send emails and tweets, write letters to the editor, organize events, register voters, help raise money, and so on. Your involvement can be as simple as putting a candidate-support sign in your front yard or hosting a coffee at your home where neighbors and friends can meet the candidate. Or, it can be as complicated as raising funds for the campaign or coordinating all the volunteer efforts. You know what your talents are and how much time you have available. Anything that you agree to do (and do well) is welcome.

REMEMBER

As a volunteer, you can carry out many valuable tasks for a campaign:

>> Research the press coverage and Internet traffic that your candidate and the opponent are receiving.

>> Contact other voters to get your candidate's message to them.

>> Organize events.

>> Register voters.

>> Raise money.

>> Get your candidate's message out to the public.

>> Do opposition research to see whether anything the opponent said, did, or voted on in the past can be held against them.

Finding your niche

When you contact the campaign, you should already have in mind several specific ways that you can help. If you call simply to volunteer, you may be put to work stuffing envelopes, licking stamps, or picking up pizza. (Not that there's anything wrong with stuffing envelopes — someone has to do it.) But if you can write press releases, schedule a candidate's time efficiently and accurately, write position papers on issues, or raise a ton of campaign money, tell someone because these talents are extremely valuable in assisting the campaign.

TIP

Campaigns are always interested in volunteers who have a knack for raising money. (Chapter 14 tells you about all the things campaigns do with that money.) If you demonstrate an ability to set a fundraising goal and meet it or — better yet — exceed it, the candidate will value you and your support. We all know how well paved the road to hell is; when a candidate finds a volunteer who can actually deliver on their good intentions, they'll ask them to do more fundraising and perhaps to expand their role in the campaign.

WARNING

Don't commit to more than you're certain you can do well and promptly. Nothing impresses a campaign manager more than a volunteer who can execute a plan successfully and quickly, but nothing is more frustrating than volunteers who call and ask for assignments and then fail to complete those assignments.

A campaign manager will be duly impressed if you call to volunteer and have specific ideas in mind on things you can do to help the candidate. For example, you can offer to take responsibility for placing yard signs in your neighborhood or a certain area of town. You can tell the campaign manager that you will obtain permission from the homeowners and place the signs yourself at, say, 50 or 100 homes.

If yard signs aren't your thing, or if the campaign you're supporting doesn't use them, think of other discreet tasks you can accomplish that will help the campaign gain momentum. One great idea is to offer to arrange several neighborhood coffee hours to permit voters who haven't made up their minds to meet your candidate.

If you want to arrange neighborhood coffee hours, here's what you do:

1. **Find people who can serve as hosts and hostesses.**

   These people should have homes that are comfortable meeting places for the candidate and the voters — in terms of both location and the layout of the house.

2. **Make the appointments with the candidate's secretary.**

   Don't forget to double-check the candidate's availability against that of your hosts' and hostesses'.

3. **Identify the voters you want to persuade.**

   The campaign manager can get that information for you.

4. **Invite the voters to attend.**

   Here's the real test of your powers of persuasion. You need to get enough firm commitments of attendance to make the meeting worthwhile.

5. **Follow up with your hosts and hostesses to make sure that the arrangements are complete, with the candidate's secretary to make sure that the date is still set, and with as many of the voters as you can to ensure their attendance.**

6. **Attend the coffees yourself.**

   Your presence reinforces the important role you played in getting these affairs arranged.

TIP

MORE, MORE, AND MORE VOLUNTEERS!

When candidates are first starting out, they rely more on volunteers than on paid staff. After all, paid staff is expensive, and new candidates are usually short on money. Even if a candidate is an incumbent or has run before, they rely more on volunteers if the office is less visible.

For example, a campaign for city council, except in a large metropolitan area like New York City or Los Angeles, probably won't have any paid campaign staff. Most city-council candidates rely on volunteers to place yard signs on the lawns of supporters. They use volunteers to distribute literature to potential voters. Volunteers call voters to tell them about the candidate and to urge them to vote on election day. A well-run campaign of this type may use 10, 20, or more volunteers.

Volunteers also play a significant role in the campaigns for more-visible offices. Most statewide candidates — those who want to succeed, anyway — try to conserve their funds for TV ads and social media, which go directly to voters. Any money they spend for staff reduces the money available to persuade voters to vote for the candidate. Most statewide or congressional candidates try to keep their paid staff to a half-dozen or fewer people. They have many times that number of volunteers.

Spending your time well

Why would you want to bother working for a political campaign without getting paid? The answer is that you *do* get paid — not with money, of course, but with experience.

>> Many people enjoy the team spirit and camaraderie that come with volunteering for a political campaign.

>> Volunteering for a campaign is a great way to meet people who care about the same issues you do.

>> Your experience working for a political campaign stands out on a resume. It shows not only that you have great organizational skills but also that you care about and get involved in your community.

>> Especially in smaller, local campaigns, volunteering is a way to make your voice heard. You may be the reason a particular candidate gets elected. And, once elected, officials are likely to consider the opinions of those who helped them get there.

TIP

You've put in a lot of work to make your candidate successful. You ought to get credit for your volunteer efforts. Don't miss an opportunity to be at an event when the candidate is present. Once they see you several times at successful events you've put together, you can be certain they will remember who you are and how much you've helped to get them elected.

Hardworking volunteers who can accomplish tasks are worth their weight in gold. But you want to be sure the candidate knows that *you* are responsible for the success of the events — not the paid staff at headquarters.

Money Talks

For some people, time is an even scarcer resource than money. You may find that you'd rather contribute to a campaign from your wallet than from your over-booked schedule.

If you decide to get involved in politics by contributing money, you may want to start with a fairly minimal level of involvement. If so, just pick a candidate you like (see the next section for help on identifying a candidate to contribute to) and make a small monetary contribution to that candidate.

TIP

What constitutes a small, medium, or large contribution in a political campaign depends on the office being sought. (See Table 4-1.) What is a large donation for a local race may not be significant in a statewide contest for governor or US Senate. Usually, between $50 and $100 is a respectable sum. In some local races, that would be a significant contribution — you could get by with $25. In some statewide elections, you need to give more to accomplish that goal. The key is giving enough to ensure that your donation is noticed.

TABLE 4-1 **General Range for Contributions in Certain Types of Campaigns**

Type of Race	Small	Medium	Large
Local (school board official, county officeholder, city or county council member, county commissioner)	$25–50	$50–250	More than $500
Legislative (general assembly member, state representative, state senator)	$50	$100	More than $250
Less-visible statewide (attorney general, state treasurer, state auditor)	Less than $100	$100–$250	More than $500
More-visible statewide (governor, US senator)	Less than $100	$250–$1,000	$1,000

If you want your donation to be noticed, always err on the side of a larger contribution. Any contribution over $100 results in invitations to most of the campaign fundraisers. Few candidates besides incumbent US senators and presidential candidates have events with a price tag of $1,000. Candidates who have events with price tags over $100 have more than one tier of giving for such an event. For example, the base price may be $100 to attend a dinner. If you want to attend the cocktail party before the dinner, the price may increase to $250 or even $500 for a statewide candidate (for a governor or a US senator).

REMEMBER

The maximum contribution that a US Senate candidate can accept is $2,800 per election. That means $2,800 for the primary and $2,800 for the general election. If you're married, your spouse can give the same amount of $2,800 per election. And $5,600 is a substantial contribution!

In many states, those limits don't apply for state races (governor, lieutenant governor, attorney general), and some wealthy contributors give much more.

The money avenue does provide you with a ready entry into virtually every campaign. How do you decide which one to enter? Well, for starters, you can read the next section.

Deciding who should get your money

You've decided to get involved by contributing money. To whom do you give?

If you already think of yourself as a Republican or a Democrat, you can rule out half the potential recipients right from the start. Then the challenge is simply to consider the various candidates running for office from your party.

>> If you like to back a winner, you pick a candidate who seems to be headed for victory. Remember, though, that nothing in this life is certain but death and taxes. There certainly is no sure thing in politics.

>> If you aspire to be a kingmaker, you pick a candidate of your party who is seen as a long shot — as long as the candidate has potential. (A *kingmaker* is someone who is content to stay in the background of the campaign. That person usually gives or raises a great deal of money for the candidate they're supporting. The kingmaker is generally regarded by the candidate as the most important person in making that candidate successful.) Look for a candidate who is telegenic, hardworking, and articulate and who also has an attractive family — a person you would be pleased to have your son or daughter marry.

TIP

Don't be afraid to trust your instincts. If you like the person, the odds are that other voters will, too. Of course, the campaign has to be run in an intelligent fashion to make the most of the attractive characteristics of your candidate. Your candidate may walk on water, but that does the campaign no good if the voters are convinced your candidate can't swim!

The decision is more complicated if you don't have a predisposition to either party. In that case, your decision about the beneficiary of your contributions may take some independent research. (See Chapter 13 for more on how to do this research.)

Putting your wallet away

If you've decided to make a contribution to a candidate or to raise money for that candidate, virtually every campaign will be eager to have you — with a few notable exceptions. If you make your money operating a brothel or have ties to organized crime, most campaigns won't touch your money with a ten-foot pole. (But then, you're not that kind of person, are you?)

Even if your sources of income are perfectly legal and aboveboard, campaigns may be reluctant to accept your contribution if taking your money creates a political problem. Suppose that you own a company that employs a substantial number of the voters in a candidate's district, but you're embroiled in a nasty dispute with the labor union representing the workers. Your candidate's opponent may use your contribution, which must be reported, to persuade those workers to vote against your candidate. As much as your candidate would like to have your money, they should refuse to accept it. Don't get upset by the refusal.

REMEMBER

If the opponent attacks your candidate because of your contribution, news stories no doubt will erupt. Those news stories will resurrect the labor union unpleasantness and speculate whether you have an ulterior motive in making the contribution. So your candidate's refusal to accept your contribution also protects you from unfavorable publicity, even if the candidate was motivated purely by self-protection.

These exceptions to the rule that money powers the political process are rare. The vast majority of the time, campaign managers jump at the chance to take your contribution or fundraising efforts.

Knowing what to expect

After you become a donor, your support is solicited during the remainder of that campaign. You get invited to events, at additional cost. If your candidate is running a state-of-the-art campaign, you receive direct-mail or email solicitations.

Your candidate considers your views on everything from their position on issues to the effectiveness of the campaign strategy. Because you helped finance the campaign, you now have a personal stake in the outcome of that election.

Which Kind of Contributor Are You?

The simple fact is that candidates need money in order to run a campaign. What's not so simple is where the money comes from and why it's donated.

The source of contributions varies with respect to the type of contributor, the amount donated, and the motivation behind the contribution. But every contributor — from the individual who gives $100 because they agree with a candidate's ideas to the special interest group that gives tens of thousands of dollars to push for certain legislation — is warmly welcomed into a campaign.

Contributors fall into a few categories based on their style of contributing and their motivation: party supporters, ideological givers (with or without a personal agenda), kingmakers (and queenmakers), and special interest groups.

TIP

What contributors expect in return for their contribution (if anything) depends on the contributor. The following sections give an overview of the contributors and their motivations, which may help you determine where you fall and what you should expect in return for your contribution.

Party backers

If you're a voter who identifies strongly with a political party, you're likely to contribute money to candidates of that party to help them win elections. You probably give over and over again to many different party candidates over the years. Your gifts are usually modest — less than $100 at a time. You're a *party backer*; you make these contributions because you're committed to the success of the party. And you measure that success by the number of officeholders a party has at any given time. Your contributions are meant to help increase the number of party officeholders.

It doesn't matter too much to you who the candidates are. What matters most is the party affiliation. People who support the party will give to almost any Democratic or any Republican candidate who asks them for contributions.

Individuals with strong party identification make their contributions in any one of a hundred ways. Here are just a few:

- ❯❯ Buy tickets to hog roasts, fish fries, and bean dinners that honor a candidate or a party.

- ❯❯ Buy buttons emblazoned with the candidate's name.

- ❯❯ Buy a raffle ticket in hopes of winning a homemade quilt or pie.

- ❯❯ Pay for a car wash performed by volunteers who give the money raised to a candidate or party.

- ❯❯ Pay dues to a party organization.

In local elections for county offices or small-town mayors, party backers may form the majority of givers. They may also represent the majority of the total campaign budget. In smaller towns and cities or rural counties, the entire campaign budget for an office may be less than $5,000, raised entirely or primarily from the party backers.

If you're a party backer and give to a candidate, you may expect that candidate to represent the party well during the campaign and, if successful, in office. Continued loyalty to the party and its people after the candidate is in office is a must. The officeholder is expected to "dance with the one that brung ya," which means that party supporters want policy and hiring decisions to reflect party affiliation. (See Chapter 7 for more on party affiliation.)

Ideological givers

If you're an *ideological giver* with or without a personal agenda, you give to see that certain laws are passed or repealed; you expect the candidates you're supporting to vote a certain way on these issues while in office. You usually interview the candidate in depth or review their records or statements before giving your support. The in-depth discussions assure you, as an ideological giver, that the candidate shares your concerns about issues of importance to you. With higher offices or with more modest contributions, you might instead follow advice given by the leadership of groups that share your goals.

Ideological groups typically expect to have the officeholders they support listen with a sympathetic ear to their arguments when legislation or policy is being decided. Contributors make their contributions with a goal in mind: for the officeholders to reflect their views when the time comes to pass laws or implement policy, whether their support was motivated by a personal agenda or not.

With no personal agenda

You may be a person who gives money for a completely unselfish reason: the desire for good government. Sometimes, a candidate's background, qualifications, or ideas excite a particular group into contributing to the candidate's campaign with no other motivation than the hope that this person will be good for the city, state, or country. If you're this type of contributor, you expect and demand high standards from your officeholders. Because you don't have a specific purpose in mind — other than good government — when you give, you usually don't expect the officeholder to provide something in return for the contribution.

If you belong to this group, you give to candidates who support the same issues you do. Ideological givers feel deeply about certain issues and want to elect office-holders who reflect those views.

An example of this type of ideological giver is an environmental activist. These activists contribute to and work for candidates who are committed to protecting the environment. They have nothing personal to gain from their support of candidates; they simply want to see that people who are committed to protecting the environment are in positions of power. The only thing they hope to gain is a cleaner, safer environment for themselves and future generations.

Other groups that fit into this category are pro-choice and pro-life givers. These individuals may never be personally involved in an abortion decision themselves but feel strongly about promoting or restricting access to abortion for others. These ideological givers donate regularly to candidates who support the pro-choice or the pro-life position in the hope of protecting or restricting these legal rights.

With a personal agenda

If you're an ideological giver *with* a personal agenda, you support certain types of candidates committed to the same issues as you. You have a more personal interest in the selection of officeholders than those with no personal agenda. You hope that the selection of candidates with a similar point of view will mean a government that shares your views and takes action consistent with those views, which will directly and personally benefit you.

For example, you might be an anti-gun-control, single-issue contributor who owns guns. If the law changes, your ability to own weapons also changes. You're committed to opposing gun control, but you also have a personal stake in the issue.

Business groups, such as chambers of commerce, support general ideological principles that will also help their members financially if they become law. For example, laws making environmental regulations more difficult to issue and legislation shifting the property tax burden from businesses to individuals reflect the members' ideology and help their bottom lines.

Labor unions give their contributions in much the same way. They want officeholders who oppose laws such as striker replacement legislation and bills that tax health benefits to union workers. They want officeholders who support the right of employees to organize.

Single-issue groups also include religious groups, which oppose government regulation of any aspect of their activities. If you're a member, you believe philosophically that the First Amendment to the Constitution makes you secure from any government interference in the way you run your church. Practically, you also have a second agenda. If you can keep government completely away from your organization, you can operate day care centers without bearing the cost of complying with governmental health and safety regulations. You believe in the issues you're fighting for, but winning the battle also has a direct benefit on your bottom line.

Kingmakers (and queenmakers)

Some wealthy contributors give to political candidates because they enjoy the power that comes from helping to create a political phenomenon.

You may be a kingmaker if you

>> Enjoy being "in the know"

>> Enjoy having calls returned by important people

>> Enjoy having your favors and contributions sought

>> Are in a position to contribute and/or raise thousands or tens of thousands of dollars for a candidate

Many wealthy contributors may like to be acknowledged by people in the know, but they may shun publicity. You may or may not seek any direct financial benefit from your role as kingmaker. You may simply enjoy the social part of your power — the invitations to special parties and receptions that come from being on the A-list of important and influential people. The pride of discovering new talent may provide enough satisfaction for you.

If you're in this category, you seek the recognition that comes with your role in helping a candidate become an officeholder. You can expect to be stroked by the officeholder, to have your counsel sought and your advice heeded, and to help influence the decisions the officeholder makes.

POLITICAL MYTH

Many times, personal financial gain doesn't play a role in kingmaking, because it's too risky for the officeholder to associate closely with an adviser who stands to gain from the association. Reporters love to write stories that detail a personal gain for a key financial backer and adviser to a visible elected official. So, if at all possible, politicians shy away from relationships with large contributors who may gain in personal, financial ways from those relationships.

Special interest groups

Special interest groups are bands of like-minded individuals who contribute to candidates in order to advance their positions or to protect themselves from assaults by other interests. Chapter 8 deals with special interest groups in more detail.

IN THIS CHAPTER

» Calling your legislator

» Speaking up at town meetings

» Writing letters to your representatives

» Getting others to join you

» Cultivating media attention

Chapter **5**

Telling Politicians What's on Your Mind

When you're no longer content to be buffeted like driftwood by the waves of political change, it's time to take the plunge and communicate with some of your elected officials.

SPEAKING UP

How you communicate depends on which elected officials you're trying to contact. Communication can be pretty informal when it comes to your local elected officials. Your city-council representative or county commissioner, small-town mayor, school board representative, and state representative are all accustomed to receiving telephone calls, emails, or other communications at work or at home from voters who express their opinions and concerns directly.

The larger the size of the official's *constituency* (the group of voters that the official represents), the more difficult that official is to contact directly, which stands to reason. Officials elected by the voters of an entire state answer to millions of voters. There are simply not enough hours in a day for statewide officials (officials whose constituency is a state's entire voting population) to speak with or respond to all the voters who want to express their views directly, even if the officials are inclined to listen.

The problem is much greater with national officials. The president wouldn't have much time to hold a state dinner for the ambassador from New Guinea or natter on with NATO if they were compelled to deal with Tom, Dick, and Mary Fenster from Des Moines, Iowa, who just called to say that they're in town and would like to talk to him about that little farm bill that might adversely affect their 120 acres of soybeans.

Reaching Out and Touching Your Representatives

If you feel strongly about a local issue, whether it's the location of a liquor store or the construction of a new jail or the level of state funding for education, just pick up your phone and call, text, or email the elected official whom you think has responsibility for that issue.

REMEMBER

Calling an official's work number is more polite than calling at home, unless the official works part-time and doesn't have an office. Believe it or not, your elected officials are people, too, with business and family demands that should be respected.

TIP

Phone numbers are listed in the government sections on the web. If you can't find a phone number for the official, call the county or state party headquarters for the official's political party and ask how to reach them. State parties and candidates have websites you can use to express your ideas or concerns.

State legislatures have hotlines to the party *caucuses*, or meetings. (See Chapter 21 for a full definition of party caucuses.) You can call these hotlines to leave messages for your state representatives and state senators who are in session and are voting on bills that you read about in your morning newspaper. You also may be able to leave messages for your state legislators by calling the main staff office for the chamber in which they serve.

You can also call the congressional office for your members of Congress. You're much less likely to speak to your national representative than to your local elected official (although it never hurts to ask). It's also less likely that the opinions of a single voter will be persuasive enough to draw the elected official's direct attention. At the very least, you can leave your name and your message with a staff person — who will bring your position to the member's attention if enough people call with similar concerns. You're more likely to get satisfaction if you want help dealing with the federal government, such as if you're seeking information about a federal program or trying to speed up a Social Security check. Each representative has at least one district office, in addition to the main office in Washington, DC.

I THOUGHT YOU'D NEVER ASK!

Many legislators and members of Congress send out questionnaires to voters in their districts to solicit their opinions on important issues or pending bills. If you're registered to vote, you probably receive these questionnaires from time to time. They usually take just a few minutes to complete. If you make the effort to return these questionnaires, the elected official conducting the mailing considers your answers.

Responding to questionnaires is a painless way for you to communicate with your elected official and let them know what you're thinking. See Chapter 15 for more on how elected officials pick your brain.

TIP

If you're not sure who your state representative or senator is, you can call any of the following places:

>> Your county election board or Board of Elections for your state

>> Your local office of the League of Women Voters

>> The local headquarters of the Democratic or Republican party

>> Your local library — ask the reference librarian

>> National groups like Turbovote (https://turbovote.org), which can also assist you in determining whether you're registered and in which districts

Many states also maintain web pages that help voters identify their state legislators. Every member of Congress has staff people who keep track of the number of phone calls, emails, and letters received on an issue. The greater the number of calls, the more likely the member will pay attention to the issue and the views of the callers.

TIP

Every year, *Congressional Quarterly* (available at your local public library) publishes a Washington information directory that gives the exact address of your district's representative and your state's senators. It also includes direct phone numbers for each office. In addition, at the start of each session of Congress, most newspapers publish addresses and phone numbers for members of Congress and US senators in their area. Cut that list out of your local newspaper and put it on your refrigerator. You never know when you may have an urge to call or write.

Here are some tips for what to say when calling your member of Congress:

>> Be prepared to state your name, address, and phone number.

>> Tell the staff person precisely why you're calling.

>> Refer to the bill you're calling about by number, if you can.

>> Tell the staffer whether you support or oppose the bill and why.

>> Be patient. If an issue is hot enough, the phone lines may be busy.

Town Meetings

In addition to being available over the telephone, many legislators and members of Congress regularly hold town hall meetings when the legislature or Congress is in session. These town meetings are conducted around the district to give all voters a chance to attend. Schedules are available from the official's office.

Town meetings allow you to ask questions directly to the officials on topics you want discussed. Because these meetings aren't always well attended, they provide a good opportunity for in-depth interaction with your elected officials. They also guarantee that your opinions won't be filtered or sanitized by a staff person. Your elected official will hear from you directly, like it or not.

TIP

If the elected official doesn't know the answer to your question during the meeting, you will be given a response later. Staff will take down your name and address if your question requires further investigation. Be sure to get their business cards so that you can follow up in case you don't hear from them.

For the most part, legislators and their staffs make a point of paying dutiful attention to constituent problems and concerns; after all, legislators come up for a job performance review with the voters every time there's an election. They can't afford to get a reputation for not getting back to constituents who call with a problem or question. Indeed, solid problem-solving work from the congressional staff is considered as crucial to a congressperson's reelection as their voting record.

If you're interested in attending a town meeting, here's what you do:

1. **Call the local office for your member of Congress and ask for a schedule of town meetings.**

or

Call the main number for your state legislature and ask to speak with your representative or a staff person. Ask for a town hall meeting (sometimes called a *third house meeting*) schedule.

2. Go to the Internet and read about the issue that you want to discuss so that you're prepared to talk knowledgeably about the topic.

3. Get to the town meeting early to get a seat where you can be sure that the congressperson can't miss you when you raise your hand for questions.

REMEMBER

Don't worry that you may not know all the facts when you express your opinion to your elected official. Don't be afraid of feeling foolish. If you've done your homework but don't know all the facts, it's because the elected official and the media haven't done a good job of communicating the facts to you. And that's certainly not your fault.

Putting It in Writing

You don't have to use the phone or attend a town hall meeting to put your opinions before your elected officials. You can always dash off a letter. If your issue is time-sensitive, using the phone or sending email may be better. Most public libraries provide access to computers if you don't have one at home you can use.

Suppose that you noticed in today's paper that Senator Smith cast a vote in favor of aid to Freedonia. You're opposed to aid to Freedonia. You want Senator Smith to know of your displeasure with that vote. What do you do?

When you've analyzed the issue and are confident that you've stated your position just the way you want, call or email the senator's office — you can also find contact information online.

TIP

While your displeasure with Senator Smith is in the front of your mind, you may want to see whether the senator's opponent in the upcoming election agrees with the vote on aid to Freedonia. Contact the challenger's campaign headquarters and get the opponent's position on the same issue.

REMEMBER

Send compliments your officials who vote the way you want them to. After all, positive reinforcement can work as well as criticism.

TALK RADIO

You can post your views on issues and candidates on social media or on popular talk radio shows. Most of the national commentators and many local ones have email addresses that they broadcast, and they regularly read the emails their shows receive.

More sometimes means less

The more local the office, the less likely that office is to receive a large volume of mail, calls, or emails from voters. If an office doesn't receive a large volume of mail, the mail that the office does receive has a greater impact. The greater the impact, the higher the probability that the elected official will answer the mail personally.

Conversely, the more mail an elected official receives, the less significant the impact of one contact. Offices that receive large numbers of contacts have staff members whose sole responsibility is to reply to those contacts. The higher the volume, the less the likelihood that the official will ever see a particular piece of correspondence or email. But staff members keep track of the number of contacts received for and against a bill or an issue and then inform the official of those numbers. Sometimes, the size of those numbers may be persuasive to an official.

TIP

You can increase the impact of a letter by writing it out neatly rather than typing it in a word processor; handwritten notes take more time and, therefore, command more concern from a legislative office.

Multiplying your opinion

If writing a letter doesn't put your views in front of your official, what else can you do? The answer is *multiply*. Elected officials pay more attention to opinions that aren't yours alone. For example, if your neighbors share your opinion that a liquor store should not be located on your corner, ask them to sign your letter in support of that position. Or, better yet, ask your neighbors to write letters, too.

TIP

The most effective way to multiply is to get others to write their own letters, in their own words. Flooding the congressperson's office with form letters and postcards, although not without its attention-getting impact, isn't considered to be as effective as that personal, heartfelt letter from the individual constituent.

Here are some more tips for getting others involved and achieving strength through numbers:

>> Ask your neighbors, friends, coworkers, and relatives to write similar letters.

>> Draft and reproduce a 1-page flyer telling people why they should care about the issue. Distribute the flyer to possible letter-writers and petition-signers.

>> Circulate petitions supporting your views to people you know.

>> Recruit others to help you organize. These people can provide the core of your team and can approach their friends, relatives, coworkers, and neighbors for letter writing and petition signing.

>> Think of all the places you go where you can approach people: church, work, Little League, the supermarket, your children's school events, and so on. Then be sure to take flyers along.

>> Posting you views on social media can have an impact. See more in Chapter 9 on the how the Internet is used in political campaigns.

The first time you try to mobilize people on an issue, it seems impossible. You may be intimidated by the thought of asking five people to help. It gets easier. Those five people may provide the core and each find five others the next time you want to make your voices heard. The next time you flex your political muscle, you may draw support from 25 others, and so on, and so on.

TIP

The key is picking an issue that you and your neighbors or friends think is important and then getting started. Before too long, you may have a grassroots movement on your hands. Now the elected official is dealing not simply with one angry voter but rather with tens, hundreds, or maybe thousands of voters, if the issue is hot enough.

WARNING

Although it's fine to be passionate about your cause, ensure that none of the letters sent to your elected official is threatening or accusatory. Making officials angry or convincing them that your votes are already lost will undercut the influence of any grassroots campaign.

If you're successful in gathering substantial neighborhood support for your position, you may be able to request and secure a meeting with the elected official to make your case in person. A personal meeting with the elected official allows you and your neighbors to convince the official that you feel strongly about the issue. Certainly, you and your neighbors care enough about the issue that you've taken time from your busy schedules to meet with the official. In other words, you mean business.

You're now in a position to prove the truth of the point I make in Chapter 2 about the nature of politics: You can make the money-versus-vote analysis that the official performs on this issue work for you. (Flip to Chapter 2 to find out what this analysis is.) You're able to demonstrate to the official that actions such as allowing a liquor store in your neighborhood will cost that official a substantial number of votes in the next election.

You can show the elected official that you and hundreds or thousands of your neighbors feel so strongly about liquor stores that this issue alone will determine your votes in the next election. If the elected official is with you, those votes are available in the next election. If the elected official disregards your views, you may exact a substantial price at the voting booth.

REMEMBER

You must realize that the elected official will feel pressure to go in the opposite direction, coming from those individuals who may think that a liquor store in the neighborhood is a brilliant idea. You won't be able to tell how strong that pressure is, so you can't know whether your side will prevail. Business groups may be behind the opening. The owners of the liquor store may have contributed to the official's campaign. You can't accurately assess the strength of the opposition, but you can make your side as strong and well organized as possible. In so doing, you ensure that your views are taken seriously. The threat of a voting bloc of that size in a local election isn't one that a successful politician is likely to disregard.

Teamwork Is the Name of the Game

If the elected official ignores your letter, has their staff intercept your calls, and instructs the security guards not to let you get close enough to the official for a face-to-face conversation, how can you make certain that your opinion reaches that official? The answer is simply teamwork.

SPEAKING UP

Teamwork means recruiting other interested parties to help you make your case to an official that you can't reach by yourself. The more people or organizations you bring onboard, the more likely representatives will listen. Reinforcements can be local organizations, local chapters of national organizations, or the ultimate big gun: the media.

Other officials

Other elected officials — particularly the more approachable ones, like your own state representative and state senator — are valuable potential team members. They can intercede to gain the higher official's attention. They may even be able to schedule you an appointment with the official you're attempting to persuade so that you can make your case personally.

The local elected official may be willing to help you out once you have convinced them that many of their voters share your concerns. When you request your local official's intercession, you're subtly letting them know that you and your allies will remember their cooperation (or lack thereof) on election day. If the local official can gain the support of a group of voters, they may help you put the problem in the lap of an elected official higher up the political food chain.

Recognized organizations

Other well-known organizations can serve the same function as a local elected official in connecting you to the statewide official. Neighborhood organizations, chambers of commerce, labor unions, community groups — any organizations with the credibility to obtain the higher official's attention — can be useful allies and intermediaries. To form a team, you must recruit organizations that share your point of view.

REMEMBER

Organizations won't assist you and your neighbors unless they share your goal. So don't try to enlist the National Rifle Association in your crusade to limit the sales of handguns in your community or ask Greenpeace to help build a toxic waste dump near a fish hatchery.

The media

Another useful ally in the fight to draw attention and get results is the media. The media love reporting on events organized by ordinary citizens trying to convince their government to do the right thing. The media are likely to cover your event if you organize it well and pick a day when not too much other news is happening.

Even television may cover your event if you remember to provide interesting and creative visuals for the cameras to shoot. Elected officials pay a great deal of attention to television coverage. If you can get the television reporters to cover your event, you may get a double hit out of it. If you indicate to the reporters that you're asking your governor, senator, or big-city mayor to do something, the reporters may go to the governor, senator, or big-city mayor and ask that person to comment on your request.

When you want media attention, you need to do the following:

>> **Pick a location that provides the television cameras with something interesting to shoot.**

 An individual sitting at a desk or standing behind a podium isn't nearly as interesting as a statement or demonstration in front of the public library if the issue is censorship of library books, or on a street filled with chuckholes if the issue is road maintenance. Television news departments like to shoot tape of images that help to convey the message effectively, and not just a picture of a spokesperson reading or delivering a statement, producing the dreaded talking head.

Be creative. Think like a television producer and figure out ways to make your message more visually interesting and appealing. Also keep in mind that, in today's fast-paced newscasts, reporters use only 10- to 15-second excerpts, or *sound bites,* from your spokesperson's statement or answers to reporter's questions. So try to keep such statements and answers brief to help make sure that the meat of the message makes the air.

>> **Pick a day and a time that make it easy for the media to attend.**

Day shift reporters and news photographers generally start work around 9 a.m. So a good time to schedule your news conference or event is 9:30 a.m., which should put it among the first stories on a newsroom's daily assignment menu. Events at this time also allow the reporter to put your story on the station's noontime broadcast in addition to the early evening news shows.

Avoid scheduling your event after 3 p.m., when reporters and photographers are plunging into their hectic (bordering on maniacal) ordeal of writing and editing their stories in time for the 5 p.m. newscast.

>> **If your goal is newspaper coverage, make sure that you find out the reporter's deadlines.**

Give the reporter time to cover your story and still make the deadline.

>> **Give the reporter as much notice of the event as possible and remind them by calling the morning of the event.**

>> **Tell the media in writing what the issue is all about. Draft a simple news release telling reporters**

- Who your group is

- Why you're having your event

- What you want officials to do or not to do

- A name and a phone number to contact for additional information

>> **Organize the event to have as many people as possible attend.**

The media view the number of supporters present as a sign of importance.

>> **If you have any documents to support your position, make copies of them available to the press.**

Journalists weigh the value of a story against the difficulty of covering it. If you make your concerns easier to document and report, you're more likely to get the desired coverage.

>> **If someone can shed additional light on the problem through personal experience, have them available to talk to the press.**

Real-life stories spice up journalistic coverage. News items with a human-interest angle are much more likely to attract the attention of a reporter's audience.

>> **Identify a member of your group who will speak with the press and answer any questions.**

Be selective in choosing a spokesperson. This person must be articulate and be able to make the necessary points directly and concisely.

>> **Limit the number of speakers to the best one or two. Newspeople have deadlines and not much patience.**

REMEMBER

Nothing is guaranteed to focus the attention of officials more quickly than a television camera in the face. With the help of the media, you can make almost any elected official sit up and take notice. One of the greatest things about the United States is that any citizen with enough determination and the right issue can become a force to be reckoned with. If you feel strongly about something, go for it. Make your officials listen to you. Tell them what you think!

3

Politics is a Team Sport

IN THIS CHAPTER

» **America's two-party system**

» **The declining power of parties**

» **How political parties serve voters**

» **Splitting your vote**

» **How parties select their candidates**

Chapter **6**

Partying with Politics

A *political party* is a group of people who organize to promote common beliefs and goals by electing officials who share their views. Parties select candidates, raise money for their campaigns, encourage participation by eligible voters, and gain power by winning elections. Parties also influence the policies of government and serve as the loyal opposition when they're not in power.

Why We Have Only Two Parties

The United States has almost always had two major parties: currently, the Republican Party and the Democratic Party. Other parties, called *third parties*, have formed in this country from time to time. Sometimes these parties are organized around a single person, such as Teddy Roosevelt's Bull Moose Party (or Progressive Party) in 1912. Sometimes these third parties form around a single issue, such as George Wallace's pro-segregation American Independent Party in 1968 or the anti-alcohol Prohibition Party, which had a candidate on the ballot in every presidential election for 100 years, from 1876 to 1976.

Third parties, such as H. Ross Perot's Reform Party, can occasionally make impressive showings. But third parties seldom receive many electoral votes in presidential elections. Perot received none in 1992. The few third-party candidates who have received electoral votes have never won. Even Teddy Roosevelt, who received more electoral votes in 1912 than the Republican nominee, William Howard Taft, succeeded only in splitting the Republican vote and electing the Democrat, Woodrow Wilson.

Third parties have been known to change the outcomes of elections, even if they don't win. Conventional wisdom credits Ralph Nader's Green Party candidacy with altering the outcome of the 2000 presidential contest because he tended to attract the sort of voter who otherwise preferred Vice President Al Gore over Texas Governor George W. Bush. In 2000, Gore won the popular vote with 48.38 percent of the votes cast nationwide. Bush received 47.87 percent of the nationwide popular vote.

In Florida, George Bush received 48.85% of the vote in 2000. Al Gore received 48.84%. Ralph Nader received 1.63% or 97,488 votes. The third-party vote for Ralph Nader was more than 180 times the margin of George Bush's victory in Florida. Winning the electoral votes in Florida gave George Bush the electoral votes he needed to reach the magic number of 271 and win the election.

In 2016, Hillary Clinton received 65,853,516, votes which is 2,871,691 more votes than Donald Trump's 62,981,825 votes. But, as you know if you're reading the entire book, the electoral vote (I discuss this topic more in Chapter 22) determines who becomes president: The pivotal states for putting Donald Trump over the top, with 304 votes, were Wisconsin, Florida, Pennsylvania, and Ohio.

A Libertarian Party candidate in Wisconsin, Michigan, and Pennsylvania, Gary Johnson, received more than the number of votes separating Donald Trump and Hillary Clinton in those key states. In Wisconsin, Gary Johnson received 106,674 votes or 3.6% of the votes cast. Donald Trump received 48.2% and Hillary Clinton 47.5%. In the closest race for president in Michigan history, Gary Johnson received 173,057 or 3.6% of the votes. Donald Trump received 47.50% and Hillary Clinton received 47.27%. In Pennsylvania, Gary Johnson received 146,715 votes or 2.4%. Donald Trump received 48.2% and Hillary Clinton received 47.5%. In short, the number of votes cast for the Libertarian Party candidate for president in these three states was many times the number of votes which determined victory or defeat and the outcome of the Electoral College vote, even though the Libertarian Party candidate did not win one electoral vote himself.

The 2016 election was also unique because a record seven electors in the electoral college defected, declining to vote for the candidate they were supposed to support.

The big-tent theory

In the United States, the two major political parties are essentially big tents: They allow room for many different approaches and policies, all under the same banner. The parties don't enforce rigid adherence to party policies by refusing to attach the party label to those members who don't agree with everything the party says and does.

The big-tent theory of parties in this country is necessary because the electoral system discourages splinter parties. Ours is largely a winner-take-all system. Members of Congress win election from districts, each of which gives a single congressional seat to whoever wins the most votes. Similarly, the presidential candidate who gets the most support in a state usually receives all of the state's electoral votes. The United States doesn't have proportional representation in Congress or the state legislatures. Under *proportional representation* systems, parties win seats in legislatures in accordance with the percentage of the vote cast for their party.

Various methods are used by states to select candidates in the general election. The most common method now used is the primary. There are several types of primaries:

>> **Closed Primary:** This method is used by 12 states and only voters who have previously identified themselves as belonging to a party are able to vote for the candidates for that party. Massachusetts permits previously unaffiliated voters to declare for a party in its closed primary.

>> **Semi-closed Primary:** In 14 states, voters may vote for one party's candidates only.

>> **Open Primary:** In 11 states, voters may vote for one party's candidate for an office and another party's candidate for other offices.

>> **Blanket or Jungle Primary:** Voters choose among all candidates for an office regardless of the candidate's party affiliation. The top two candidates for any office will then be on the ballot in the general election. Washington, California, Alaska, and Louisiana use this method, but not for Presidential primaries. In Louisiana, if a candidate for an office receives a majority vote, he or she wins the office — no general election is held.

A handful of states choose their nominees by caucus and do not hold primaries. For more on caucuses, see Chapter 20.

A winner-take-all system discourages third-party candidates and third parties. It also limits the options available to the voter. Because success is limited to one of two parties, the parties must select candidates with the broadest possible appeal. Controversial candidates with bold ideas aren't favored under this system. Parties seek candidates who represent the lowest common denominator of appeal to voters — that is, the broadest possible appeal with the lowest potential for alienating voters. Single-issue candidates, like controversial candidates, are disfavored.

WHEN IN ROME . . .

Although the United States practices winner-take-all elections, the experience in other countries is different. Many other countries allow proportional representation of the political parties in their legislative bodies.

Proportional representation increases the likelihood that smaller parties will win some elected offices, which permits smaller parties to be players. When ruling coalitions are formed to piece together a majority in the legislative body of a country, smaller parties that have won seats by way of proportional representation have bargaining power. That ability to have political power encourages smaller parties to continue playing the political game.

In Italy, for example, putting together a government may take a coalition of seven, eight, or more parties. Each of those parties bargains for something from the coalition leader in exchange for the party's support. The party may have a minister or two selected from its ranks for service in the new government, and so on. The parties can have influence even though they received a tiny percentage of the popular vote in the election.

This system permits the formation of small, well-organized parties that advocate one issue or a small group of issues. Proportional representation and coalition-building permit these parties to play a role in government and policy that isn't available in the American system.

Third parties

The odds against third parties winning the presidential election are so great that it's difficult for them to get a toehold. Campaigns are so expensive that third-party candidates must have a huge amount of personal wealth to launch a national campaign.

Ross Perot spent tens of millions of his own dollars in his two efforts to run for president. He managed to get about 19 percent of the votes cast for president in 1992, but he received none of the electoral votes. His support dropped in 1996.

POLITICAL STUFF

Perot may have run under the banner of United We Stand, a campaign organization that resembled a political party, but he was, in reality, an independent candidate. (*Independent* candidates are different from third–party candidates in that they're running purely on their own views and merits, not as representatives of an overarching group or party.) No one organized an effort to run other United We Stand candidates. Perot later converted his organization into an official political party, the Reform Party, but it had only moderate success in the late 1990s.

The 19 percent of the popular vote received by Ross Perot is the largest percentage received by a third-party candidate for president in US history. Many political pundits regard his impressive showing, despite his on-again, off-again candidacy, as a symptom that the two major parties aren't meeting the needs of the voters.

Many political commentators think that the United States will see more successful third-party candidates during this era of voter alienation from the political process. But the odds are that a third party will probably have no more to show for its efforts to elect candidates than some considerable expenses or spoiling the results for one of the two main party candidates. Presidential elections in the United States are winner-take-all, even without a majority, and that system definitely favors the two party system. Occasionally, an independent candidate can be elected if the circumstances are right, but that's an individual candidate, not an entire slate of candidates running under the banner of a third party. (See the following section for more on independent candidates.)

REMEMBER

Dominance by two political parties doesn't mean that the same two political parties will always dominate. It's possible that a third party could gain momentum by advocating the right issue at the right time and eclipse one of the two major political parties. The names and perhaps the philosophies of the two political parties might change under those circumstances, but the number of major political parties would probably remain the same.

Independent candidates

Being elected as an independent is considerably easier in theory than in reality. Independent candidates must build the structural support that parties otherwise provide for their candidates. They must raise the money to get their message across on their own. Unless the candidate is independently wealthy, running as an independent is a *difficult* proposition.

If all the stars, the sun, and the moon are in alignment, it's possible for independent candidates to win elections. But don't bet your farm on the outcome — you might have to move in a hurry.

Departing from the party

Parties in America are entirely different animals than parties in other countries. Candidates, not parties, drive the American political process. The American electorate, by and large, votes for the candidate, not for the political party the candidate represents. Sometimes, if a popular candidate belongs to an unpopular political party, that candidate deliberately downplays their party affiliation. Often, the candidate's ads may not even mention the party. The candidate may refuse to appear in advertisements or printed campaign material with the party's candidates for other offices. Campaigns in America these days can be largely solo performances rather than team competitions.

Voters value independence

In the United States, *straight-ticket voting,* or voting for all the candidates of a single party, has declined as a number of states have changed their laws to eliminate it. Eleven states have changed their laws on straight ticket voting in the last 20 or so years. (See "Straight-Ticket Voting versus Ticket Splitting," later in this chapter.) Candidates seek opportunities to demonstrate their independence, which can extend to becoming mavericks within their own political parties. Voters view independence as a positive, not a negative, characteristic.

Officeholders relish nothing more than opportunities to show that they can't be ordered around by anyone. Voters value officeholders who show a willingness to "stand up" and swim against the tide. Voters aren't impressed by party discipline or team players.

Legislation requires cooperation

Getting elected because of your independence is one thing. Doing anything after you're elected is another. The attitude that a candidate is their own person and not answerable to anyone, which may help them get elected, works *against* their being able to pass legislation, where the emphasis is put on teamwork.

When you're dealing with Congress, getting those majorities involves convincing quite a few representatives and senators. It takes 218 votes for any legislation to pass the House of Representatives, and it takes another 51 votes for anything to pass the Senate. (In fact, in the Senate, some key bills require 60 votes to pass.) For a bill to become law, it must pass both houses of Congress — usually, with a majority vote. That means 217 other mavericks in the House and 50 in the Senate must agree with the legislation that the representative or senator is attempting to pass. If all the officeholder has done during the session is demonstrate independence by swimming against the tide, why should any other legislators bother to help that person pass legislation? Why should other members of Congress take risks for someone who won't take risks for them?

REMEMBER

Compromise and consensus are the essence of good legislation. No representative or senator can accomplish anything alone, other than to gain the reputation of a maverick. Any legislation needed by a district or state, or any public policy sought to be enacted because it benefits voters, must have the support of a majority in both houses of the legislature.

Only Nebraska has a lone legislative house. All other states have two houses that must pass legislation before it can become law. Even in Nebraska, a majority of the 49 elected representatives must vote to enact legislation.

Those Were the Days

Before candidates began to use television and social media to speak directly to voters, they were identified by their parties. In your parents' or grandparents' day, parties had a much greater influence on candidates — as well as more power over them.

Television, cable, and social media are such pervasive parts of the culture that it's difficult to imagine life without them. In earlier eras, parties were the vehicles by which candidates communicated with other voters. Party workers contacted their *constituents,* those voters they were responsible for representing, personally. They distributed literature to help voters make decisions. Parties needed volunteers to make those contacts, but little else. Candidates relied on the parties to help with their campaigns. The parties provided the only effective way of reaching the people and persuading them to vote a certain way. Because candidates and officeholders needed the parties in order to win elections, the parties had influence with them. They could use that influence to encourage elected officials to do things voters wanted — things that the officials might otherwise be reluctant to do.

Party officials who knew the ins and outs of politics followed closely the actions of elected officials. Those party officials knew precisely what an officeholder had to do to ensure passage of a bill. They weren't fooled by the fancy footwork or double-talk of an elected official and understood the issues and the procedural maneuvers involved in bill passage. They followed what happened on important issues and took retaliatory action if officials failed to live up to their commitments.

In short, there was accountability. An elected official was directly responsible to someone other than large contributors. In the "old days" (not to say the "good old days") of party bosses the system had its flaws. For example, before the widespread use of primaries, party bosses chose candidates for many offices, and these candidates were chosen because the leaders were comfortable with them. But once the candidates were elected, they were required to keep commitments. If an officeholder failed to keep a commitment, the party could deny that person the party's nomination for reelection.

Television and the decline of party power

The advent of television in political campaigns changed the dynamic of campaigning. Today, parties are no longer monolithic structures that control political life in America. Now, with the help of the old boob tube — and even more with the rise of social media — candidates take the issues directly *to* the voters and draw their power directly *from* the voters. This process creates problems.

The cost of campaigning

In today's politics, candidates can buy network television, cable TV, radio, social media, and online time to talk directly to you. They can hold town halls and press conferences and appear on television and radio talk shows. They can send email to lists or tweet their ideas to reporters or constituents. All these options guarantee candidates the media coverage to take their message over the heads of the party members and into the homes of the voters.

"What's wrong with that?" you may ask. Shouldn't candidates and officeholders communicate directly with the people who elected them? Isn't that what a democracy is all about? Of course they should. The issue isn't *whether* they should communicate; the issue is *how* they communicate.

REMEMBER

Network television and targeted cable television are effective ways to communicate, but they're also costly. In a contest between a candidate with money and a candidate with party support, the candidate with money usually wins. That person becomes the nominee of the party, whether the party leaders like it or not. The truth is, money limits the field of candidates in statewide and congressional races. Either candidates must be rich enough to finance their own campaigns or be able to persuade people with money to make substantial contributions.

Today, party leaders can't control who runs as their candidate, and candidates no longer need party leaders in order to communicate with you and other voters.

Officeholders have the power of incumbency to raise large sums of money for reelection. Those large sums give them further insulation and protection from accountability to the political parties.

Contributors gain the upper hand

Television has not only undermined the ability of party organizations to enforce accountability — it has also tremendously increased the cost of campaigning. Candidates must spend enormous amounts of time raising money to enable them to communicate via network television, cable TV, radio, direct mail, and social media and online time. To raise the enormous amounts of money required, officials must court those individuals and groups that can make substantial campaign contributions.

WARNING

Those individuals and groups that help the officials raise the necessary amounts of campaign money seldom do it solely out of a desire for good government. These contributors do hold the officials accountable — for their own agenda of interest, that is. It's no accident that incumbents have a significant advantage in the fund-raising area. After all, if you're a contributor interested in influence, the office-holder is a proven winner. That person is in a position to help the contributor's agenda, at least as long as they keep winning.

This is accountability of a sort. Now officials are listening more to a few contributors and less to the Tom, Dick, and Mary who comprise the voters in their districts. Ask yourself who is more likely to represent your interests on these issues and votes: wealthy contributors or Tom, Dick, and Mary?

REMEMBER

Perhaps it's not in your interests to allow the decline of party influence to continue. Maybe it's time you and your neighbors got involved in the party of your choice.

Voters can be duped

Now, you may say that all elected officials are ultimately accountable to the voters, so what's the problem? Don't the voters have the final say in this process? Isn't that the final check on abuses in the system?

In theory, that's true. However, today's society is so complex and fast moving that it's totally unrealistic to expect you, the voter, to follow each issue as closely as necessary to make officials accountable. Of course, in this modern age, numerous citizen groups spend extensive amounts of money and effort to monitor this complex system. They alert journalists when public officials are misbehaving, and journalists usually pass that story on to their audience. But so few voters keep current on public affairs that this indirect monitoring system may not give voters the control they should have. Clever officeholders may be able to have their cake and eat it, too.

WARNING

Elected officials, particularly legislators, can position themselves to claim to have supported both sides of an issue. To do this, an official may vote on a procedural matter to kill a proposal and then vote for final passage of the measure. The official can then "legitimately" claim to one group of constituents that he was *for* the measure and then, to another group of constituents, claim to have voted *against* the measure. Given this ploy, how can voters be expected to hold their officials accountable?

Not every elected official pulls this type of stunt, but it's much too common. An official who does try it, and who has enough money to get their message out in a campaign.

You can't possibly monitor all the nuances of an official's voting record on any and all issues. After all, you have enough to do already with work, home, children, parents, and perhaps church or Little League. Anyway, you'd have difficulty getting the type of detailed information necessary to assess the importance of every vote even if you had the time.

Some organizations do track every vote of interest to the group. These special-interest groups then publish the results to their membership and sometimes to the public. Senior citizens' groups, business groups, environmental groups, chambers of commerce, labor unions, citizen watchdog groups, and the like watch every procedural and substantive vote on their issues and attempt to hold elected officials accountable for their votes. If the group is large enough or influential enough in the elected official's district, accountability can be enforced.

On issues not followed by such groups, accountability is absent. Officials can talk out of both sides of their mouths without serious consequences.

Straight-Ticket Voting versus Ticket Splitting

Perhaps as a consequence of the increased polarization of the electorate, voters seem more willing to vote for all the nominees of the party of their choice. The idea that voters choose to vote for the candidate and make independent decisions about their choices seems to be a thing of the past.

Ticket splitting — that is, voting for the nominees of one party for some offices and the nominees of another party for other offices — had been declining in part because a number of states had changed the practice of requiring a voter to choose a party before being able to vote for any candidates. However, in the 2018 general election, every state that elected a Republican senator voted for Donald Trump in 2016. Every state that elected a Democratic senator that year went for Hillary Clinton in 2016. In one recent estimate, in 2018 the number of straight-ticket voters in elections has actually increased in a number of states to 50 percent or higher.

The increase in straight-party voting affects all offices. For example, Professor Steve Rogers of St. Louis University claims in a study that the single most important factor in state legislative races is whether the voters approve or disapprove of the president of the United States. If they approve, they vote the party of the incumbent president. If they disapprove, they vote the opposite party.

That means political parties may nominate up-and-coming candidates for lesser political offices with the confidence that their party affiliation alone would carry those candidates to victory in the election. Voters don't need to be educated about the qualifications and issues in these lesser offices, because the party identification alone would ensure that sufficient votes were cast to elect these people on the coattails of the top of the party's ticket.

Political Parties Serve a Purpose

Despite the fact that the majority of voters call themselves independents, political parties still serve as vital components of the political system in America. They provide various important civic services that are essential to the election process. (The "independents" aren't really that independent, either, since they tend to vote the same way year after year.)

Ensuring a fair election

Political parties and their supporters choose the candidates from whom you pick when you vote in the general election, but they also perform many other functions that enable elections to occur without much controversy.

Political parties are responsible for finding people to work everywhere that voters cast their ballots on election day. Volunteers monitor voting places and count and record ballots. In short, the political parties provide workers to guarantee that elections are held in as open and fair a manner as possible.

Watchers

Each political party must provide *watchers* to ensure that elections are conducted according to the law. Those workers make certain that their candidates' right to an election free of fraud and intimidation is respected.

POLITICAL STUFF

As many states move to centralized voting made possible by computers, fewer watchers are needed than when everyone voted in their own neighborhood. Nonetheless, each party is entitled to an equal number of watchers at every voting place. The precinct committeeperson or chair of the local party appoints the watchers for each voting place. Each candidate on the ballot is also entitled to a watcher at every polling place. The campaign manager for a candidate issues a piece of paper that identifies the volunteer as a watcher for a particular candidate.

Let the party find the people

Candidates are free to provide their own poll watchers for each voting place in the district in which they're running. Few candidates do so. Finding the number of volunteers necessary to cover each voting place is difficult. Having each party do it for all the party's candidates makes more sense than having 10 or 15 candidates finding volunteers to cover all the voting places necessary.

Counting ballots

Although the number of states using electronic voting machines is rising, a few places still use paper ballots. In those jurisdictions, the parties provide workers to count the undisputed ballots and record the disputed ballots so that election boards or courts can determine whether those ballots should be counted.

Precinct workers have several alternatives when counting paper ballots. They may agree to

>> Count a ballot because, although there may be mistakes, it's clear whom the voter wanted to vote for

>> Count a ballot partially — that is, to count it for some offices where the voter's intent is clear but not for one or more offices where it's unclear what the voter was trying to do

>> Not count a ballot

At the precinct level, the workers need only count the paper ballots they agree on and put the others aside. Most of the time, the workers at the precinct level resolve all disputes as fairly as they can.

If the representatives of both political parties can't agree, the ballot is disputed. State law determines whether a disputed ballot is ultimately counted.

Ballots are disputed for various reasons, as in these examples:

>> The voter voted for two people for the same office.

>> A ballot contains marks that might identify the voter. (All paper ballots are cast anonymously.)

>> The voter used a paper ballot for the wrong legislative or congressional district.

>> The results of a ballot scan are indefinite. Some punch card ballots require that voters use a stylus to punch out a piece of cardboard held at four places. If voters don't sever all four corners, the optical scanner that counts votes will

read the card differently each time the ballot is scanned. This problem was the source of the infamous *hanging chad* that you heard about *ad nauseam* during the Florida 2000 presidential recount.

Increasingly, however, states are using electronic machines that read the paper ballot completed by the voter and tally the number of votes cast for each candidate.

TIP

If you're interested in helping on election day, contact the precinct committee-person for your political party. If you want to work on election day to help a particular candidate, call the campaign headquarters for that candidate and let the staff know that you're willing to volunteer. Your political party will be delighted to train you; it never has enough good election-day workers.

Getting out the vote

In addition to ensuring a minimum of shenanigans at the voting places, parties perform what is commonly referred to as grassroots activities. *Grassroots* political activity begins with registering people to vote and continues with polling voters and making voting as easy as possible.

Registering voters

If you volunteer for grassroots activities, you may find yourself going door-to-door to register people to vote and identifying them as sympathetic to or opposed to your candidate or party. You don't usually get paid for performing this important function, but it's a way for you to be involved in politics and meet your neighbors at the same time.

REMEMBER

Although government employees register voters who come into government offices, they don't provide this service in people's homes. Door-to-door registration is usually a volunteer effort by civic-minded people like you.

Polling a precinct

After registering all potential voters, conscientious party people begin to poll their precinct. *Polling a precinct* means canvassing voters in that precinct in person or by phone to determine which party's candidates the voters are likely to support.

A precinct poll is unlike a poll by professional pollsters. A precinct poll doesn't consist of a randomly drawn sample of registered voters from the district where demographic information, but not the identity of the individual voter, is important. A precinct poll is designed to identify each and every voter in the district by name. Party workers need to know which voters they should be encouraging to vote on election day.

Volunteers canvass by knocking on doors or calling people on the phone, identifying the party or candidate they're working for, and asking a few simple questions. The approach goes something like this:

Hi! I'm Bill Monroe. I'm your neighbor just down the street, and I'm taking a voter poll for the Democrats. Do you mind if I ask you a few quick questions?

>> Are you registered to vote?

>> How many others are registered to vote in this household?

>> Do you consider yourself a Democrat, a Republican, or an independent?

>> This November, our city will have an election to choose a mayor. Do you plan to vote in that election?

>> The candidates are Democrat Joe Blow and Republican Mike Smith. For whom will you vote?

Volunteers are trained on how to react to the different responses they may get when conducting a precinct poll:

>> If the voter tells the Democratic pollster that they plan to vote for the Democratic candidate, the pollster asks how the other voters in the household feel. He asks whether the voter needs an absentee ballot or any assistance in getting to the voting place on Election Day.

>> If the voter tells the pollster that they haven't made up their mind, the pollster gives them literature about the candidate and perhaps talks to them about their party's nominee to help persuade the voter to vote for their candidate.

>> If the voter tells the Democratic worker that they're a Republican who's supporting the Republican candidate, the pollster politely thanks them for their time and leaves.

Polling a precinct is a time-consuming project for which the party worker usually isn't compensated. That poll can provide candidates with useful information about voters whom they need to persuade. It also helps the party worker do their job of turning out more voters who will vote for their party's candidates.

Making it easy to vote

Party organizations are service organizations. They want to help you, the voter, by making it easier for you to vote . . . and, in particular, to vote for their candidates. Political parties can do some specific things for you. They can

>> Tell you which district you live in and who your candidates are

>> Tell you the location of your voting place

>> Assist you in obtaining absentee ballots and rides to the polling places

Individuals who are ill, disabled, out of the state on election day, or away at college are all prospects to vote by *absentee ballot.* Such voters can mail in their ballots. Or, in the case of a shut-in voter, election representatives go to the voter's home with a paper ballot for the voter to fill in.

SPEAKING UP

Not every party organization has its act together; you may ask for something and not get it. But you never know whether your local party organization can help you until you try to use it. Call a party when you have a question or need help. Most party organizations have a headquarters with telephones. If yours doesn't, find out the name and phone number of the county or city chairperson for your party and call the person at home. If you don't ask, you won't receive!

Reminding you to vote

The party and its workers also help the candidates remind citizens to vote on election day. Motivating citizens to vote in nonpresidential elections is a difficult, time-consuming, and expensive task. The party organization can help candidates by making the person-to-person or neighbor-to-neighbor contact. These efforts can turn out an additional five or ten votes per precinct.

Providing information

Political parties can even help you decide which candidate to vote for in the election. If you want to make direct contact with a candidate, the party can tell you how to contact them. If you have a specific question about a candidate, the party can help you get the answer to your question. For example, parties can give you voting records of incumbents to allow you to judge for yourself where they stand.

WARNING

Keep in mind that the information a party provides you about its candidate is drafted to persuade you to vote for that candidate. The material that parties provide voters isn't objective; or, in political terms, it's *partisan.* A party's literature tells you all the good things about that party's candidates without educating you on any flaws its candidates may have. That is to be expected, but you should be aware when you read it that you're receiving only one side of the story. Before you make up your mind, ask the opponent's party to give you the other side.

A SINGLE VOTE *DOES* MAKE A DIFFERENCE!

The extra votes that a party volunteer tries to squeeze out can make the difference between winning and losing an election. When John F. Kennedy was elected president in 1960, his margin of victory over Richard M. Nixon was less than one vote per precinct nationwide. In 2000 when George W. Bush defeated Al Gore by a single electoral vote, George Bush won because he carried the state of Florida: 5,963,110 votes were cast in Florida in 2000. George Bush's margin of victory in Florida was 537 votes!

When Donald Trump won the electoral college in 2016 by carrying Pennsylvania, Wisconsin and Michigan, the combined total of votes by which he carried all four states was 54,000. Think about that. Almost 129 million votes were cast and the difference between winning and losing was 54,000 votes in these states. If 54,000 voters had changed their votes proportionally in the three states, Hillary Clinton would have received 278 electoral votes and be the president. Who says each vote doesn't count?

Amplifying your voice

Making elected officials listen to you can be difficult if you're the only one talking. When other people join you in making noise, you're much more likely to gain attention. Political parties can turn a single voice crying in the wilderness into a chorus.

US parties may not enforce rigid party discipline and require their members to support a particular ideology, but they can help to clarify issues and to simplify your choices on election day. Parties can also help you make your voice heard. They can help to focus attention on issues or policies that mean something to you.

Many Americans join or identify with political parties in order to magnify their influence on the political process. One voter on their own has a tough time changing policy or the political process. But that one political voice (or vote) crying in the wilderness can have an impact if others join it. Just as your modest contribution to the candidate you support can multiply when you solicit your friends, neighbors, relatives, and coworkers (see Chapter 5), your lone vote can have a multiplier effect. When you join with others who feel about the issues as you do, your voice becomes loud enough to be heard. You can make your voice so loud that officeholders and candidates ignore it only at their own peril.

Of course, you can always form your own coalition of citizens who think as you do on an issue and bypass political parties. That approach requires organizational skill, time, and effort, but it is possible.

Choosing the Candidates

On election day, you may ask yourself, "How did these two alternatives wind up on my ballot? How come I get to choose only the lesser of two evils?"

Party nominees

Parties in America are the main vehicles for selecting nominees for office. Parties and voters supporting political parties have the responsibility of weeding through the large number of candidates who may file for a particular elective office.

There's no real secret to candidate selection: Party people prefer to select their candidates from among those people they know and know well. Party people are no different from the rest of us. We are all more comfortable with things and people we know.

Party people get to know a candidate in one of two ways: They have either been active in the party organization itself or have been a candidate in the past.

Choosing one of their own

Nobody likes to nominate a candidate for an important office who hasn't earned political spurs first. Candidates are first expected to work for the party organization, performing a variety of functions from precinct work to fundraising. Would-be candidates are also expected to have labored in the vineyards of other campaigns. Both of these activities demonstrate to party people that the would-be candidate is *really* a Democrat or Republican. After a candidate puts in an apprenticeship, party people recognize that it's the candidate's time to run. A common expression is "It's their turn."

Party workers like candidates who demonstrate commitment to the party team. After all, party people value the functions performed by party organizations. Because they value the party's work, it's natural that activists would expect candidates to value that work, too. A candidate truly demonstrates their regard for the party and its work by performing those tasks, preferably for some length of time, before becoming a candidate for office.

Recycled candidates

Another way party activists know would-be candidates well enough to nominate them for office is when the candidate is *recycled*: That is, the candidate ran in the past, for either the office in question or another office. The level of comfort that comes with a recycled candidate encourages many of the same people to run over and over again for the same or another, comparable office.

POLITICAL STUFF

TERM LIMITS AND RECYCLED CANDIDATES

It isn't unusual for one person to serve at different times in different county-elected offices. In a political career, a candidate may serve as county treasurer, county assessor, county auditor, and/or county clerk. Ironically, this recycling of candidates occurs because of term limits. For years, many local governments have imposed term limits on the number of times a candidate may be elected to a particular office. For example, in some jurisdictions, a person may be elected county auditor, assessor, clerk, or sheriff for only two terms. But the statutes are silent about the total number of years or terms an officeholder may have in all elected offices.

Term limits were designed to keep officeholders from becoming arrogant and complacent. Advocates for term limits believe that taxpayers receive better service from officeholders who have a definite term of office to complete their improvements on the office and make their marks as officeholders. New blood is introduced into the election process at regular intervals. These new candidates are supposed to invigorate elected offices by generating new ideas and creating fresh approaches to public service.

Some people feel that officeholders should serve for brief, distinct periods as elected officials before resuming their careers in the private sector, rather than having office holder who are career politicians. The country doesn't have many citizens serving their communities for brief stints in elected offices. Ordinary citizens interested in public service aren't being nominated on anything approaching a regular basis. We have *career officeholders:* The same recycled candidates move from one position to another as the term limits expire, in an elaborate game of musical chairs.

Other people believe that officeholders who serve for substantial periods of time bring a level of expertise and experience to the position they hold. You should decide for yourself whether experience or newness are the qualities you want in a candidate.

Does the complacent county assessor who views the office as a personal fiefdom become an exemplary public servant by moving two doors down the hall in the county office building and changing their title? Of course not! The title may change, but the quality of service for the taxpayer stays the same.

Recycled candidates are more likely to be nominated by conventions or caucuses because the party activists who attend them prefer recycling. When ordinary voters like you don't participate in primary elections to select the nominees of the parties for office, the party activists who do vote have more influence because fewer votes are cast.

Candidates will continue to be recycled until you get involved and convince party activists to set their sights higher for candidate selection.

Some of the more influential party workers may be currently, or may have once been, employed by the recycled candidate when they were an officeholder in the past. These influential party workers have a vested interest in the candidate.

The party workers may know that the recycled candidate won't set the world on fire. The recycled candidate may not be the best candidate the party could put forward, but the person probably isn't the worst candidate, either. The party workers know what they and the voters are getting with a recycled candidate. That knowledge raises the party workers' comfort level. It's the unknown that is frightening, after all. These are the factors that party workers think about when choosing a candidate. (See Chapter 13 for some things you may want to consider in selecting candidates.)

Primaries

The primary allows parties and the voters who identify with these parties to choose the candidate who will be the nominee of that party for each office in the next general election. Either directly (by way of primaries) or indirectly (by electing delegates in primaries who go to state conventions and vote on the nominees), the primary determines your choices on the ballot in the next general election.

Voters increasingly use the primary to select candidates for office. When primaries were first used, they were viewed as a democratic alternative to the control of the nominating process by party bosses sitting in smoke-filled rooms. Now primary selection is more common than convention or caucus selection for nominees. That is particularly true for the office of president. Voters express their preference for presidential candidates by primary in 41 states. However, in some states the political party of an incumbent president may decide not to hold a presidential primary or caucus, on the assumption that the incumbent will be nominated again. In 2020, for example, four state Republican parties have decided not to hold their presidential caucuses, or primaries on the assumption that Donald Trump will be nominated again. In 2012, several state Democratic parties did the same, assuming (correctly) that Barack Obama would be nominated again. The distribution of delegates to the national conventions of the parties where the president and vice president are chosen are proportional to the showing of the candidates in the primaries.

REMEMBER

Most states have what are called *closed* primaries. That means voters who are registered to vote as Republicans may vote only for Republican candidates (and registered Democrats can only vote for Democratic candidates). An open primary method allows voters to vote in either primary, regardless of their registration or past votes. Whether the primary is open or closed, voters must choose one ballot. They may not vote for a Republican candidate for one office and a Democratic candidate for another in a primary election. There's too much opportunity for mischief if Democrats can help pick Republican candidates and vice versa.

Caucuses are held in the following states: Iowa, Alaska, Nevada, North Dakota, Kansas, Wyoming, Hawaii, Maine, Washington, (Democratic only), and Kentucky (Republican only). See Chapter 21 for more on caucuses.

Primary elections are seen as a reform because they allow more people to participate in the selection process for candidates. In primary elections, even if only 25 to 35 percent of those eligible to vote in a statewide primary do so, you're still talking about reaching hundreds of thousands of voters.

WARNING

Unfortunately, primaries increase the cost of campaigning significantly. Primaries are a much more expensive method of selecting candidates than conventions. If you're concerned about the rising cost of campaigns, you should be aware that primaries are one reason for the higher cost. You can decide whether the increase in the cost of a campaign is worth the opportunity for more people to participate in the nomination process.

Conventions

Those delegates you elect in primaries go to the state convention of your political party and choose the party's nominees for other, less visible statewide elected offices, sometimes called *down-ballot offices* too. In states that elect an attorney general, a secretary of state, a state treasurer, a state auditor, and so on, nominees for these offices are usually selected by the state conventions of the political parties.

Convention selection for down-ballot positions is a less expensive method of choosing candidates for less-visible offices. A candidate running in a convention doesn't have to spend as much money campaigning to reach 1,000 or 2,000 delegate votes as they would have to spend to reach a majority of voters in a primary election in the entire state.

TIP

You can have a role to play in the selection of convention nominees by either running as a delegate yourself or asking the delegate candidates, who want your vote, whom they're prepared to support at the convention. You can then vote for the delegate who will support the candidate you want nominated.

Any voter who declares their party affiliation can run for election as a convention delegate. See Chapter 20 to find out how you can become a delegate.

REMEMBER

Conventions are cheaper for the candidate to run, and they're also less expensive for taxpayers. It costs taxpayers millions of dollars to conduct a statewide primary. Convention or caucus selection costs the taxpayers nothing.

The role of ideology in candidate selection

Background plays a more significant role than ideology in the selection of nominees for local offices. How candidates for county clerk feel about the balanced budget amendment or abortion is less important than how candidates for Congress feel about those issues.

Ideology doesn't have much impact at the local level, where the main function of an office is administrative. But when an office involves setting public policy, ideology plays a vital role in the selection process for both parties. Party activists choose these candidates in significant part because of their ideology, whether such a choice may cost the party support in the general election or not. Many party people are active in politics because they feel strongly about policy issues. They have policies they want to see implemented, and they have policies they want to see undone. They do their work to elect candidates because they want to make a difference in their community, state, or nation. If you understand why many activists become, and remain, involved, you will understand that policy considerations play an important role in the selection of candidates for policy-formulating offices.

When you understand that background, you can appreciate the fact that candidates must support certain litmus-test issues in both parties if they're to stand a reasonable chance to be nominated by party activists. A *litmus-test issue* is one which, by their support or rejection of that issue alone, candidates prove themselves to be ideologically in line with their party. In other words, other party members won't regard someone who fails that litmus test as a true member of their party.

The parties try to enforce ideological conformity on their candidates by requiring commitments to certain key policies supported by most party activists. The parties require these commitments even though making such commitments may not assist candidates in the general election. They require these commitments and leave the candidates to assume the risks associated with supporting these positions. The commitments aren't meant to help or hurt their candidates' chances for election; they're so required because they're important to the party activists.

REMEMBER

To make certain that the litmus tests are few in number and reflect your views, you need to participate in the candidate selection process. The old adage is an accurate one: If you want to make sure that something is done right, do it yourself! The only way you can be absolutely confident that your alternatives on election day provide you with good choices is to choose those alternatives yourself. You need to get involved in the selection process for candidates early.

Chapter **7**

Taking Sides

You're in a position to decide whether you want to associate with a political party. You can choose to join the Republican Party, the Democratic Party, or a third party. You're the only one who can decide which party you should join and what joining it means for you. Reading this chapter may help you decide.

Putting Parties in Their Place

As early as the 1790s, political parties had influence on the electoral college. In those days, the electoral college consistently played a much more important role than the official role it usually has today. (For more on the electoral college, read Chapters 22 and 23.) Of course, the electoral college *did* play a determining role in the 2000 and 2016 presidential elections, when the losing candidates won the popular vote but lost in the electoral college.

POLITICAL STUFF

Every president in this nation's history has had the support of one of the major political parties of their time. No candidate from a third or minor party has ever been elected president of the United States.

Although this country has had two major political parties at all times, the names and the groups supporting these political parties have changed over the years. The positions the parties have taken on issues have also evolved. It's not important for you to know all the twists and turns the parties have followed in becoming what they are today. Here are the only two things to know (so that you can casually mention them at parties):

>> The Democrat-Republicans of Thomas Jefferson's day became the Democrats of Andrew Jackson's time, and that party is today's Democratic Party.

>> The Grand Old Party (or GOP), as the Republicans are known, is actually the younger organization. It formed just before the Civil War, taking the place formerly held by the Whigs and, before them, the Federalists.

For the past 130 years, the two major parties of this country have been the Democrats and the Republicans. These two parties compete to win elections and the support of voters.

Identifying by Political Party

Joining a political party definitely has its advantages. You can

>> Enjoy a more substantial role in selecting the candidates you get to choose from in the general election.

>> Help shape issues for your party and its elected officials. Your voice is louder when you belong to a group of people who think about the issues the same way you do.

>> Begin working, as a party activist, to restore accountability for elected officials.

So, how do you become a member of a political party? You simply declare yourself a member. Call yourself a Democrat or a Republican and then you are one. You won't find a master list of all Democratic Party and Republican Party members. They have no pledges to sign or membership cards to issue, and no dues or bizarre initiation ceremonies. You are what you say you are — with certain limitations. You can increase the likelihood of being identified as a political party member by

>> **Voting in a primary election:** In some states, you're viewed as a member of a party by voting for the party of your choice in a primary election. When you do that, voting lists in your county and state show the party for which you vote.

WARNING

Some states discourage voters from voting in one party's primary one year and another party's primary the next. Check with your county or state election board to see whether your state has any rules in this regard. You'll want to know if those rules can affect you. After all, you never know when the other party will have a more interesting primary — you may want to vote in that one instead.

>> **Declaring your party preference when you register to vote:** If you do this, which is permitted in certain states, you're automatically listed on the voter files by the party label you provided — regardless of whether you ever vote in a party primary.

>> **Contributing to the party's candidates and the party organization:** Even if your contribution is too small to be listed in the campaign finance reports, the government requires campaigns and parties to keep a list of your name, address, and contribution. After you give money, the party to which you gave regards you as one of its own!

Registering as a Democrat or Republican

When you publicly identify yourself as a Republican or a Democrat by officially registering as such, that disclosure has consequences for you. Would it perhaps be better to play your cards close to your vest and say that you're an independent? After all, our country has a secret ballot so that you don't have to tell anyone how you voted if you don't want to — why give hints?

Advantages

If you declare yourself a party member, chances are that a number of good things will happen. Here are some of the doors that party registration can open for you:

>> **Candidate literature:** During the primary election season, you may receive information from candidates eager to win your vote for the primary election. Receiving (and, of course, reading) this information makes it easier for you to cast an informed vote.

>> **Primary elections:** You become eligible to vote in primary elections. Few people, often as few as 25 percent of the eligible voters, vote in party primaries. If you're one of the 25 percent, your vote carries a lot of weight. It carries a lot more weight in the primary, when candidates are selected, than it does in the general election, when the candidate is elected, because the number voting in the general election is more than double that of the primary turnout. (See Chapter 20 for more about primary elections.)

>> **Caucuses:** You also become eligible to vote in the caucuses that may be held by your party if your state uses a caucus selection system for candidates. (See Chapter 21 for more discussion of caucuses.)

>> **Volunteering:** You may be asked to work at the polls on election day as a poll watcher or a get-out-the-vote volunteer. (*Get-out-the-vote* volunteers identify people who are eligible to vote and who are likely to vote for the candidate or party for whom the volunteer is working.) This volunteer makes sure that

those people are registered and then vote on election day. The volunteers may canvass a precinct door-to-door or make telephone calls to identify and turn out these voters.

Serving as a volunteer is an easy way to become more active in politics. It provides a means for you to meet the party activists and most of the local candidates who visit the polls on election day. You have a chance to interact with these people when you attend the party's training sessions to learn your new task — and learn to function on coffee and doughnuts, which help fuel such activities.

>> **Delegates:** You also become eligible to run for delegate to the state and national party conventions. These conventions adopt the state and national platforms for the respective parties and nominate candidates for a variety of offices, including president and vice president. (See Chapter 21 for more on delegates.)

REMEMBER

Regardless of whether you declare a party affiliation, you're completely free to vote for whomever you like in the general election. Republicans can vote for Democratic nominees for any office and vice versa.

Disadvantages

Declaring your party affiliation also has a couple of disadvantages:

>> **Courting:** You probably won't be courted by either party's candidates. You probably won't receive direct mail or phone calls. Both parties assume that you will vote the way you have declared. (Of course, you may view this neglect as an advantage!)

>> **Everyone knows your politics:** Once you declare an affiliation, you have told the world, or at least the part of the world that wants to look, which way your politics lean.

WARNING

Many states require political balance for appointments to boards and commissions appointed by state governments. If you're seeking appointment to a board or commission, the government looks to your party preference stated by declaration or via primary voting to determine whether you're eligible.

Asserting your independence

You can choose not to affiliate with a political party. Approximately one-third of the voting public takes this approach. Being an independent also has pluses and minuses.

Advantages

>> People don't know your politics unless you want to tell them.

>> The candidates from both parties woo you, trying to persuade you to vote for them. You'll probably receive direct mail and phone calls from both sides.

Disadvantages

>> In most states, you'll probably not have a vote in the nominating process. You may find yourself choosing the lesser of two evils on the final election day.

>> Your opportunities to become active politically by volunteering are limited to supporting a particular candidate. In those states where the parties count the votes on election day, you'll be unable to participate.

Joining a third party

Nationally and in many states, third parties are active. In fact, in 2016 the following third parties nominated candidates for president:

>> Reform Party

>> Green Party

>> Libertarian Party

>> Constitution Party

>> Party for Socialism and Liberation

>> Independent

Third parties tend to be organized around an issue or a philosophy. They're less interested in winning elections than in focusing attention on issues or policies of importance to their membership. Predictably, third parties don't generally receive many votes in any election. The system of government in the United States is set up to accommodate only two parties — anything extra lacks the perks or the opportunities of a dominant party.

ADVANTAGES

>> If you feel strongly about an issue — and you're more interested in making your feelings known than in winning elections — a third party may provide the answer.

TIP

>> If you feel that neither major party reflects your views, you may be more comfortable joining a third party.

>> If you think that the time has come to shake up the political process and you're just now getting involved, membership in a third party may be the way to make waves.

>> If you're just now becoming active and want prominence and responsibility in a hurry, you may find it easier to obtain them in a third party.

DISADVANTAGES

WARNING

>> Staying involved and working hard in election after election is difficult when it's almost a foregone conclusion that all your candidates will lose.

>> Third-party members have no say in the selection of Democratic and Republican nominees in many states.

>> Raising money for third parties that have almost no chance of winning is a difficult proposition.

>> Third parties generally form around a few ideological issues of importance to the members of the third party, but the public may not feel as strongly about these issues and may wonder why you're wasting your time and effort "tilting at windmills."

Separating the Democrats from the Republicans

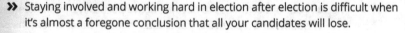

To understand how to separate the Democrats from the Republicans, you must understand some general conditions of their histories, their evolutions, and their memberships.

Historically, the Republican Party emerged in the northern United States. Many members were evangelical Protestants who favored abolition of slavery, prohibition of alcohol, and harsher immigration laws. Until the turn of the century, they were the party of northern financial interests. In Teddy Roosevelt's era, though, the GOP developed a strong "progressive" wing that opposed big business. The Republicans supported antitrust legislation to break up monopolies, and Roosevelt himself was strongly pro-conservation.

The Democratic Party, on the other hand, supported states' rights. It wasn't at all eager to abolish slavery or provide the newly emancipated African Americans with rights. The Democratic Party identified with the steady stream of immigrants who flooded US shores in the second half of the 19th century and into the 20th century. It was also the party of poor farmers in the south and frontier west.

Over time, the policies advocated by both parties changed. So did the membership of the parties. Knowing which is the chicken and which is the egg is always difficult. Did the parties change their positions to win more voters to their banners, or did the people who called themselves Democrats and Republicans change their views, leaving the parties to adjust their philosophies? Whatever the reason, the two parties undoubtedly have changed over time. For example, during the Great Depression and the terms of Franklin Roosevelt, the Democrats enacted more federal government programs to protect the poor and elderly. The Civilian Conservation Corp and Social Security were examples. The Republican party, on the other hand, identified more with big business and opposition to government spending.

REMEMBER

The state and national platforms can provide insight on what the parties believe and what their goals are. The platforms are supposed to represent the views of all party members. When the parties viewed themselves as big tents, encompassing everyone who wanted to wave the party banner — including liberals, conservatives, and moderates — drafting the platforms to obtain majority support at the national and state conventions was difficult. (See Chapter 21 for more on platforms.)

In recent years, groups have tried to move their parties in certain ideological directions. In the Republican Party, it is the religious right that wants firmer statements of ideology and goals than some Republicans are comfortable with. In the Democratic Party, the tension comes from the liberal wing pushing the party more to the left than many members want to go. These attempts lead to spirited debates about the drafting and content of party platforms and have put more emphasis on ideological purity and less on ensuring that all party members live happily under one big tent.

POLITICAL STUFF

WHY THE DONKEY AND THE ELEPHANT?

Since 1831, the donkey has been the national symbol of the Democratic Party. The symbol was popularized by the famous cartoonist Thomas Nast of *Harper's Weekly* during the 1880s. Nast first used the symbol in a political cartoon showing Andrew Jackson riding a donkey and beating it to support his veto of the US Bank recharter.

The elephant was first coined as the Republican Party symbol by the same political cartoonist, Thomas Nast, in 1874. Nast depicted the Republican elephant stomping Tammany Hall (the New York Democratic political machine) tiger. The elephant has been used to symbolize the GOP ever since.

Running with the elephants

If you're considering whether to join the Republican Party, you should be aware of several general points of agreement among those who identify themselves as Republicans. Remember, not every Republican feels the same way about each issue, but this discussion should give you an overview of some basic Republican philosophy.

In today's political world, Republicans lead the charge for states' rights. They want the states, not the federal government, to manage as many issues and programs as possible, including enforcement of environmental regulations, welfare, nursing home standards, and Medicaid. Republicans favor smaller government and want to get the federal government "off the backs" of the states, businesses, and individuals. They oppose gun control. They see little role for the federal government aside from foreign policy and national defense.

Republicans do see a role for the federal government in fostering what they call family values, such as sexual abstinence, prayer in public schools, taxpayer support for alternatives to public education, an abstinence-only approach to sex education, and restrictions on abortion.

There are exceptions to every rule, but here are some characteristics shared by many members of the Republican Party:

>> Higher income

>> Self-employed

>> Business oriented

>> College-educated

>> More small-town than big-city

>> Male

>> White

>> Fundamentalist or evangelical Christian

>> Protestant

EVOLVING CONSTITUENCIES

Certain subgroups in the population identify more with one party or the other. It's fair to say that upper-income people, businesspeople, suburbanites, and White males are more likely to count themselves as Republicans. Lower-income people, union workers, high school graduates, African Americans, other minorities, and women are more likely to consider themselves Democrats.

Party identification doesn't necessarily stay constant. It can evolve over time. Women and African Americans used to associate themselves more with the Republican Party. From the Civil War to Franklin Roosevelt's second term, African Americans voted Republican. From the time women received the vote nationally in 1920 until the 1980s, women were more likely to vote Republican. These days, both groups are more likely to identify with the Democratic Party. More women identify themselves as Democrats by a few percentage points, and African Americans overwhelmingly self-identify as Democrats.

Joining the donkeys

Unlike Republicans, Democrats believe that the federal government should play a role in assisting citizens whom they consider to be disadvantaged: the poor, the elderly, and the disabled. Democrats are more willing to see the federal government intervene and propose solutions to problems. They lack the same inherent faith in the ability of state governments to manage complex problems that Republicans have and are less willing to turn over federal dollars to the states to administer. Democrats generally favor gun control, affirmative action, and higher taxes. But Democrats generally have less faith than Republicans in the ability of government to foster a system of personal values in this country and prefer to leave churches and families to perform that function. Democrats are opposed to prayer in public schools. They're generally pro-choice on abortion issues.

With the same caveat about exceptions to every rule here, here are some common Democratic characteristics:

>> Less-educated and highly educated (graduate school)

>> Working class

>> Minority (especially African American and non-Cuban Hispanic)

>> Female (especially unmarried)

>> Jewish or (to a lesser extent) Catholic

>> Urban rather than rural

This list and the list for Republicans (refer to the earlier section "Running with the elephants") are intended as general guides. It's not necessary for you to fit all or most of the characteristics described here. Some voters feel more comfortable in a party where they don't fit the profile. They may determine their party affiliation on the basis of a single issue that they feel strongly about and ignore the other parts of the profile. When or if you choose to join a party is definitely a decision that you should make for yourself.

Making Your Own Choice

Okay, you're sold on the advantages of belonging to one of the two major parties — but which one? Maybe you don't feel comfortable picking a party according to the types of people who belong to it. Maybe you want to decide based on what they believe. How do you determine which party reflects how you feel about the issues and which party's candidates you want to see in office?

Evaluating the platforms

The first thing to look at in determining which party you're more comfortable supporting is what the parties stand for. You can look in several places to determine for yourself which party more closely mirrors your views of government.

Each state and national party drafts a party platform that their state and national conventions adopt. The national party adopts a platform every presidential election year. The state parties may adopt platforms more frequently, usually every other year.

REMEMBER

You can request copies of these platforms from your Republican and Democratic state committees. The state committees usually have an office in the state capitol. They may also have offices in the state's largest city. Call the state committees and ask for copies of the most recent state party platforms.

You can do the same with the national party committees in Washington. The addresses are

>> **Democratic National Committee:** 430 South Capitol Street SE; Washington, DC 20003 (https://democrats.org)

>> **Republican National Committee:** 310 First Street SE; Washington, DC 20003 (www.gop.com)

TIP

In addition to asking the state and national committees for copies of their platforms, ask to be put on their emails. The state and national committees will send you information and newsletters that can provide you with a great deal of insight on which issues the parties support and why. Reading the material produced by the state and national committees for both parties should assist you in choosing which party to join.

Listening to the candidates

Another way to determine which party you're comfortable joining is to watch and listen to the candidates the parties put forward for election. See which party's candidates reflect how you feel about the issues. See who else supports the candidates and determine for yourself whether you're comfortable traveling in the same circles.

TIP

When you decide which party to join, you should consider the following checklist of issues. Determining where the parties stand on these issues compared to your views can help you determine which party to associate with.

>> **Tax policy:** Do you think taxes are too high or too low? Do you prefer taxes that impact everyone equally, or taxes that are heaviest on particular groups (such as the upper class or corporations)? Do you think tax breaks should be used to encourage particular forms of desired behavior, such as saving for education, buying insurance, or using childcare?

>> **The role of the federal government:** Do you regard an active federal government as a social problem or as the solution to social problems? Do you think the federal government has an obligation to assist those in need, or should it stand out of the way of private behavior?

>> **Social issues:** Do you see a role for the government in shaping values and morals? Do you think the government should permit abortion and forbid prayer in public schools? Do you think only students who attend public school should receive government funded educations, or do you think those in parochial schools should receive government aid as well? Do you think government should take affirmative steps to improve the lot of racial and ethnic minorities? Which party approaches crime and justice in the way that will make your world a safer place?

>> **The environment:** Do you feel that government has a role to play in preserving the environment and forcing businesses to observe standards, or do you feel that environmental extremists have created a bureaucratic nightmare that hinders the growth of jobs and the profitability of businesses?

>> **Foreign Policy:** Do you think the US should be seeking allies and be involved around the world or do you think the US does not need allies and should concentrate on the problems in the United States?

Compare your positions on issues like these with the positions of the parties and the parties' candidates to decide whom you would be more comfortable associating with.

Differences within a party

Both the Democratic and Republican parties have conservative, moderate, and liberal members. American parties don't generally conduct litmus tests for ideological purity, as some foreign parties have done. In the Soviet Union under Stalin, failure to agree with Stalin's (often changing) opinions on any issue could result in being ousted from the Communist Party. Democrats and Republicans may disagree among themselves, but no procedure exists for drumming an ideological maverick out of either party.

POLITICAL STUFF

Sometimes, elected officials switch and declare themselves members of the opposition party. For example, Senator James Jeffords, from Vermont, decided to leave the Republican Party in 2001, giving control of the US Senate to the Democrats by a single vote. Renunciation of party affiliation by an individual is not the only way to leave a party. The parties don't have formal mechanisms for purging their ranks of members who are no longer in the mainstream of party ideology, but a party can attempt to purge itself of members perceived as disloyal by refusing to provide campaign services otherwise available to candidates or by running an opponent in a primary against a member perceived as disloyal.

For both parties, the tent encompassing membership is quite large, and the requirements of membership are quite vague. (See the section in Chapter 6 about the big-tent theory.)

Differences between the two parties

Despite the fact that the major political parties tolerate opposing views, general differences do exist between the parties in attitude and ideology. Those differences translate into different groups that support one party rather than the other.

When you're deciding which party to join, you need to see which party, as a general rule, is closer in approach and philosophy to what you feel the role of government should be and how you feel about the important issues of the day. The only real test is whether you're comfortable with your choice. You are the only person who needs to be pleased by your selection.

Chapter **8**

Joining a Special Interest Group

Races for the legislature in the 50 states are financed in part by party givers (as described in Chapter 4). But legislative candidates also receive money from groups that are interested in the legislature and, perhaps more important, in the laws enacted by the legislatures. These groups, sometimes referred to as *special interest groups,* band together to pursue their common interest in passing, protecting, or repealing laws.

Special interest groups are large, organized groups that work together because they share common interests or goals. They exist to protect what they have *from* government action and to get more *through* government action. These groups lobby and exert political pressure to get what they want from elected officials.

Special interest groups

» Want laws that benefit them to be passed and those that hurt them to be repealed

» Want the government to make decisions that help them and their causes

» Want laws passed that will change the behavior of other private individuals

REMEMBER

Not all groups are self-interested. Some are issue groups, which want to change the behavior of others.

Special interest groups work to find common ground with other special interest groups so that they can form temporary alliances to increase their numbers and their strength on particular issues. When they're larger and more powerful, they may have an easier time getting what they want from elected officials.

Identifying Special Interest Groups

You may hear much discussion about the influence of special interest groups on the political process. You may think that, whoever these special interest groups are, they have more power and influence than you do. Perhaps that worries you.

TIP

Many different groups qualify for the title of a special interest group. They may be ideological groups with no personal agenda or those whose members do have personal agendas. Because of the vast number of special interest groups, you probably belong to one or more yourself. Are you

>> An employee of a corporation or an industry that can be defined as a special interest (steel, pharmaceutical, hospital, nursing home, mining, utility, insurance)?

>> A member of a profession that lobbies (bar association, trial lawyer, doctor, dentist, accountant)?

>> A member of an educational group (teacher, school superintendent, school board, university)?

>> A member of a consolidated group (chambers of commerce, manufacturers associations, retail associations)?

>> A member of or contributor to groups that lobby for specific issues or programs, including these:

- *Not-for-profit, such as associations for veterans, people with mental health problems, and people who are deaf or blind or who have other disabilities*

- *Arts funding or public broadcasting*

- *Outdoor recreation, such as bicycling*

- *Parent-teacher association*

- *State university*

>> A union member?

>> An environmentalist who contributes when groups solicit door-to-door?

If so, you may have met the enemy, and it is you. Of course, you may not agree with all or even many of the policies of the group to which you belong. You may have joined the American Association of Retired Persons (AARP) for travel or medical discounts rather than to support it in lobbying for seniors, for example. If you aren't typical of the group to which you belong, you don't view the special interest that claims you as a member as working for you. Even if you are typical, you may still view the influence of special interest groups with grave concern.

REMEMBER

One person's membership and support of a group may seem like special interest politics to someone else. Your attitude toward special interest groups depends on whether you're working with the special interests or from the other side of the issue. If you're part of an interest group that's trying to exert influence to change votes or minds, you probably see nothing wrong with trying to use the numbers and money of a special interest group to effect change. If the issue you support is being attacked by special interest groups, you may view the attack in a much different light.

Enlisting Lobbyists

Although the term *lobbyist* has a legal definition under state and federal law, generally speaking, lobbyists are people who are paid to represent special interest groups primarily before the legislative branch but also before the executive branch of government. Lobbyists are paid because they make it their business to know and schmooze officials and their staffs. They also know how the government works, inside and out.

Special interest groups pay for the services of lobbyists in a variety of ways. Corporations and unions simply pay out of their operating budgets for lobbying services. Groups with large memberships may use a part of the fee charged to members to pay for these services. Some of the dues you send each year to organizations to which you belong may be used to provide lobbying for those organizations' legislative or political goals.

THE HISTORY OF LOBBYISTS

The term *lobbyist* comes from the special interest representatives who gather in places frequented by representatives of government to discuss the special interest agenda. Lobbyists have been around since the earliest days of our government and go back as far as the seventeenth century in England. There's an urban legend that says that the term dates from the Grant administration, when President Grant, who liked to enjoy brandy and a cigar in the lobby of the Willard Hotel in Washington, would be subjected to the attentions of special interest lobbyists. What began as a few people's informal method of buttonholing members of Congress to discuss pending legislation has mushroomed into a multimillion dollar industry with thousands of people registered as lobbyists before federal, state, and local governments.

What a good lobbyist does

A lobbyist working in a state legislature or Congress is familiar with the rules of procedure of the body in which they lobby. They know the personalities of the supporters and the enemies of the legislators, and they know how to

>> Get a bill killed

>> Amend a bill to make it more acceptable

>> Amend a bill to make it unacceptable to legislators

>> Push the hot buttons of elected officials

>> Form alliances with other special interest groups to pass or defeat a bill

For example, lobbyists develop relationships with particular legislators or members of Congress. They spend a great deal of time and money getting to know the people who vote on legislation. Lobbyists socialize with legislators — provide tickets for sporting events, pick up the tab on dinners with legislators, sponsor fundraisers for the campaigns of legislators, and so on. All these activities are designed to ingratiate the lobbyist to the legislator who's being cultivated so that when the lobbyist needs a favor, the legislator grants it.

There *are* some laws regarding limits to the types of gifts officials may receive. The National Association of State Legislators maintains a website of state-by-state ethics laws regarding gift giving by lobbyists and reporting of lobbying expenditures at `www.ncsl.org/research/ethics/50-state-table-gift-laws`. The laws are all different in the amounts which may be given, how often or whether reporting is required, and the penalties for violations of the law. You can check your own state to see whether the legislature is serious about its ethical requirements or simply trying to look like it is serious.

One favor that a lobbyist can ask for is a poison pill amendment to a bill that the lobbyist is against. (A *poison pill amendment* is a provision that's so unacceptable to segments of the legislature that an otherwise acceptable bill containing this provision is doomed to failure.) The lobbyist doesn't have to openly rail against the bill that they're opposing; instead, they can change the debate to the poison pill amendment and, in so doing, kill the bill anyway. This ability results from the efforts of the lobbyist to cultivate the legislator to be able to call in favors when necessary.

In short, a good lobbyist knows the ropes much better than a freshman legislator or congressperson.

Lobbyists are paid to protect the special interest groups from laws that may hurt them. They carefully watch all the bills introduced and all amendments proposed to those bills to make certain that nothing will have a negative impact on their clients' interests — and to sound the alarm when something will have a negative impact.

A lobbyist's success doesn't depend on their speech-making ability or whether they look good on television; it's determined by what passes or fails to pass a legislative body. The future clients of the lobbyist and the amount of money a lobbyist can charge are directly related to the lobbyist's success.

It's not uncommon for a high-powered lobbyist to represent numerous special interests at once, although lobbyists avoid representing interests that may compete against each other in the legislature.

Special interests and the government

Special interests follow lots of strategies and ask the government to do a wide variety of favors. For those groups primarily seeking material benefits, however, their tasks when lobbying the government fall into three categories:

>> **Interests that do business with the state and federal governments**

An example of groups that do business with state governments and the federal government are healthcare providers: nursing homes, pharmaceutical companies, hospitals, and so on. Lobbyists for these groups try to get favorable reimbursement rates from Medicare and Medicaid for their clients.

Medicare is the federal program to provide healthcare to the elderly. *Medicaid* is the federal program that provides healthcare to the poor, some of whom are elderly. It's jointly funded by federal and state tax dollars.

Due to the increasing cost of healthcare — and more and more individuals qualifying for inclusion in the Medicaid program — the cost of Medicaid is growing by double digits for state and federal budgets. Combined, these programs have caused health services to become the largest category of spending in the federal budget.

>> **Interests that are funded by the state or federal government**

Lobbying for these groups includes persuading the legislators to give them more money from the state or national budget or allowing them to raise fees or borrow money. School corporations, universities, mental health facilities, the National Endowment for the Arts, the Corporation for Public Broadcasting — all these groups lobby legislators for a bigger share of the state or federal budget.

>> **Interests that are regulated by the government**

Special interest groups that are regulated by states lobby the legislature and state agencies for more favorable regulatory treatment. Insurance companies, utilities, banks, and other financial institutions fall into this category.

POLITICAL STUFF

CONSERVATIVE LOBBYISTS AND GAS TAXES

You can find an example of how lobbyists band together for a common purpose and look out for their clients' interests in the alliance of groups favoring highway construction.

Representatives of architectural and engineering firms, asphalt paving companies, concrete companies, and trucking companies are ordinarily pro-business and anti-taxes. In other words, they favor conservative fiscal policies by their governments — with one big exception.

These group can band together to urge state and federal governments to increase gas taxes, joining with environmental groups which may also be pro- gas tax. These groups would not be considered normal legislative allies, but in this effort they have a common goal. Although the revenue from higher gas taxes goes to road and bridge construction, the environmentalists will hope that some of the gas tax will go to public transportation or that the higher price of gas will be incentive for more people to use existing public transportation. The higher price of gas may also spur demand for more fuel economy in cars. Both of these results may results in improved air quality in cities.

USING LOBBYISTS TO PROTECT PRICES

A special interest group may pay lobbyists to lobby the executive or legislative branch of government to receive favorable treatment in order to protect its profits.

An example at the federal level is the discussion about the price of prescription drugs. Candidates for president in 2020 are raising the issue of the high cost of drugs in the United States compared to other countries such as Canada. In an attempt to prevent any federal action that might affect the prices pharmaceutical companies receive for their products, pharmaceutical groups spent a record $280 million for lobbying efforts in 2018, according to Open Secrets, a nonpartisan, independent research group tracking money in politics.

REMEMBER

Many lobbyists represent special interest groups that work to support or change policies that they think are good for the country or themselves. These groups work to change laws and regulations at the state and federal levels on a variety of issues with no thought of monetary gain. These groups support or oppose issues dealing with the environment, gun control, smoking, the developmentally disabled, and abortion, to name a few.

Making Political Contributions

Successful special interest groups mount campaigns on several fronts to protect and promote their interests. Lobbying, maintaining political clout, and organizing campaigns designed to rally public support for their positions are all part of successful campaigns to advance their interests. But making political contributions is one of their best-known tactics.

A key factor in a politician's decision on which position to take is whether special interests with money to contribute care about the issue. Special-interest contributions can be a big factor in a politician's analysis of what's at stake. Picking the "right" side of an issue can result in large special-interest contributions. Picking the "wrong" side of an issue can mean that the special interests give to the candidate's opponent or run an independent campaign to defeat the candidate.

REMEMBER

Special interests don't contribute large sums of money to a campaign — particularly, a campaign to enact certain legislation — purely out of a desire for good government. Sure, *you* may make contributions to a cause and expect nothing in return, but your contributions are relatively modest. When a group invests thousands of dollars in the political process, it wants something in return. Of course, just because a group benefits from a law doesn't mean it's a bad idea. The group may want government to abolish a bad tax, drop a regulation that's unnecessarily costly, or alter a part of the legal code that helps foreign competitors steal business away from American companies. Nevertheless, the "something" these contributors want usually has a direct financial benefit to them.

Sometimes special interests use their money to mail information to their membership and urge those members to vote against a candidate or for their opponent. The money spent doesn't go directly into the campaigns of a candidate or the opponent, but it has an indirect effect on the outcome of the campaign if enough special-interest supporters follow the advice of the special interests and vote in the election.

Getting action with PACs

Special interest groups form *political action committees* (PACs) so that they can contribute to legislative candidates and political parties. Because the federal government and a large number of states prohibit corporate contributions as well as contributions from labor funds, many corporations and unions form PACs to enable themselves to contribute to political campaigns. Associations of trial lawyers, defense lawyers, educators, doctors, and more also form PACs to maximize the impact of contributions from individual members. PACS may also receive contributions from individuals in excess of the federal limits on individual contributions to candidates' campaigns. A PAC may spend the money it has received to benefit a candidate and not be subject to the limits imposed by law as long as the PAC does not coordinate with the campaign it is trying to help.

PACs can make substantial ($5,000) contributions to federal and many other officeholders every election cycle. Some states permit PAC contributions larger than $5,000 per candidate per election. PACs contribute money to incumbents who support them and to incumbents whom the PAC can persuade to support them. PACs also invest in challengers to incumbents who have opposed their stand on issues.

Some states permit direct contributions from corporations to candidates and political parties. In those states, the corporate contributions are supplemented by PAC contributions.

PACs have become common features of modern-day political campaigns, and they come in all shapes and sizes. Many PACs are formed at workplaces by employers or unions. Others are formed by people who share views about issues. When many small contributions are pooled to support a candidate, these small contributions can be substantial enough to attract any candidate's attention.

PACs MEAN BIG MONEY

PACs consist of groups of like-minded people who are often employed by the same company or are members of the same union and who pool their contributions to maximize their impact. PACs are equivalent to labor unions and operate under the same principle — a large number of people, when organized into a group, can speak with a louder voice and change their lives.

The larger PACs not only talk loudly — they carry very big sticks. Here are two examples of how much PACs contributed to Democratic and Republican candidates in the 2018 election cycle:

- The National Association of Realtors contributed $3,444.276 to candidates.

- The National Beer Wholesalers Association contributed $3,433,500.

Both PACS divided the contributions relatively evenly between parties.

Not surprisingly, candidates certainly do regard the PACs as serious political players.

Here are some reasons that PACs are formed:

>> To support women and African American candidates

>> To support the pro-life or the pro-choice cause

>> To support candidates who are sensitive to environmental issues

>> To support the anti-gun-control or pro-gun-control cause

>> To support the causes of employers or unions at various workplaces

>> To support the causes of the healthcare industry

>> To support the causes of the tobacco industry

REMEMBER

If you ask around, you'll find numerous opportunities to join and contribute to PACs — and that will help you increase your political clout.

Joining a PAC or forming your own

You may already be a member of one PAC or more through your work and community involvement. If you're a member, you can seek appointment or election to your PAC's committee that decides where the PAC makes its contributions. The people who make those determinations for PACs can be influential in determining who wins and who loses various races for office. Those PAC committee members have substantial political clout — now that dollar signs are attached!

You can form your own PAC. If you care about a particular issue and have some friends who feel the same, you can create your own PAC, raise money, and decide who will receive the contributions. Keep in mind that you will also have to comply with state or federal reporting requirements for PAC activity. Your state election board and the Federal Election Commission (FEC) can provide you with the information you need to comply with the law. You can call the Federal Election Commission at 1-800-424-9530 or log on to www.fec.gov.

PAC regulations

Since the decision by the Supreme Court in *Citizens United v. FEC*, the ban on corporations and unions making uncoordinated expenditures for or against candidates was lifted. As long as corporations and unions don't give directly to the campaigns of candidates, they now may give unlimited contributions to PACs who make such campaign expenditures. The Federal Election Commission says that in the 2017–2018 election cycle, 1,823 corporate PACs spent over $312 million, and 278 labor PACs spent over $210 million helping to influence the outcome of midterm elections.

Each state has its own rules on who may give to state and local candidates and how much can be given. If you want to give and are unfamiliar with your state's laws, you can call your state election board or secretary of state's office and ask for a copy of your state's campaign finance laws. Your state library has a copy of them, too. This information is usually provided free of charge.

PAC money and clout

Knowing which organizations gave money and to whom is important because it helps you understand what's going on. If a PAC is supporting or opposing an issue that you're interested in, you need to know whether your elected official has received contributions from this PAC. If the PAC you're interested in is federal — because the elected official is a member of Congress — you can consult the reports at the Federal Election Commission at https://classic.fec.gov/finance/disclosure/norindsea.shtml or check out www.opensecrets.org/pacs.

If the PAC is active with a state official, you can consult your secretary of state or state election board for a copy of the reports of the PAC or the elected official.

The evolution in PACs since the Supreme Court decision in *Citizens United v. FEC* has created super PACs. As mentioned, *super PACs* can accept money in unlimited amounts from unions, corporations, and unaffiliated individuals as well as from not-for-profit organizations, which don't have to report the source of their funding. Although super PACs cannot coordinate with the campaigns they're supporting or give directly to candidates, many super PACs are run by persons associated with the candidates whose campaign they're supporting. The candidates can help the super PACs raise money by appearing at fundraisers, as long as the candidates don't ask for contributions in excess of the $5,000 annual limit. So the candidates cannot ask, but others associated with the super PACs can and do ask. Individuals supporting presidential candidates through super PACs have written checks for millions of dollars. If the money is given to a not-for-profit and then given to the super PAC, the names of the contributor on the report is the not-for-profit organization and not the person, union, or corporation that actually gave the money!

If your political official is taking money from a PAC whose views are different from yours, you have to organize enough voters who feel the same as you do about the issue to counter the impact of the contribution on your elected official's behavior.

Of course, the elected official may strongly support the PAC's position from the get-go, which is why the PAC gave the person money in the first place. In other words, the legislator's position may be the chicken and not the egg. If that is the case, the officeholder may not be willing to change their position regardless of how much pressure you bring to bear.

If the PAC's contribution is the chicken, though, you need to convince your elected official that voting the way the PAC wants will cost them votes in the next election. You need to counter the money analysis that the elected official will perform with a vote analysis that you've created. (Chapter 2 explains the money-versus-vote analysis in detail.) You need to convince your elected official that it's better to lose future contributions from that PAC than to lose all the votes you can mobilize against the person at the next election. Demonstrate to the official that not only large contributors can have political clout — voters can have political clout too, even without the dollar signs attached. (Chapter 5 tells you how to communicate your arguments to the official.)

Contributing to nonlegislative candidates

Legislative candidates aren't the only beneficiaries of special interest contributions. Mayors and city or county councilpeople of large cities, federal candidates, and governors also benefit. Mayors and governors can propose legislation. They can usually sign into law or veto legislation, and they make many decisions on awarding grants or funding to new or existing businesses. Theirs is usually the final word on awarding city and state contracts. Large-city mayors and governors are the types of elected officials whom special interest groups cultivate with campaign contributions and support.

I'll help you if you help me

Special interest groups usually see a direct relationship between their contributions and the goals they're seeking. That isn't to say that they're foolish enough to demand a commitment from a candidate to vote a certain way on a bill in return for a political contribution. That approach is too direct — and illegal. Besides, if the officeholder changes their mind, there's no way for the special interest group to enforce the commitment it had from the officeholder. No, approaches by special interest groups tend to be subtler.

The representatives of the groups and the candidate meet to discuss matters of concern to the group and see whether they share a common understanding of the issues. The group may ask for and receive a general commitment of support, but that's all.

What the special interest groups receive in return for their contributions is all-important: They receive access! (*Access* means an opportunity to make their case directly to the legislature and their staff.) If they give enough money, their calls will be returned. When they give election after election, their requests for meetings with officeholders are honored. That access permits lobbyists for special interest groups to make their case for or against proposed legislation directly to one or more of the officeholders casting votes to decide the issue.

If these special interest groups give to many different legislators, their access increases dramatically. If they give generously to the leadership of the legislative bodies or the caucus fundraising efforts, they can count on being received courteously at the highest levels of power.

POLITICAL MYTH

Contrary to popular belief, access may not guarantee the special interest groups the results they want. Competing special interest groups may be exerting counterpressures on the official. Or the public outcry over the legislation may make it politically difficult or impossible for the legislators to deliver what the special interest groups want.

Access by a special interest may not be a foolproof way to gain support but it provides an advantage. The ability of special interest groups to make their arguments directly to lawmakers gives them a leg up on the competition. That competition can include you, the average voter, as explained next.

Getting the Same Access as Special Interest Groups

What you, as an individual, want is the same access that special interest groups enjoy — to explain your position on issues of importance to you. Some access is available to you already. Your state legislator may return your phone call when you call to tell them what you think. Of course, the call may come after the vote is cast. You may even receive a letter or a call from a staff person for your member of Congress in response to your call or letter.

But gaining access to the leaders of your state legislature or Congress is much tougher. You don't have the same ability as an influential lobbyist for a special interest group to call the chairperson of the House Ways and Means Committee in Washington to get listed on his calendar for a lunch appointment. To make your voice heard in the halls of leadership, you need to multiply your clout. See Chapter 4 for suggestions on how to do that.

It's obvious that the special interest groups that contribute can make their cases to these important people in person — and you can't. Campaign contributions in large quantities translate into access for those making the contributions. That's why many special interest groups give in the first place.

TIP

Keep in mind that, if you're a member of a special interest group that has contributed generously and often, your group's representative may be able to have lunch with these legislative leaders even if you yourself can't. That's fine from your point of view, as long as you share the viewpoint of the special interest group to which you belong.

Are Special Interest Groups Contributing Your Money?

The answer is *probably*. If you buy from a corporation that can make direct contributions to PACs, you have helped make those contributions possible. If you buy power from a utility company or insurance from a company that can make direct corporate contributions to candidates and political parties, you helped make those contributions possible. The influence purchased with that money may or may not be exercised on your behalf.

If you participate in a PAC yourself, you're contributing your own money directly to political campaigns and political parties. If you work for a corporation that has a PAC and you make voluntary contributions to that PAC, you're contributing your own money. The PAC committee may decide how the money is spent, but *you*'re contributing.

You may not realize that simply purchasing from a corporation with a PAC helps to make its contributions possible. Your money may not be used directly by the corporation to fund its political PAC, but your money can be used to pay the salaries of the management personnel of the corporation. In turn, people in management are encouraged by their bosses to participate in a voluntary corporate PAC. They're asked to make voluntary payroll deductions to fund the corporate PAC out of the salaries that your purchases helped pay.

Union PACs work the same way. If you belong to a labor union and participate in a PAC, your money is used to fund the PAC's political contributions. Some states permit unions to use a part of their union dues money for political contributions over and above union PAC contributions. If you belong to a union, you're helping to fund contributions in those states that permit the use of union dues money for political contributions, even if you don't participate in the PAC.

In short, you may be part of the financing for the special interest that you've been blaming for contaminating the political process in recent years! Well, everyone's a special interest these days. You can't avoid involvement completely, but you can take a few steps to try to make the PACs you're associated with reflect your views. After you're aware of what a special interest with which you're associated is doing and decide that you don't agree with it, you can either stop your contributions or make direct contributions to the side of the issue or election that you want to support.

You can also avoid purchasing the products or stock of companies whose executives or PACs support candidates and issues with which you disagree.

Finding out who contributes

When a special interest group or PAC makes a contribution to a political candidate, that information gets reported two times: The candidate must report it in their campaign finance report (Chapter 19 has more information on campaign financing); in addition, the special interest group PAC must report all its expenditures to the government.

Special interest groups must file federal PAC reports with the FEC in Washington. You can access the information at the FEC website `https://classic.fec.gov/finance/disclosure/norindsea.shtml`.

When you examine the special interest PAC report, you may find out who contributed to the PAC as well as every candidate who benefited from the PAC's generosity.

Local races

In most states, the campaign finance reports for local candidates and political parties are filed in the offices of the county clerk or the county election board. These reports tell you how much special interest money a local candidate or campaign has raised and from whom. The reports also tell you how a campaign has spent its money and how much it has left on hand as of the filing date. These reports don't tell you all the contributions a special interest has made to other political candidates, but they do tell you whether any local candidates or parties, whose reports you look at, received anything from a particular interest. You might want to visit https://votesmart.org/elections/offices/IN - .XVWbxVB7nUo for more information.

TIP

In an election year, most states require local candidates up for election and their party organizations to file several reports. These reports cover set periods in the election cycle. You can probably examine preprimary or reconvention reports as well as reports filed a month or six weeks before the election is held. Some states also require candidates to disclose large contributions received late in the campaign within a short period after they're received by the candidate.

State races

Many states require candidates for statewide office and state political parties to file their campaign finance reports with the state election board or secretary of state's office. In a year when the candidates are on the ballot, they must file their reports several times at key points in the election cycle. You're free to examine any of the reports for statewide candidates to see who gave money to these candidates, how much, and when. Each report you examine gives you a part of the picture on how a particular PAC is spending its money. You might check out www.followthemoney.org.

REMEMBER

These reports don't give you a complete picture of how a special interest is spending its PAC money. For that, you must look at the special interest PAC reports in your state. Check out the FEC's website, which reports PAC contributions. (See the later section "Federal races.")

TIP

Many states maintain campaign finance reports on line which you can access through your state election board or Secretary of State's website.

Federal races

If you're interested in a race for US Congress, you can check two different places for these reports:

>> They're filed with the state agency responsible for keeping the records. States generally use the secretary of state's office, the state board or registrar of elections, or the lieutenant governor's office to file these records.

>> The records for all federal campaigns are also kept by the FEC in Washington, DC.

>> Online resources like www.followthemoney.org can help you find the information you want.

TIP

The information that the FEC has available includes

>> Contributions by individuals, PACs, and party committees

>> Financial status reports on all federal candidates and committees, including latest total receipts, disbursements, cash on hand, and debts owed

>> "Top 50" rankings by the FEC of campaign finance activities, which indicate facts such as the 50 campaigns that raised the most or spent the most or received the most PAC money

REMEMBER

The FEC website can be a valuable tool for any citizen wanting to learn what's really going on with campaign contributions. You can find out who is giving money to the candidates you're interested in and how the special interest groups raise and spend their money. These reports can also tell you whether groups you belong to are making contributions that include your money to candidates or political parties.

TIP

If the task seems too overwhelming, you can simply read and pay attention to media reports of campaign contributions. Many groups interested in campaign finance reform publish their findings from analyzing the reports of many different candidates. These groups follow the most visible and controversial special interest group contributions. Sometimes, the groups also follow the voting records on the special interest issues of elected officials who are the beneficiaries of the contributions. These evaluations can give you a greater understanding of what's going on with your elected officials and/or the special interest groups you're watching. See Chapter 12 for more on how to find this information.

POLITICAL STUFF

SOFT MONEY

Soft money can't legally be given directly to a federal candidate. It either exceeds the federal limit for individual contributions of $2,800 per election or the PAC $5,000-per-election ceiling; or it's direct corporate money, money from PACs that aren't federally qualified, or labor union dues money.

These contributions must be donated to state and national parties rather than directly to the candidates to avoid legal limitations.

The parties then spend the money on activities that benefit the candidates. However, candidates can't coordinate how the party money is spent.

Chapter **9**

Getting Political Online

hen the first edition of this book came out, in 1995, this chapter began by noting how much personal computers had changed the world in just 20 years. Back then, the Internet was still a relatively new phenomenon — one that promised to change the world in new and exciting ways. But it's hard to believe that anyone could have predicted just how much change it would bring in another 20 years.

For starters, computers are no longer just bulky boxes that sit on your desk. Your phone — which no longer hangs on the wall but fits neatly in your pocket — is a computer. If you're like most Americans, your phone is your primary device for accessing the Internet. And because your phone is probably in your pocket, that means you almost always have immediate access to just about any information you could possibly want.

It's not just the devices people use to connect to the Internet that have changed, though: Nearly every aspect of our daily lives can now be done online: banking, shopping, buying groceries, watching TV, and even turning off the lights in your house. Just like everything else, politics has also been transformed by the Internet.

But one thing remains the same: Back in 1995, this book told you, "Your computer can be your ticket to becoming more politically involved without leaving the comfort of your own home." That's truer than ever today.

Understanding Politics on the Internet

The idea that the leader of the free world could instantly transmit random thoughts whenever he wanted to virtually every person on the planet sounds like the plot of a 1950s sci-fi novel. Yet in 2019, President Donald Trump's prolific use of Twitter accomplished exactly that. What's more: You can respond to what he says with a question, and he might give you an answer within minutes.

This direct access you have to politicians best sums up how most people think politics has been changed by the Internet. But it works the other way, too: Politicians now have direct access to you.

In the past, an elected official could send out a press release to make their opinion known on an issue. As the name *press release* implies, that opinion wasn't sent directly to constituents — it was sent to the press. The press might write a story about the press release, but they would probably add information or quote a politician with an opposing view. What most Americans read in the paper might not be exactly what the politician hoped they would read.

The Internet changes that arrangement. Because they no longer have to communicate with citizens by way of the press, politicians gain just as much from the direct access of the Internet as you do. Here are some examples of how politicians can now directly engage with voters:

>> They can put press releases on their own websites for anyone to read.

>> They can use other platforms, like Facebook or Twitter, to share their opinions with individual voters.

>> If you sign up for the politician's email list, they don't need for you to visit a website in order to send you a message about where they stand.

Government Websites versus Campaign Websites

If you go to www.whitehouse.gov, you see the website for the president of the United States — Donald Trump, at the time this book was written. You can read about his actions as president, but you won't find any information about his next campaign rally or how to make a donation to his campaign. For those sorts of activities, go to www.DonaldJTrump.com. But once you get there, you'll notice that there are no links to other government agencies you might be interested in. Wouldn't it be less confusing to have just one website for the president?

Or, maybe you've noticed that your local member of Congress or US senator has two different accounts on Twitter or that they seem to use two different Facebook pages. You might be tempted to believe that one of them is fake, but chances are good that they're both legitimate. So, how do you know which one you should engage with?

There's a good reason that many elected officials have two websites or two accounts on other sites: Federal and state laws prohibit government resources — like money, staff, websites — from being mixed with resources that are supporting a political candidate. As a taxpayer, you probably want your money to fund government services and not political campaigns (especially for candidates you oppose).

Yes, it can make things confusing online when you aren't sure which website or account to use. But once you understand the reasoning, it's a lot easier to figure out. For example, here are situations where it makes more sense to use a government website or account:

>> You want to voice your opinion on a piece of legislation.

>> You need help connecting with government services or agencies, like Medicare or the IRS.

>> You're visiting your state capital or Washington, DC, and you want to tour government buildings when you arrive.

However, it makes more sense to use a campaign website or account when you want to

>> Volunteer for a political campaign or attend a campaign rally

>> Make a donation to a candidate for office

>> Complain about a mudslinging TV ad that was run against an opposing candidate

How can you tell whether an account or a website is for a government office or a political campaign? For a home website, if the address ends with .gov, it's definitely for a government office. Beyond that, there are no set-in-stone rules, but there are usually some telltale signs.

If the website address or name of the account contains the name of the office as a title, it's probably for the government office. If the word *for* is part of the website address or account name, especially before the name of the office, it's probably for a political campaign. If no office is even listed, it's probably for a political campaign, or it's a personal account. (Though personal accounts can sometimes be used for both governmental and political reasons, most politicians choose not to, to avoid breaking any rules.)

Here are some examples of how real-life politicians have named their different accounts. See if you can spot the telltale signs for government offices or political campaigns for each one:

>> Former President **Barack Obama** used the Twitter account @POTUS44 (for 44th president of the United States) for his government office and @BarackObama for his political campaigns.

>> US Representative **Jim Banks** uses the Facebook page "Congressman Jim Banks" for his government office and a "Jim Banks for Congress" page for his political campaigns.

>> Illinois Governor **J.B. Pritzker** uses the website address gov.il.gov for his government office and www.jbpritzker.com for his political campaign.

>> President **Donald Trump** uses the Twitter account @realDonaldTrump because it's a longtime personal account, so he does both governmental and political business with a single account. Those tweets that are only governmental in nature are archived by the account @POTUS.

Engaging with Elected Officials and Candidates Online

After you understand the difference between government and campaign websites, you also have an idea of why you might interact with one or the other. But how can you find the politicians you want to engage with across all the different platforms that exist?

Though you can choose from dozens of possible platforms, just a handful of platforms are universally adopted by almost all politicians:

>> A home website you can visit

>> An email list you can subscribe to

>> A Facebook page you can like

>> A Twitter account you can follow

Let's take a closer looking at these four methods of engaging politicians. For each, I'll talk about how a government official might use it, how a political candidate might use it, and how you can use that information to make sure your voice is heard.

Visiting a website

Most politicians have dedicated websites that contain all the information about them or their office that you might want to know, including how to contact them offline or where you might be able to meet them in person:

>> **Government official:** The websites for government officials usually focus primarily on how the office can assist you in obtaining government services, but the sites usually also contain information about the officeholder, such as a biography, policy initiatives or legislation they've authored, positions on policy or legislation, and news coverage. You can usually also find press releases sent out by the office. Finally, you should see clear contact information to reach the office, including a phone number or an email address. But you may also see a form, which is sent by email to the office, on which you can type your comments or questions.

>> **Political candidate:** Websites for political candidates focus almost exclusively on a candidate's biography and policy positions, but you should also be able to find information on getting involved with the campaign, donating money to the campaign, and attending upcoming campaign events. You'll also likely find lots of pictures and videos (many of which are current TV ads).

The easiest way to find the website you're looking for is to use a search engine, like Google. Typically, all you need to type is the name of the person you're searching for and perhaps the name of the office they hold or seek, and then you can find their home website(s) within the first few results. For government officials, you can find the official page in other ways. For a member of the US Senate or US House, you can find all home websites by going to www.congress.gov and clicking the Members link at the top right of the page. The names of all members of Congress, either House or Senate, are listed by state and if you click on the name you want, it will take you directly to the member's home page. For state-elected officials or legislators, you can type the state's 2-letter abbreviation followed by .gov and then look for listings of elected offices. So, for Alabama, you type **al.gov**; for New York, you type **ny.gov**; for Wyoming, you type **wy.gov**.

REMEMBER

If you need help connecting with government services or you want to research or weigh in on legislation that is being considered, you definitely want to find the website for a government office. Especially if you need government services, it's important not to go to a campaign website and fill out a contact form, because the campaign may be prohibited from sharing information with the government office. But if you want to get involved with a political campaign in some way, or research the people on your ballot, or even find a campaign ad you saw on TV, you'll definitely want to go to a political candidate website. In either instance, if you use a contact form or an email address, expect a response from staff, not from the politician.

WHY AM I SEEING ONLINE ADS FOR A PARTICULAR ELECTED OFFICIAL OR CANDIDATE OVER AND OVER?

Ever notice that when you look at an item on Amazon that you don't buy, you start seeing online ads for that product everywhere? That's not a coincidence. Amazon puts a small file (called a *cookie*) on your computer to keep track of all the products you view. Then it spends money to run online ads for those products, but only when the right cookie is on the computer. Politicians can do the same sort of thing when you visit their websites. Chances are good that if you visit the page for a political candidate, you'll start seeing their online ads everywhere. But even if you've never visited the page, you may still see the ads. That's because your computer, much like your house, has an address, known as an *Internet protocol,* or *IP,* address. And much like your house address, your IP address is roughly based on your location. That means a local politician can also place ads that show up for you because they know you live in their district. Best of all: You don't have to constantly search for new information — it's sent right to your email inbox

TIP

Look for icons linking the elected official or candidate on other social media platforms, such as Twitter, Facebook, or Instagram.

Subscribing to an email list

>> **Government official:** A government official is likely to use an email list to send out regular newsletter updates weekly, biweekly, monthly, or infrequently. However often the newsletter is sent out, it's likely to highlight positive press coverage, new policy announcements, recent accomplishments, and photos of the official traveling around the district or state.

>> **Political candidate:** A political candidate is much less likely to have a set schedule for emailing a list, and is somewhat less likely to regularly update the newsletter. Instead, you should expect sporadic emails at least once every few weeks, but possibly multiple times within one week. Right before an election, you might get multiple emails a day. The content will likely highlight a single news story, a single policy position, a new campaign ad, an invitation to an upcoming campaign event, or a fundraising solicitation. Because most campaigns must report the money they've raised at the end of each quarter, you should expect to see a lot of fundraising emails at the end of March, June, September, and December — usually, with a message that underscores the urgency of the deadline.

If you've already found the website of the person or office you're looking for, you're probably pretty close. Look for the box to submit your email address and click the Submit or Sign Up button.

WHY DO CANDIDATES SEND FUNDRAISING EMAILS ASKING FOR $3?

If you sign up to receive emails from political candidates, you'll notice that they continually email you to ask for money and that many ask you to donate just $3. What's so special about $3? Why not $5 or $10 or $25? First, $3 is a relatively low amount that many people don't mind donating. Second, most people who donate once will probably donate again later. That can add up quickly to the $50 or $100 (or more) that many people might not donate all at once. Finally, and perhaps most importantly, campaigns these days spend a lot of money on online ads trying to entice people to sign up for newsletters. Generally speaking, most campaigns consider it a success if they spend an average of $3 or less per email address on their list. So, if they can persuade someone to donate $3, that person has paid for themselves.

Email lists from politicians are a great way to stay current on what's happening in government or in a political campaign. If you're more interested in policy and the happenings of government, sign up on a government office website. If you're more interested in politics and elections, sign up on a campaign website. *Remember:* You aren't limited to email lists from elected officials or candidates only in your area. Signing up for the email list of elected officials in other parts of your state, or for candidates you might have seen on TV in other states, is a great way to gain multiple perspectives and stay up-to-date.

WARNING

If you don't want to sign up for an email list, be cautious about signing any petition or taking any survey on the website of an elected official or a political candidate where you're asked to enter your email address. Generally, such tactics are aimed more at collecting new email sign-ups than signing the actual petition or survey.

Liking a Facebook page

The *Facebook* social media platform allows users to write messages, share photos and videos, and discuss innumerable topics with other users in an easy-to-follow manner. Users subscribe to the posts of public officials and candidates by "Liking" their accounts:

>> **Government official:** Many government officials use their Facebook pages to share press releases, photos, links to government services, and statements on current events and legislative debates. In some sense, government officials tend to use their Facebook pages to share a lot of the information you might find on their websites, but it's more continually updated.

>> **Political candidate:** Political candidates usually focus more on sharing news stories, commentary, and statements about current events and policy positions. They also tend to share more videos than government officials because political campaigns often have professionals on their teams to make their TV ads.

If you can't find a link to the Facebook account on the politician's home website, log in to your Facebook account. After you're logged in, you can type the name of the politician you're trying to find in the search bar at the top of the screen. Generally, the account you're looking for will be one of the first results.

The same rules about visiting websites applies to Facebook: If you want to read or leave comments about government services or legislative issues being debated, look for the governmental account. If you want to weigh in on a certain aspect of a campaign or ask questions about how to get involved, find the political campaign account. But realize that in most cases, it's governmental or campaign staff who are helping to manage the Facebook page. So, although it might look like you're interacting with a politician, you might be interacting with their staff instead. Some politicians comment on their own pages, though, and they often clearly specify who's speaking. If you aren't sure, it doesn't hurt to politely ask which person you're interacting with.

REMEMBER

Many elected officials have two accounts on websites like Facebook and Twitter — one for their government office and the other for their political campaign. With multiple accounts under the same name, how can you be sure you're following a legitimate account? Look for the Verified checkmark — a blue circle with a white checkmark next to accounts that are verified by the account holders. This icon is especially useful to ensure that you're following real-life politicians.

HOW ARE ONLINE ADS ON FACEBOOK DIFFERENT FROM OTHER ONLINE ADS?

Though a lot of the online ads you see may be based on what webpages you've visited, Facebook is a little bit different. When you create your account on Facebook, you can enter in a lot of information about yourself: Where you live, what religion you are, what your political beliefs are, and so on. Additionally, every time you "Like" a page you're revealing more information about yourself. Facebook lets advertisers, including candidates, show ads just to people who have entered in certain information, or who like certain pages. For instance, if you say that your political beliefs are Republican, then you will probably see a lot of ads on Facebook for Republican candidates. If you "Liked" the page for Hillary Clinton, you will probably see a lot of ads on Facebook for Democratic candidates.

Following a Twitter account

The *Twitter* social media website allows users to post short thoughts (or responses to the thoughts of others) in no more than 280 characters. You subscribe to the posts of others by following their accounts.

>> **Government official:** Government officials often use Twitter as a way to offer thoughts on policy or legislation ahead of a vote, or they may give updates as they travel around their districts or states. These officials usually place less emphasis on government services on their Twitter accounts as compared to other platforms, and more emphasis on current events. They may also break up large press statements over multiple posts, and they frequently link to press releases or other content on their websites.

>> **Political candidate:** Political candidates usually focus heavily on sharing and providing commentary on news stories, especially when it's relevant to their election. They also tend to engage other users, especially other politicians and reporters, more than government official accounts might do. Because of the 280-character limit on tweets, political candidates tend to sound a bit more informal on Twitter than they do on other platforms.

OTHER WAYS TO CONNECT WITH ELECTED OFFICIALS

I describe in this chapter four ways that you can find politicians on the Internet, though usage beyond these platforms isn't universal. Still, you may have luck finding politicians you're interested in on other platforms. The same general rules on how to find politicians, and when to interact, apply:

- **YouTube:** A site for sharing videos of nearly any length, which politicians use to share speeches they've given or TV ads they're running

- **Instagram:** A social media site that is used solely for sharing pictures

- **Snapchat:** A social media app for your phone that allows you to share short videos and pictures

- **Medium:** A website that allows users to publish essays, which many politicians use to share items such as opinion columns they write for newspapers

New Internet platforms pop up all the time, so be sure to check the websites of politicians to see where you might find them.

As with Facebook, look for a link on a politician's home website first. If that fails, log in to your Twitter account and enter the name you're looking for into the search bar at the top of the page. You should usually see the name in one of the first search results.

Again, some of the same rules apply when determining whether to interact with a governmental or political account. But whereas a Facebook page is likely managed by staff, politicians much more commonly use their own Twitter accounts. Again, it doesn't hurt to ask politely if you aren't sure, but Twitter is the platform where you're most likely to be able to interact directly with an elected official or candidate.

Don't assume that a politician has seen a post from you on their page. Because Twitter is limited to 280 characters per message, users see more messages, and conversations can move *fast*. Sometimes you may have to post several times before you receive a response, especially if several people are all trying to attract the politician's attention.

Sample resources

To help get you started on contacting or following your elected officials and candidates online, Table 9-1 lists some politicians and organizations you might want to look into. To become politically engaged online in no time, start visiting these pages and subscribing to their email lists, liking their Facebook posts, or following their Twitter accounts.

TABLE 9-1: Politics Online

Politician or Organization	Type	URL
President Donald Trump (government)	Website	www.whitehouse.gov
Donald Trump (candidate)	Website	www.donaldjtrump.com
Donald Trump (government)	Twitter	www.twitter.com/POTUS
Vice President Mike Pence (government)	Facebook	www.facebook.com/VicePresidentPence
Mike Pence (candidate)	Facebook	www.facebook.com/MikePence
US House Speaker Nancy Pelosi (government)	Twitter	www.twitter.com/SpeakerPelosi
Republican National Committee	Website	www.gop.com
Democratic National Committee	Website	www.democrats.org

4

It's All Marketing

Chapter **10**

Harry Handler Meets Carly Candidate

To understand any campaign, you need to remember that it's all about marketing, pure and simple. The product is a candidate — not soap, cornflakes, or cars — but the technique is essentially the same, with one critical difference: You can purchase soap, cornflakes, or a car anytime you want to (provided you have the money). But in a campaign for election, the sale and purchase of the product take place on only one day in an election cycle.

WARNING

Either you make your purchase on the first Tuesday after the first Monday in November, or someone else makes the purchase for you. In some elections, the date may be different, but the principle is the same. The purchase occurs with or without your input.

It may be a little insulting to suggest that a political candidate's campaign is, in essence, the same as selling soap, cornflakes, or cars, but the analogy is accurate. A candidate is packaged, marketed, and sold to the voters. Citizens use their votes as the currency to "buy" the candidate of their choice. Not every voter receives their choice, but all the currency is spent (or else it's valueless).

Handling a Campaign

Who decides how the candidate — I'll call her Carly Candidate — is packaged? Who calls the shots about marketing strategy, such as what Carly says and when she says it? In high-visibility elections for important offices, those decisions are usually made in consultation with professional political consultants, also called *handlers.*

The handler makes all the important decisions about when the candidate conveys her message and how the money for the campaign is spent. (Other professionals specialize in raising the money.)

Examining the profile of a political handler

Professional handlers usually follow similar career paths. I'll use the fictional Harry Handler for the purpose of this discussion.

Starting as a volunteer

Harry probably enters politics as a volunteer in a local campaign. He works for his state or national party while learning the ropes of the political world, or for an elected official in his state or in Congress. (See Chapter 4 for how to volunteer your time in a campaign.)

Getting paid as a staffer

Next, Harry becomes a paid staffer in a political campaign. He is expected to work long hours for very little pay. He is young and, fortunately, has incredible amounts of energy — a necessary commodity for campaign work.

Working in a high-visibility campaign demands a total commitment of his time and effort. Harry has no life outside the campaign as long as the campaign lasts — no vacations, no leisurely dinners, no time for romance. Harry measures success and failure by the amount of money raised and the press coverage for a particular day; a day with the fundraising quota met and with good press coverage is a good campaign day. It's fair to say that a political campaign consumes the lives of the staffers and handlers as well as the candidate.

Some campaign staffers remain active in their state in subsequent elections. They may have other jobs that they leave to come back to campaigning. But Harry remains in politics full time, graduating to the level of handler.

WHY DO PEOPLE DO THIS TO THEMSELVES?

Campaign workers put in their long, poorly compensated hours because they like the work. As crazy as that may seem, some individuals truly enjoy the demands that a campaign imposes. They enjoy working closely with others to achieve a common, higher goal: the election of the person they view as the better candidate.

This goal, coupled with the excitement of being part of a campaign, is what initially encourages young people to get involved. It takes a certain personality type — and a unique combination of ability and luck — to stay involved and make it into the small circle of successful, well-compensated Harry Handlers.

If you're thinking about becoming a handler, remember that it's a risky business. If you lose a couple of campaigns in a row, you may need to find another line of work. You also should realize that handling a campaign is seldom compatible with a healthy family life and children.

Becoming a handler

After rising from the ranks of the young, poorly paid campaign workers to the rarefied atmosphere enjoyed by handlers, Harry is now much better paid. It may still be a labor of love, but, for political handlers, campaign work is well compensated.

Harry is friendly with a lot of other handlers. He and his associates probably reside in or around Washington, DC. Other handlers are more like nomads, wandering from state to state and working in election after election.

Moving around within the party

Many professional handlers move from state to state and from campaign to campaign like migrant farm workers. But, usually, these handlers choose political sides — they work exclusively for Republican or Democratic candidates. Party affiliation may be the only criterion for employment. They work for conservative, moderate, or liberal candidates from the party of their choice. They are particular only as far as the party label; to work for both sides of the political fence could hurt their credibility and make them less marketable.

Working for a common goal

The handlers for the candidates defend their candidates and verbally attack the opponents during the campaign. Each believes in their own candidate and thinks it best for the voters if that candidate wins. But all handlers share a commitment to win.

>> They conduct hard-fought campaigns based on different approaches to issues, which may or may not be real.

>> They exploit every weakness of the opposing candidate.

>> They use whatever tactics (usually within the law) to gain support for their candidate.

>> They launch attacks on opponents so that the candidates themselves can stay above the fray.

POLITICAL STUFF

Shared respect for the political process can sometimes overcome the antagonism that comes from being on opposite sides in an election. Look at James Carville and Mary Matalin. During the 1992 presidential campaign, Carville was a handler for Bill Clinton, and Matalin was a handler for George H. W. Bush. Though they were on opposite ends of a major political battle, they didn't let it interfere with their long-term romance, and they were married after the election was over. Now, they may be joined in marriage, but still not in politics. Carville still works for Democrats, and Matalin remains a Republican.

Developing a Marketing Strategy

Carly Candidate relies on her consultant, Harry Handler, to devise a strategy for winning your votes. Harry's marketing strategy spans all facets of Carly's candidacy:

>> Your reaction to the candidate's appearance

>> Your image of the candidate

>> The message you hear from the candidate

Checking out the candidate's appearance

When Harry Handler is brought in to manage a highly visible campaign, he looks first at the candidate's appearance to see whether improvement is necessary or possible. Does the candidate dress correctly for the image that the campaign is trying to project? For example, if the campaign wants to project the candidate as a no-nonsense businessperson, Harry may decide not to dress the candidate casually, choosing a dark business suit instead. Harry may bring in a fashion consultant to help with the dress, hairstyle, and makeup. The fashion consultant's job is to suggest clothes and hairstyles that reinforce the desired image. A candidate's look may change over the course of the campaign, as different issues or different swing voters become central to the results.

Judging a book by its cover

Appearance is a vital part of any campaign. Many voters see the candidate only once or twice, for short periods, in the course of the campaign. First impressions may be the only impressions. They're extremely important, so it's not surprising that a great deal of thought goes into the candidate's appearance.

Small changes in dress or grooming can result in subtle changes in the manner in which a candidate is perceived. Remember when Dan Rather, of CBS News fame, began wearing sweaters under his sports jackets on the nightly news? Some fashion consultant decided that wearing sweaters would make Dan seem more approachable and likable. If more people liked Dan, the CBS News ratings would go up — obviously, Dan and CBS News were willing to give it a try. Don't dismiss the importance of small changes to a candidate's appearance.

POLITICAL MYTH

Also remember that no Harry Handler, no matter how good, can create a silk purse from a sow's ear. The changes I'm talking about are relatively minor. Fine-tuning is the order of the day. Smoothing out rough edges is the goal more than fundamental change. Should the candidate wear contact lenses instead of glasses? Is a body wave for his hair appropriate? Is the hair color acceptable? Could they lose ten pounds? Do they need a red tie or accessory to spice up their image, or a light blue tie or accessory to make them seem calmer? These are not wholesale changes. A handler can't (yet) alter the candidate's genetic makeup. No matter how much the handler would want it, the candidate won't turn into Chris Evans or Jennifer Lawrence for the duration of the campaign.

Still, the press always treats these changes as newsworthy, even though most of the changes a handler requests are nothing more than what you would do to get ready for your 25th high school reunion. If you go in for a makeover and change your appearance, are you being manipulative?

Opening the family album

When Harry Handler is reviewing the candidate's appearance, he also considers the appearance of the candidate's family. Does the candidate's wife wear her skirts too short? Does she otherwise dress in a way that reveals too many of her physical endowments? If the candidate is a woman, how does her husband look? How does he dress? Does he wear too much flashy jewelry? Do the candidate's daughters suffer from big-hair disease (too much hair going in too many directions all at once)? Do the candidate's sons dress like extras in a rap video?

A nice-looking family can be an asset to a candidate. Their appearance can reassure the voters that the candidate can be trusted — for example, she's a nice, ordinary family woman, just like the voter. But if the appearance of a candidate or family member strikes a discordant note, the voters may hesitate to support the candidate. That's unfair, of course — anyone who has raised teenagers knows about the constant battle to make them leave the house dressed as full-fledged members of the human race. Sometimes, you just shrug and suspend hostilities in the constant war about what a teenager may wear, but even though you may be lax yourself, you expect more from your elected officials. After all, if a candidate can't manage their own family, how can they hope to manage a city, state, or nation?

Improving a candidate's image

In addition to physical appearance, handlers concentrate on the candidate's image. To gain voter's support, the candidate must come across as a leader and inspire confidence and trust. Voters want to be enthusiastic about their leaders. They want a good person — a person of honesty and integrity. People want to feel secure that the candidate is mentally, physically, and morally ready to hold an important government office.

Getting on TV

Handlers work to create situations that reassure voters on all the fronts I just mentioned. They try to arrange situations where the television coverage of a campaign event reinforces a positive image for the candidate.

Campaigns work hard at developing those visual images because more and more Americans get their political information and news from the media. Most of them trust what they see on TV more than what they read in the newspapers. That's why presidential campaigns work hard on the free media visuals that you see on the nightly news or on the web. The campaigns also spend most of the money they raise for the campaign on television commercials and social media.

Employing image-boosting gimmicks

Handlers have made an art of manipulating the images of their candidates. If you know the methods handlers employ to market candidates, you can recognize those methods when a campaign directs them at you. You can decide whether you're impressed. Or not. You can cut through the glitz and slick marketing devices and decide whether this is the candidate you want to support. You can see through the techniques and base your decision on issues and substance rather than on good marketing strategies.

IMAGE VERSUS REALITY — SOMETIMES, REALITY WINS

When George H. W. Bush was running for president, his handlers decided that they needed to show that Bush was not the haughty patrician he seemed to be, but was really just a regular guy. They wanted to demonstrate that voters could trust him because he was just like they were. He worried about the same things and spent his time the same way they did. How did they demonstrate how regular Old George was? They put him in a pair of jeans and sent him into a bar in Texas to talk to the customers. He ate pork rinds. The national news ate it up.

In 1988, when Michael Dukakis's handler decided that the Democratic nominee for president had to reinforce his image as a candidate who strongly supported the military, he had Dukakis pose for photographs in a tank while wearing a helmet. Dukakis's "Harry" sorely misjudged the situation. The picture he created was of a short, uncomfortable candidate very much out of place in a military setting. Although the Dukakis campaign had other crippling issues, the "Dukakis in a tank" image contributed in no small part to his eventual defeat.

Sometimes, Harry's right. Sometimes, Harry's wrong.

Whenever a handler alters a candidate's appearance or puts them in a setting where they would not normally appear, the handler is manipulating appearances to win you over to the candidate's side. You don't have to reject a candidate who resorts to these tactics, but you should be aware enough to recognize them for what they are.

WARNING

To move beyond the slick marketing, be aware of some common techniques used to market candidates:

>> **Warm fuzzies:** Shots that create a happy or comfortable feeling — posing with the family or the family pet, holding a baby, speaking with an elderly person while holding her hand — all designed to make you like and trust the candidate

>> **Patriotic themes:** Shots that inspire feelings of national pride — flags in the background, parades, patriotic music — all designed to make you identify the candidate with patriotism

>> **Informal poses:** Shots of the candidate in a flannel shirt, with a suit jacket slung over the shoulder or a tie loosened, designed to persuade you that the candidate is a regular guy, just like you

>> **Testimonials:** Testimonials about the candidate by relatively unknown third parties who tell you good things about the candidate's background or record, designed to reassure you that other people like you are also supporting the candidate

>> **Action shots:** Shots of the candidate in motion — talking to voters, viewing the manufacturing process up close, talking to children in the classroom — and designed to show the candidate on the move, working for constituents and working on the issues they're worried about, such as jobs and education

>> **Staged events:** Shots of occasions where campaign staffers have worked hard to turn out as many people as possible, designed to demonstrate the candidate's popularity

The event may take place in a room that's too small, in order to make the crowd appear larger than it actually is. The staffers make signs that look as if the audience created them spontaneously. Other visuals, like balloons and red-white-and-blue bunting, are used to create a festive atmosphere.

POLITICAL STUFF

OPPONENT MAKEOVER

At the same time that campaigns work to establish a positive image for their candidates, they are not above creating a negative image for the opponent.

In the 1988 campaign, George H. W Bush's consultants told him that Democrats would not vote for Dukakis if he were seen as soft on crime and unpatriotic. The Bush campaign decided to redo Michael Dukakis's image. By the time they were finished, the Willie Horton ad (an ad that concentrated on a repeat offender named Willie Horton and the concept of jails with revolving doors) and the debate over whether schoolteachers should be required to recite the Pledge of Allegiance had remade Dukakis's image and the election was decided in Bush's favor. (For more on the Willie Horton ad, see Chapter 18.)

In the 2000 presidential contest, Vice President Al Gore needed to shake off an image that he was stiff and robotic. The campaign was desperate to make him seem more "warm and fuzzy." First, Gore was dressed in sweaters of various shades of brown to portray him as a regular guy. Then when he was nominated at the convention in Los Angeles, he and then-wife Tipper engaged in a prolonged, congratulatory kiss onstage that created quite a stir in the media. That action may have improved his image, but unfortunately for him, the improvement was short-lived.

Another method used in 1994 to make over the image of the opponent was *morphing*, which is the technique of fading from the opponent's photo to a photo of an unpopular but recognizable third party. The object is to make voters associate the opponent with the unpopular third party. This technique was used in many congressional races around the country by Republican candidates for the House of Representatives. They would morph the Democratic candidate's face until it turned into President Bill Clinton's. (For more about campaign techniques that focus on the opponent, see Chapter 18.)

These techniques convey visual images designed to sway you into supporting the candidate. They're good marketing strategies because you think positive thoughts about the candidate when you see them.

But a good marketing strategy is not a sound reason to choose an elected official. You need to recognize this strategy for what it is and move on to substance before you decide how to cast your vote. After all, most candidates have a family and some friends willing to say nice things about them. Candidates are patriotic folks, and flannel shirts are comfortable.

REMEMBER

A candidate is free to use these marketing techniques as long as they aren't the sum and substance of the campaign. Make sure that the candidate gives you a sound, tangible reason — something other than slick packaging and marketing — before you give them your support. (See Chapter 11 for more on how to decide which candidate to support.)

Identifying the message

Perhaps the biggest step in the marketing campaign is to identify the message. Many factors go into deciding what message Carly Candidate will spend the campaign communicating to you:

>> Carly starts with some ideas that she wants to discuss or issues that she thinks need to be addressed.

>> You and the voters have issues or problems that you want Carly to talk about.

>> Carly and her opponent may have records to promote or defend.

>> Groups of voters may be clamoring for positions on issues of importance to them.

>> Even the media may have ideas about what the campaign should include.

All this goes into the mix when Harry Handler determines Carly's message.

Focus groups

If Harry Handler has enough campaign money, he conducts *focus groups* to discuss your responses to issues and approaches the campaign wants to take in depth before or after the first poll is taken. Campaigns use focus groups to gain in-depth knowledge of the voters' concerns and attitudes. That is, they do if they can afford focus groups — which cost tens of thousands of dollars each.

"IT'S THE MESSAGE, STUPID"

In the 1992 presidential campaign, Bill Clinton preached a simple message, which was displayed on the wall of campaign headquarters in Little Rock: "Change versus more of the same. The economy, stupid. Don't forget healthcare."

"The economy, stupid" mattered to the voters. They were worried about the national recession, which had appeared under the Bush presidency. Clinton's simple message carried the day.

In the 2000 election, George W. Bush's message was equally simple: Bush was not Clinton. Bush was a family man who would not engage in sexual activity with an intern in the Oval Office and then lie about it. Al Gore had a more populist message that attempted to identify with average Americans in fighting against the powerful moneyed interests that Gore said Bush was representing.

In 1980, Ronald Reagan's message was a question: He asked voters whether they were better off in 1980 than they had been in 1976. The answer was no, and that answer translated into votes for Reagan on election day. He defeated the incumbent, Jimmy Carter, with that message.

In 2008, in the throes of the biggest recession since the Great Depression, Barack Obama's message of "Yes, we can" appealed to voters looking for a hopeful sign for the future.

In 2016, Donald Trump's message was Make America Great Again — and build a wall on the border between the United States and Mexico. That message resonated, and it proved to be a winning formula for him.

At most, Carly can emphasize two or three issues in a campaign. Picking the right issues can mean the difference between winning and losing. Harry doesn't rely on his instincts or the instincts of Carly Candidate to refine the content of the message that Carly will deliver; he checks it out first with you, the voter. Harry touches those bases with you and the other voters by conducting focus groups and polling. (See the two later sections "Focus groups" and "Benchmark polls.")

Harry wants Carly Candidate to be successful. You, the voter, are the key to that success. Harry and Carly must know what's on your mind — what you want the candidates to talk about. Harry Handler tries to find out what you think about the following:

- **Carly and her opponent:** Help Harry decide how to make Carly's case and whether to attack her opponent.

- **Carly's ideas and proposals:** Help Harry decide which two or three of Carly's ideas or proposals to emphasize in Carly's message.

- **Proposals that Carly's opponent is making:** Help Harry decide whether to ignore the opponent.

- **Carly's record:** Assuming that Carly has established a record, do her actions impress or offend you?

- **Her opponent's record:** Assuming that the opponent has established a record, do their actions impress or offend you?

Focus groups bring in a random, representative sample of the voters in a candidate's district. The people in the sample are paid to spend a few hours discussing the candidates, the issues, and their attitudes in great depth with Harry Handler or a facilitator.

If a candidate is running for statewide office and wants to use focus groups, more than one focus group needs to be held, because different regions may have different ideas about the issues. For example, a focus group in the northern part of a state may list economic development and jobs as their primary concern because a plant just closed in that area of the state, putting thousands of workers out of work. Another area of the state may list crime as the number-one issue because a vicious murder just occurred in that area. Holding more than one focus group permits the campaign to understand regional differences in emphasis. (See Chapter 5 for more on focus groups.)

Benchmark polls

Harry Handler orders a professional *benchmark poll* as early in the campaign as money and campaign research permit. (See Chapter 15 for more about benchmark polls.) Money is important because a statewide poll can cost between $25,000 and $40,000. Campaign research is important because the campaign needs to know what questions to ask in the poll.

Consider a candidate for governor who wants to talk about their program for capital improvements in the state's highways and bridges. (A *capital improvement* by government is an expenditure designed to improve long-term productivity, such as sewer, highways, bridges, or dams.) They may think that this program is an important way to appeal to voters. No candidate in a high-visibility race discusses such a program or how to pay for it without first determining, via polling and perhaps focus groups, whether the voters in the state share their ideas and are willing to vote for them because of those ideas.

For example, a poll that asks whether the state highway or bridge system could stand improvement will receive an overwhelming response of *yes*. Voters always agree that the situation can be improved. The trick for a pollster is to measure the depth of that support for improvement. Are the voters willing to see improvements made in highways and bridges if they have to pay for those improvements?

Sometimes voters want it all. They may be enthusiastic about suggested highway and bridge improvements, but that enthusiasm disappears when asked which tax they are willing to raise to pay for the improvements. The poll will test the level of enthusiasm as well as the most palatable method of financing the capital improvements, if any. If the poll shows that the public is unwilling to pay for the improvements, Carly discards the highway and bridge improvement program. In this political climate, no candidate who wants to be elected proposes a tax increase that does not have broad, popular support.

WARNING

An unscrupulous candidate may raise a proposal requiring significant new public spending, even if polling shows that voters don't want to finance it. When pressed for a financing mechanism to pay for the capital program, the unscrupulous candidate may duck and weave. The candidate may deliberately understate the cost of the capital program or propose a funding source that they know is inadequate for the task.

Remember this old adage: If something appears too good to be true, it probably is. Unscrupulous politicians are not above making false promises to gain politically. You need to ask yourself whether that's the type of leader you want in office. Are you willing to vote for a candidate who promises you the moon with no chance of delivering? The choice is yours.

A leader or a follower?

Harry Handler completes the research, the focus groups, and the polling, all to find out what you want the candidate's message to be. Harry is trying to identify those items that you want discussed and the proposals you want to hear more about. This entire exercise is performed to capture your interest and, ultimately, your vote for Carly Candidate.

If your opinion on an issue changes, Carly Candidate can change her message. You may change your mind because events occur and receive media coverage. For example, the capital improvement program for highways that Harry Handler decided not to frame as an issue may suddenly get new life when a bridge collapses and a series of news stories about the condition of the state's bridges alarms the public. Or, the opponent may launch an unanticipated attack that requires a response. Campaigns may have a game plan and a message, but they must remain flexible if they want to win. At this point, you may be troubled. The behavior of candidates as described here may sound sneaky or even scary to you. You may say that a candidate who would shift with the winds isn't good enough for you. You want a candidate who doesn't need to look to you and other voters to determine how they feel about an issue or what they want to propose to improve the situation. You may say that you want to vote for a *leader* to represent you — not a parrot who mimics what you and the other voters are thinking and feeling. Perhaps you want an elected official who will tell you what you need to hear even when the message is unpleasant. After all, you don't want to choose someone whose only goal is to get reelected.

Just as a candidate who is merely a follower isn't good enough for you, being merely a leader isn't good enough, either. Do you really want a candidate or an officeholder who doesn't pay attention to what you and the other voters think? Are you comfortable with a candidate who is so sure of herself that she doesn't want or need input from you? Of course not — you have a right to be heard, especially because you've become politically involved and know what is going on.

A better approach is to elect a candidate who has a reason for running other than winning. You want a candidate with ideas about what needs to be done and how it should be accomplished — a leader, but not only a leader. You have a right to demand more. You have a right to demand a candidate who will lead and, at the same time, listen. You're entitled to elect an officeholder who doesn't think that they must be the originator of every worthwhile idea or program — someone who is aware that they haven't cornered the market on brains or creativity, regardless of what their handler wants you to think. You deserve to elect someone who wants to do what you want but isn't afraid to propose ideas and suggestions of their own — someone who knows that they were elected to represent you.

Finding that type of candidate isn't easy — Chapter 11 shows you how to select a candidate. But once you absorb enough information from this book to become politically aware, you'll have a better shot at recognizing a candidate of that caliber when you see them. You'll also know what to do to get them elected and what to do when they're in office to keep then on the straight-and-narrow path of leading and following so that they can be the type of official you want and deserve.

Responding to a Handler's Controls

How should you react to the ways in which Harry Handler controls Carly Candidate's campaign? You can view them as smart marketing moves to win you over. You can view them as deceptions designed to manipulate you into voting a certain way. Or, you can view them as somewhere between the two extremes, as described in this list:

>> **Smart marketing moves:** Many of us voters don't worry too much about candidate makeovers, because we do the same thing all the time ourselves. We've all changed our hairstyles. We go from long to short, from sophisticated to casual, from curly to straight hair. Many people even change their hair color every couple of months. Almost everyone changes their clothing style and eyewear. We're used to changes of this nature because we all try to look our best, and what constitutes our best changes with the styles and over time. Because you make these sorts of changes yourself, you shouldn't view them as manipulative. You should consider them good marketing or packaging techniques.

>> **Between the two extremes:** More voters are concerned when Carly's *image* is changed. We are more skeptical of changes like these because we don't have experience with them ourselves. Whether you view these as legitimate marketing techniques or blatant attempts to manipulate you into voting a certain way probably depends on whether you think they're sincere.

Take, for example, the situation where Harry softens Carly's image. If Carly is a caring person who has a warm, loving relationship with her family, it's fair to portray her that way. Harry is trying to counter an unfair perception of Carly as a tough, self-centered person with visual evidence of the true facts. On the other hand, Harry may be trying to create an image that doesn't exist. Carly may *be* a tough, self-centered individual who doesn't have a warm, loving relationship with her family or anyone else, in which case Harry is skillfully using visual images to create a false impression in your mind to influence how you vote.

TIP

How do you decide which is which? The answer is that it isn't easy. You must be alert to these tactics. When they occur in a campaign, recognize them for what they are. When you begin seeing Carly on television night after night in warm images that aren't what you associated with her, your baloney-detector antennae should go up. Read about Carly and talk to people who knew her before she became a candidate. Then you can decide whether Carly is the type of person you want in a position of power.

>> **Manipulation:** When Harry tries to control the *message* Carly delivers, voters are even more worried about being manipulated. On one hand, we want Carly to talk about the issues *we* think are important. On the other hand, we want to know the instincts that Carly will follow on new issues when they appear before her. We don't want her to use focus groups and polling to tell us only those things that we want to hear. We want her to be responsive to us, *and* we want her to be a leader. Our fear is that Harry will control the flow of information from Carly to us, and we won't receive the type of information we need in order to cast an informed vote.

TIP

If you don't hear any new ideas from Carly Candidate, you should wonder why. If she can't tell you why she's running for office, you should be skeptical. If you hear Carly identify problems but propose no solutions, you should be concerned. If Carly talks about diversions and not important and complex issues, you should listen carefully (see Chapter 16 for more about diversions). If Carly focuses on complex hot button issues with raw emotional appeal and reduces her solution to a slogan which fixes blame on a segment of the population, you should consider whether you're being manipulated.

It's up to you to determine whether a candidate's campaign is a good marketing strategy or a dishonest attempt to manipulate your emotions to get you to vote for them. If you decide that you're being manipulated, you should ask yourself whether you're comfortable with a candidate who is willing to use such tactics in a position of power.

Chapter **11**

Selling the Candidates, Warts and All

No candidate for any office is perfect — that stands to reason, doesn't it? After all, candidates are people, just like the rest of us. They don't come from some genetic laboratory that harvests just the right combination of intelligence, appearance, personality, and ambition to create the perfect candidate. Candidates come in all shapes and sizes. Some candidates are intelligent; some aren't. Some candidates are articulate; some can't string two sentences together to complete a thought. Some candidates look great in front of a camera; some candidates have faces made for radio.

This chapter deals with how professional campaign consultants, called *handlers* (see Chapter 10 for more on handlers), identify a candidate's flaws (I call them *warts*) and selling points (I call them *beauty marks*) to best market that candidate to you.

Fixing the Warts: A Nip Here, a Tuck There

One of the most important things that Harry Handler must do to devise a campaign strategy is determine what types of problems Carly Candidate has. Now, you might think this task would be easy — Harry should just ask Carly what flaws she has. The problem with this approach is that Carly may not realize what her flaws are. And if she's a first-time candidate, she may be uncomfortable even discussing flaws, not realizing how devastating a creative attack by an opponent can be.

If Harry can't rely on Carly for this information to devise his strategy, what should he do? The answer is *internal opposition research*. Harry then can find out everything he needs to know about Carly — even people, places, and events that Carly has forgotten. Internal opposition research tells Harry where the attacks will come from and what he has to do to keep your support.

Let's get personal: Personal questions

Internal opposition research for the first-time candidate relies heavily on the memory and candor of the candidate. The handler grills the candidate on a variety of issues:

>> Arrest record, for both the candidate and family members

>> Tax returns

>> Lawsuits (either on the receiving end or the filing end)

>> Ordinance violations

>> Overdue debts

>> Overdue property taxes

>> Bankruptcy

>> Published written work (even while as a student, or letters to the editor on a controversial topic)

>> Anyone with private knowledge of the candidate who may bear a grudge

>> Employment (Is there anything about the employment that would cause bad feelings among voters? Does the candidate operate a business that has been accused of polluting the area?)

>> Relationship problems with a spouse

>> Children who may cause trouble

When Harry Handler has the answers to these questions, he can devise a strategy to win and keep your support for Carly Candidate.

POLITICAL STUFF

SEX, LIES, AND POLITICS

The Harry Handlers of old didn't have to worry so much if Carly Candidate had some secrets about her personal life to conceal. The topic of a candidate's sexual life didn't get reported in the press unless it was an unusual situation. Here are two notable exceptions from the 19th century:

- Andrew Jackson's wife, Rachel, was labeled a bigamist. Her divorce from her first husband was not finalized, as they believed, when Andrew and Rachel married. They had to remarry two years later. Her marital status was an issue in Jackson's 1828 campaign.

- Bachelor candidate Grover Cleveland was accused of fathering a child out of wedlock. He acknowledged the child, but his opponents didn't let the issue die. They used a song to remind the voters of Cleveland's misconduct: "Ma! Ma! Where's my Pa! Gone to the White House! Ha! Ha! Ha!"

Long after their deaths, it was revealed that presidents from Harding through Johnson had led interesting personal lives that could have presented political problems if revealed by the press.

In the past, the press ignored rumors about candidates or officeholders unless doing so was impossible. For example, in the 1970s, stories about drinking and other activities by Congressman Wilbur Mills, chairman of the Ways and Means Committee of the House of Representatives, didn't make the news until Representative Mills appeared on a burlesque stage and then waded in the Tidal Basin in front of the Jefferson Memorial with Fanne Foxe, his stripper girlfriend. That type of activity was too public for the press to ignore. Mills admitted having a drinking problem, was stripped of his powerful chairmanship, and did not seek reelection.

Another, more recent example of changing press attitudes involved Senator Gary Hart, who was a married candidate for president in 1988. The *Miami Herald* followed Hart in an attempt to catch him spending the night with his girlfriend. Catch him they did, and Hart withdrew from the race. The *Miami Herald* justified its decision to tail Hart by saying that he invited the scrutiny with his famous quote, "If you think I am fooling around on my wife, follow me." What the *Miami Herald* didn't tell anyone was that they were following Hart before he ever made that comment.

Many of the incidents involving the sexual conduct of persons in high places have been the subject of public testimony and, therefore, press coverage. Take, for example, the Congressional hearings where Donald Trump's former personal attorney testified.

(continued)

(continued)

The testimony revealed that, shortly before the 2016 presidential election, the attorney paid women substantial sums of money on behalf of Donald Trump. The money was paid to these women to keep quiet about the sexual relations they said they had with Donald Trump. Some of that information became public before the election, but it did not affect the outcome.

All the coverage about the sexual exploits of elected officials pale in comparison to the extraordinary coverage given to President Clinton's activities with Monica Lewinsky. His involvement with her, a young, White House intern, and his refusal to admit his misconduct led to an impeachment trial in the US Senate in 1999. The impeachment trial was only the second time in the nation's history that a sitting president was impeached. Richard Nixon resigned from office before Congress could complete the process of impeaching him. President Andrew Johnson was the only other president to be tried in the Senate, and he, too, was acquitted.

Just for the record: Officeholder record

If Carly Candidate is an incumbent or former officeholder, Harry Handler needs to research the record of Carly's term in office. In addition to all the personal questions, he must ask these professional questions about Carly's term in office:

>> Did she increase the size of the office staff?

>> Did the budget for the office increase substantially?

>> Did she take extravagant trips to conventions or seminars at taxpayer expense?

  Even if these trips were perfectly legitimate educational seminars, can you blame taxpayers for feeling angry when such trips are held in exotic or attractive locations where many ordinary citizens can't afford to travel on vacation?

The nature of the office held, or formerly held, by Carly affects how extensive the additional internal opposition research must be. Here are a couple of sample questions:

>> **Did the office award contracts or make purchases?** If so, Harry Handler takes the time to find out whether any of these were awarded to friends or contributors of Carly's and then makes sure that you know about it through a media splash. Carly may not have awarded or purchased on that basis, but that won't stop the charge from being made.

>> **Did Carly hire the offspring of friends or contributors to work in the office?** Even if the employee was perfectly qualified for the position, the hiring may be an issue that you want to consider in the campaign.

REMEMBER

A wart that doesn't appear so bad at first blush can be made to look worse by an opponent eager to exploit a weakness. For example, a simple mistake on a campaign finance report filed by an inexperienced campaign treasurer can be made to appear much more sinister than it is by a creative and aggressive opponent. It's important to hear all sides of a charge and its defense before forming any conclusions. The truth in emotionally charged campaigns is usually somewhere between the positions of the candidates.

Oops — I forgot about that: Illegal warts

It goes without saying that any type of illegal conduct creates substantial problems for any candidate. A conviction for evading taxes or smoking marijuana, even while the candidate was in college, may be a fatal flaw. Even if voters agree that the candidate has paid the required price for their conduct, they see no way to view illegal activity as an asset. No amount of cosmetics can hide the wart of a criminal history. Except in certain circumstances, a candidate with a criminal history is dead on arrival (DOA).

But I'm innocent!: Legal warts

The fact that illegal activity creates fatal warts for candidates isn't surprising. What is surprising is that *legal* conduct can do the same.

For example, candidate Barney Bankrupt had financial problems once upon a time in his career and took a perfectly legal route out — creating potentially fatal candidate warts. Barney declared bankruptcy in the past and now finds himself exposed to criticism by the opposition and the media. The argument goes something like this: "If Barney Bankrupt can't manage his own finances, how can he handle taxpayer money?" The situation may be completely different — Barney may have resorted to filing bankruptcy because of factors beyond his control. But those factors don't matter to the media or the opposition. The stigma attached to the inability to pay one's debts attaches to the candidate as well. That stigma may be sufficient in some voters' minds to torpedo the candidacy. Of course, the fact that Donald Trump declared bankruptcy multiple times did not prevent him from being elected president of the United States!

A candidate who is sued in a civil action may also develop substantial or even fatal warts. Even if what's at issue in the lawsuit has nothing whatsoever to do with running for office, the opposition may jump on the lawsuit allegations.

If the lawsuit claims that the candidate, a former businessperson, defrauded a consumer by selling the consumer a poor product, the opposition may create a commercial that says, "You can't trust candidate Fred Fraud. He will say or do anything to get elected. A customer of the widget store that Fred used to run says Fraud defrauded him out of $10,000 of his hard-earned money. Is this the type of person you want representing you in the state legislature? Vote for Sally Straight-narrow on election day!"

This attack by Straightnarrow on Fraud may not be fair. Maybe Fraud did owe the customer money, but then again, maybe not. These allegations are just pleadings in a lawsuit and are not proven. Unfair it may be, but this strategy is certainly effective. If an opponent can make a charge in 30 seconds, and it takes you five minutes to explain why the charge is unfair, you have lost the debate. Too many voters listen to the charge without hearing or understanding the explanation. Unfairly or not, candidate Fraud has a substantial wart.

Some professions are just wart-filled

Some professions give candidates so many warts that potential candidates who recognize that fact don't even run for office. Legalized gambling, bail bonding, and abortions providers are all examples of professions that don't lend themselves to producing wart-free candidates.

One profession that is the wart-developing equivalent of kissing frogs, though it produces many candidates nonetheless, is the legal profession.

Prosecutors and district or state attorneys

Prosecutors and district or state attorneys are almost guaranteed a difficult time in running for other offices. These elected officeholders can be held responsible for everything that occurred in their offices. Every plea bargain for too small a sentence or every case lost because of poor trial preparation or poor police work can be laid at the feet of the elected prosecutor or state or district attorney. Opponents can make political hay just because cases aren't disposed of fast enough. Only the toughest-talking, hardest-hitting prosecuting attorneys overcome their positions to attain elective office.

Most prosecutors' or district attorneys' offices plea-bargain the vast majority of their cases. They *have to* plea-bargain: The sheer volume of cases precludes trying them all. There are not enough lawyers, courtrooms, judges, or juries to allow all cases to go to trial. Plea bargains may be an essential part of the US criminal justice system, but they have a negative connotation in today's society.

Many people think that when a prosecutor or district attorney agrees to a plea bargain, the defendants are released from jail. In reality, many plea bargains give the defendants substantial amounts of time in prison. But just the term *plea bargain* causes problems for incumbent prosecutors and district attorneys.

Heaven help the prosecutor or district attorney who plea-bargained a case and released a defendant, for whatever good and legitimate reasons, who went on to commit a heinous crime after release. The original charge that was plea-bargained may not have been serious, but that fact won't matter. The subsequent charge will be the one generating all the publicity. The opposition — recognizing a golden opportunity — will say that the second crime was the fault of the prosecutor or district attorney. If a family member of the victim will consent to go on camera, the opposition may win on this issue alone.

Criminal defense attorneys

Criminal defense attorneys also have a difficult time getting elected to office. Fairly or not, a defense attorney can be identified by the clients they have represented in the past. An opponent may run an ad saying that accused child molesters, rapists, and murderers were put back on the street because of the criminal defense attorney's work. Such an ad is particularly predictable if the defense attorney is seeking elective office as a prosecutor, district attorney, or criminal court judge.

You may question whether this technique — identifying the criminal defense attorney with their client or the arguments they made in defense of their clients — is fair. After all, you may say, the criminal defense attorney was merely doing their job and had an ethical duty to give each and every client vigorous representation.

If the position that the criminal defense attorney is seeking has nothing to do with criminal justice, that association is probably unfair. If they're running for county commissioner or school board official, their professional representations are beside the point. You can decide for yourself whether the candidate who raises the issue in the context of one of these types of offices is simply trying to prejudice you unfairly against the criminal defense attorney. If you conclude that that's what the candidate is doing, you can decide whether you want to penalize the candidate by voting for the criminal defense attorney.

REMEMBER

On the other hand, when you're choosing a prosecuting attorney or another officeholder associated with the criminal justice system, you may find the criminal defense attorney's background to be relevant information for you to consider. The criminal defense attorney can still be a good prosecutor, but many voters would want assurance that the person can easily make the transition from defending to prosecuting. Many voters would consider the candidate's background in the overall decision on who would make the better prosecutor. They would not penalize the candidate raising the issue.

Preparing for the Worst: Handlers Dig for Dirt

Internal opposition research is tough to do. It's embarrassing for the candidate and for the candidate's family. Any candidate who undergoes this type of inquiry is understandably defensive. It's extremely difficult to put your entire professional and personal lives under a microscope to look for vulnerabilities. But as painful as this process is, it's much better for the candidate to be prepared. When a handler is aware of the worst attacks that the opponent can launch against their candidate, they can be confident that they have done the best possible job of preparing the candidate's defenses.

Anticipating the worst that the opposition can throw at a candidate may permit the handler to devise a strategy to minimize the impact of the opposition's bombs. With some creativity and preparation, the opposition's nuclear bombs may become grenades. The handler can seldom, if ever, turn a wart into an asset or a grenade into confetti, but minimizing the impact of an attack can at least turn a silver bullet into pellets from a BB gun.

Beware of Your Opponent: Fending Off Attacks

A candidate who has to defend against wart-based attacks by the opposition has four basic strategies to choose from. Campaigns use one or more of these defenses when the warts are exposed, or about to be exposed. All these defenses are designed to prevent you, the voter, from transferring your support to the opposition.

Ignore the attack

One defense is to ignore the attack. Some campaigns take this approach because they don't know what else to do. Ignoring attacks by the opposition in a campaign is rarely a good idea. The opposition is attacking because polling tells the opposition's campaign that the voters find the attack persuasive.

Ignoring the attack doesn't guarantee that it'll go away. More likely, it makes voters wonder why the candidate can't answer the charges. Voters tend to believe attacks that aren't rebutted. The first option in a campaign is always to do nothing. But when doing nothing means allowing the opposition to score points by highlighting a candidate's flaws, it may be tantamount to giving up the election.

Tell the rest of the story

Another option for the candidate who's under attack is a spirited defense pointing out that the opponent didn't tell the voters the entire story. Every issue, or wart, has at least two sides — sometimes five or six. When Carly Candidate tells her side of the story, she can raise doubts about the opponent's credibility in your mind, either directly or indirectly. You may decide not to vote for anyone who would distort Carly's record as much as her opponent did (or appeared to do).

Even if Harry Handler and the media personnel who produce Carly's advertisements can't turn the attacks on her into a positive, they may be able to prevent her from suffering a negative impact by muddying the waters sufficiently on the issue. When charges and countercharges are flying back and forth, many voters tune out the entire issue. The candidate's wart is lost in all the rhetoric. The issue never becomes the silver bullet for the opposition.

The danger in this approach is that when charges fly back and forth, voters become disgusted by the campaign and blame Carly. Harry Handler must weigh the risk of having voters view Carly as a negative campaigner against the risk of having them believe the opponent's accusation.

Diffuse the wart

Another option for the campaign of a candidate with large warts is to diffuse the potential issue that the wart may create. The handler can diffuse the issue in one of two ways: Take the initiative and make the issue public or attack the opposition for waging a negative campaign.

Self-disclosure

Self-exposure of a candidate's warts — that is, raising the issue before the opposition does — is a risky business. After all, the opposition may be incompetent and not find the warts. Or the opposition may not have sufficient resources to advertise about the warts often enough to ensure that the voters are aware of them. You never want to underestimate what opposing campaigns will do to each other, but you don't want to overestimate what they can do to each other, either.

For this strategy to work, the wart must be a unique one — one that's almost sure to reach the public. If a candidate has such an offense in their background and it's too late to back out of the campaign, the handler may decide to acknowledge it before the opposition can attack. If it isn't too late to back out, Harry Handler may even advise Carly to leave the race altogether and look for another career.

An example of a wart that Harry Handler would consider making public is Carly Candidate's drunk driving conviction. Convictions are matters of public record and available to any citizens who want to find them. The odds are reasonably good that a competent opponent will find such a conviction, even if it occurred in another location. After all, Carly Candidate can't conceal her former addresses. She has to list on her resumé the college she attended and where she lived in the past or in response to media inquiries.

If Carly stays in the race, Harry may advise her to run an ad telling voters that she has learned some hard lessons in life; one of the hardest lessons was to accept the consequences of her actions. When she was young, she made a mistake. She drank too much and embarrassed her family by being arrested and convicted for drunk driving. Now Carly asks you not to hold that youthful indiscretion against her in the election. She tells you that she took responsibility for her actions and was never so irresponsible again. For the past 15 years, she has worked hard to be a better citizen. Now she wants to put her knowledge and experience to work for the voters of the district or state.

The analysis of whether to disclose an attack in advance is trickier when there's no conviction on record. Voters aren't reluctant to penalize candidates whom they see to be mudslinging. Without proof, if the alleged illegal conduct happened long ago or is completely unrelated to the office the candidate is seeking, raising the issue can cause a backlash on the attacking candidate. As the 2000 presidential election shows, candidates are more cautious with potentially explosive allegations and less willing to bring them into the campaign. Neither the allegations of Gore's use of marijuana or Bush's use of cocaine were used by the opposing campaigns in 2000.

REMEMBER

Carly's campaign obviously would be better off if it never had to deal with her drunk driving conviction. Such an issue can never help a candidate's campaign; it never wins voter support. The best that Harry Handler can hope for is that you won't reject Carly because of it. Harry hopes that Carly's candor about her background will demonstrate to you that she is honest and can be trusted despite having made a mistake. Maybe, as a result of Carly's self-disclosure, the campaign will be on life support instead of at the funeral home preparing for burial.

Counterattack

Another way a handler diffuses the issue created by a candidate's wart is to attack the opposition for waging a negative campaign. The attack on the opposition goes something like this: "Candidate Sleaze doesn't want you to know that, as an elected official, he permitted his office budget to double. He doesn't want you to know that he took five trips a year at taxpayer expense to vacation spots *you* can't afford to visit. Sleaze doesn't want you to know these things about him. That's why he's attacking Carly Candidate. He thinks that running a negative campaign will divert your attention from his record. Don't be fooled by Sleaze's negative campaign!"

REMEMBER

Harry Handler is trying to muddy the waters here. He hopes that with charges and countercharges swirling around, you'll forget or dismiss the attack that Sleaze is unleashing on Harry's candidate, Carly. Harry's strategy isn't risk-free, because you may get irritated by the constant barrage of attacks. If you and the other voters blame both candidates, voter turnout may suffer, but the outcome of the election probably won't change because of Harry's approach.

Take the offensive and attack first

The final option for a campaign facing wart exposure by the opposition is to attack first. Whatever silver bullet a campaign thinks it can use to fell the opposition can be used before a campaign is on the defensive. The theory in political campaigns is that the best defense is a good offense. If the opponent is forced to respond to the campaign's attack, they may change their strategy. The opposition may become so rattled by an unexpected attack that it fails to launch its own attack. Even if the opponent stays with their game plan, the message may be so muddled by the charges and countercharges that it lacks the punch it otherwise would have. If the attack lacks punch, you may not be persuaded to change your vote. This strategy has risks, too. The key risk is that Carly may be labeled a negative campaigner because she went on the attack first.

Insist that candidates should always tell the truth

Whichever alternative Harry Handler employs to deal with his candidate's warts, he'd better tell the truth. Harry's first instinct may be to deny the charges or attacks from the opposition. It's only human to try to avoid unpleasantness by denial. But if the charges are true, Harry's denial is a fatal mistake. It's morally wrong to lie, and it's political suicide. When Harry denies a charge made by the opponent, he creates an *issue*, which is another way of saying that Harry has created a factual dispute. One side is saying that something is true; the other side is saying that it's a lie. When an important issue arises in a campaign, the media investigates and decides who is telling the truth: the candidate or the opposition.

When that happens, the debate no longer consists of only charges and counter-charges between campaigns. The press examines the charges and denials, determines the truth, and tells you and the other voters who's lying. If the investigation by the press supports the attack from the opposition, Harry Handler has not only his candidate's wart to defend but her credibility as well. The media may determine that the facts as presented by the opposition are true. The media may also determine that Carly Candidate has been less than candid with the voters and the media. If that happens, she may as well draft her concession speech. The campaign is over.

TIP

Why Carly Candidate lies or doesn't lie isn't important. What *is* important is that if she lies and you find out, it's fair to show your disapproval by voting against her on election day. How can you trust Carly to be a good elected official when she lies to you to gain your vote?

Highlighting a Candidate's Beauty Marks

The process of disguising or obscuring the warts that a candidate brings to a campaign can be thought of as minimizing the negative to keep you, the voter, from defecting to the opposition. But candidates also bring *positive* characteristics to a campaign, and it's a handler's job to market these to you as well.

The first trick in marketing Carly Candidate's beauty marks, as with her warts, is to identify them. What events in Carly's background would you find most persuasive as a reason for voting for her? It isn't enough that people have positive things to say about Carly. Almost any candidate's mother will go on television to tell voters that her child would make a wonderful legislator, mayor, or member of Congress. But the positive aspects advertised by a candidate like Carly must persuade you to choose her over the opposition, not just convince you that she's a nice person. Otherwise, spending money talking about the beauty marks is a waste of time and campaign money.

Determining which beauty marks will convert to votes for Carly Candidate takes some work on the part of Harry Handler. Harry must resort to exhaustive research to determine which events in Carly's background or which proposals in her bag of ideas may persuade you to select her over the opposition.

Celebrating a candidate's upbringing

The obvious place to start looking for beauty marks is Carly Candidate's upbringing. Does she have a story in her background that will appeal to you and show you that Carly shares your values and goals? Harry Handler can get that point across by using the simplest of messages.

For example, maybe Carly worked through high school and college so that she could afford a good education. The jobs themselves may not be so important, but the simple fact that she was working will seem important. Many voters held jobs to pay for college, but even those without college degrees and those who didn't have to work much while in college probably can find something to admire in the story. Harry's presentation of a rather unremarkable feat in Carly's life tells you that Carly shares your experiences and your values. You can trust her with decisions affecting your life because she is like you.

Harry Handler looks for anything in Carly Candidate's background that will appeal to voters and demonstrate that Carly is a regular person who thinks and feels the same as voters do about life. After all, they want officeholders who will approach problems and solutions in the same manner they would. Voters have confidence that people who share their values and opinions can be trusted to make political decisions affecting their lives.

Making the most of a candidate's parents

Just as Harry Handler examines Carly Candidate's past, he looks for similar simple, appealing stories about Carly's parents. "Carly's father worked hard all his life. He never got anything handed to him on a silver platter. He worked for the same company for years. Then the company went bankrupt. After 40 years with the same company, her father has no pension to secure his retirement. Carly understands the importance of protecting social security as a safety net for people like her father. Carly can understand voters' anxiety about old age and self-sufficiency. She's experienced the anxiety on a personal level. She can be trusted to protect our interests."

Even if Carly Candidate was born with a silver spoon in her mouth, Harry Handler can make the silver spoon a way for voters to connect with her. Here's one approach: "Carly realizes how lucky she has been. She wants to give something back to the country that has been so good to her and her family. She won't take any raises while she's in office. She won't take any contributions over $100 from supporters. She won't be anyone's governor but yours. Carly's parents may have been wealthier than most, but she realizes that those benefits create a special obligation to us voters. You can trust Carly Candidate with your vote."

WATCH OUT FOR ROSE-COLORED GLASSES

If Carly Candidate's office record or message is more of a wart than a beauty mark, Harry Handler may hope that you will fall for an inspiring but simplistic message about her upbringing or parents and not take the time to look at what she's done in office or what she stands for.

Whether you accept Carly's portrayal of her upbringing or her parents depends on whether you think that the image she's trying to create in your mind is accurate or a blatant attempt at manipulation. Are these Carly's true values and attitudes? You can judge for yourself — based on what you know about Carly and what people you trust know about Carly — whether you're being told the truth or being manipulated.

If you decide that Carly is like you because she shares your values and experiences, you can decide to vote for her. If you conclude that she really feels strongly about a certain pension issue, for example, and wants to get elected to do something to protect her fellow citizens, you can identify with her and reward her with your vote. If you conclude that this issue and her attitude are attempts at manipulating you — orchestrated by Harry Handler — you can punish Carly Candidate by voting for her opponent.

Remember: You make the decision. You cast the vote.

How important are beauty marks?

Mentioning family and upbringing are fine as far as beauty marks go. Voters feel more comfortable with candidates they feel they know a little more about. Voters' comfort level also increases if the things they find out about Carly convince them that she's a real, live person with emotions and experiences similar to those that voters feel and have. You don't have to base your decision for whom to vote on beauty marks alone, however. You can consider all the beauty marks the candidates have and still ask them where they stand on particular issues of importance to you.

You have many ways to find answers to your specific questions on issues. See Chapter 5 for more information about how to get elected officials and candidates to answer *your* questions. You don't have to settle for the beauty marks that Harry Handler uses to persuade you to vote for Carly Candidate. You have a right to know Carly's position on specific issues of importance to you before you cast your vote.

Chapter **12**

Truth in Advertising

Yes, you should care about knowing the truth, yet separating the wheat from the chaff in political advertising can be difficult. How do you identify the truth in the mass of charges and misinformation traded back and forth in the heat of a political campaign?

As difficult as it might prove to be, your goal should be to find out which charges or countercharges are fair and which are not so that your choice among candidates is an informed one. You don't want to vote for someone who has gained your support by unfairly attacking an opponent. You don't want to be persuaded by underhanded tactics or manipulation. Otherwise, your approach to voting is guaranteed to fail — the candidates most likely to win your support will be the sleaziest rather than the best.

Truth Plus Truth Doesn't Always Equal Fact

Many times, ads for competing campaigns seem to make opposing statements. One campaign says that the candidate lied on his taxes. The other campaign says that the candidate reported his taxes truthfully.

If all the information is accurate, can they both be telling the truth? The answer is yes.

Drawing a false conclusion

Even when a campaign is making truthful charges, the manner in which it presents the facts may still create a false or incomplete picture — without actually lying.

A paid advertisement shows you 1 + 1. The 1 + 1 are facts that are accurate. But the campaign doesn't stop there. The campaign's ad tries to show you that 1 + 1 = 3. The conclusion that the ad draws from two accurate facts isn't accurate. That's where the ad is unfair or inaccurate. See the nearby sidebar, "The case of the soft attorney," for an example of how this trick works.

THE CASE OF THE SOFT ATTORNEY

Suppose that Jane Dillon, a candidate for prosecuting attorney, attacks the incumbent's handling of a particular domestic violence case. The candidate cites this poor handling as an example of incompetence or, worse, a soft bent on crime.

Candidate Dillon describes the case this way: A woman was beaten by her husband. The police were called. No charges were filed by the prosecutor's office, so the defendant was released from jail. The defendant returned to his wife after he was released and then beat her a second time. She died from the second beating, killed by the defendant, who was out on the streets because charges hadn't been filed.

Candidate Dillon obtains pictures of the defendant and the victim and uses them in a television ad. Dillon comes to the simple conclusion in her ad: If the prosecuting attorney had been doing his job, the victim would not have been killed. The prosecuting attorney failed to help the victim. The prosecuting attorney shouldn't be reelected.

Dillon has the facts right, but she's not telling you the whole story. The fault may not be entirely, primarily, or in any way the prosecutor's. Here's another side of the story in this scenario: It was the neighbors who called the police. After the defendant was arrested, the victim called the prosecutor's office to demand that charges be dropped. The victim did not want the defendant, her husband, to go to prison.

Legally, the prosecuting attorney could have compelled the victim to testify and sent the defendant to prison. Practically, he needed the victim's cooperation. If she were forced to testify against her will, she could have gone on the stand and said that she started the fight. She could have said that she and her husband were in love and that the incident would not be repeated. She could've made it clear that she didn't want the defendant to go to prison, that their children would suffer if he were incarcerated. No jury would send someone to prison with that type of testimony.

The prosecuting attorney knew that, without the victim's cooperation, he would lose the case; filing the charges would have been a waste of everyone's time. So, after arguing with the victim at length, he told the court that the state had no case against the defendant and that the court should free the defendant.

The outcome of the case — the wife's death at the hands of her husband — was tragic, but it wasn't the prosecuting attorney's fault. He was prepared to prosecute the defendant and protect the victim from harm. He even argued with the victim to try to convince her that she was being foolish. All to no avail.

In this case, the prosecuting attorney was not at fault. But Candidate Dillon's ad implies otherwise. All her facts are accurate, but her conclusion that the prosecuting attorney did something wrong is not accurate. The charge that the prosecuting attorney deserves to be defeated because he's soft on crime is unfair.

The art of set-up legislation

In addition to implying faulty conclusions, another way that a candidate can create a false impression is by setting up a vote, in advance of an election, that is sure to win disfavor for the opponent.

For example, members of the minority party in the state legislature may introduce a bill that they know will make a good campaign issue in the next election — an election in which their candidates are challenging incumbent legislators. They bring this issue to a vote, knowing that it won't pass and perhaps even knowing that it would be a bad idea if turned into law. They may refuse to compromise with the majority party on the bill, ensuring its defeat. They offer this extreme, doomed proposal for symbolic reasons — to put incumbent legislators *on the record* against the goals of a particular group and to put themselves on record in favor of that group's goals. (Putting a legislator *on record* means making the legislator cast a vote to create a record of the legislator's position on an issue.) Then they use that record to campaign against the officeholders in the next election.

WARNING

A common example of setup legislation is when a legislator introduces a bill calling for a substantial cut of an unpopular tax, such as the property tax. That idea has tremendous popular appeal to voters because everyone wants to see their property taxes cut. But it may not be a realistic option. (See the nearby sidebar "The case of the taxing legislator" for an illustration of this point.)

THE CASE OF THE TAXING LEGISLATOR

Bill Moose, a legislator, introduces a tax-cutting bill that he knows won't pass. In fact, it cuts taxes so sharply that not even Moose would want it to pass. He knows that if it did, the state would be unable to fund elementary and secondary education adequately. Its passage would create tremendous fiscal problems. Schools would face severe budget shortfalls, delaying needed improvements or shortchanging teacher salaries.

Bill knows that his bill is fiscally irresponsible, but he isn't worried, because it will never become law. Bill Moose knows that most members of the majority party in the legislature oppose property tax cuts anyway, so he might as well make the proposal more generous than government can really afford.

After Bill Moose and his party force the majority party members to vote against a popular bill, they use that vote to campaign against the majority party incumbents in the next election.

Here's the pitch:

> *A generous plan for property tax relief was introduced, one that would have returned a large sum of money to families. Jan Incumbent voted against it. Jan Incumbent is a tax-and-spend liberal who is willing to spend your hard-earned tax dollars on fraud and waste. Vote against Jan Incumbent on election day.*

The facts are accurate, but the conclusion may not be. The equation is

(Fact)	1	A property tax relief bill is introduced.
	+	
(Fact)	1	Jan Incumbent votes against it.
	=	
(Conclusion)	3	Jan Incumbent is too tax-oriented to represent you.

Jan Incumbent opposed Bill Moose's idea. That is a fact. One reason for her vote may be that she supports much higher tax levels than her constituents. Another more likely reason is that she could anticipate the lost social services that Bill Moose's bill would cause. If most voters would've done the same thing in Jan Incumbent's place, given the information she possessed, then Moose's ads create a false impression that Jan Incumbent is fiscally irresponsible with the taxpayers' hard-earned money.

The Media Can Help You

If two ads can have conflicting messages and both still be accurate, how do you know who's telling "the truth, the whole truth, and nothing but the truth," so help you, voter? The media can provide assistance in determining the truth in political advertising. For a number of reasons, reporters are in a position to get the information they need for their analyses:

>> They have easy access to the facts and the candidates.

>> They can get transcripts of the commercials.

>> They can demand and obtain any underlying documentation that supports or refutes a candidate's charges or claims.

>> They can receive a response from the opposition and then check out the opposition's response, too.

>> They may have instant access to third parties — those who have no axes to grind in the political campaign. These third parties can sometimes shed a great deal of light on the claims and counterclaims made in advertisements.

POLITICAL STUFF

THE PRESS KNOWS WHERE TO LOOK

For an example of how the press might investigate a political advertisement, suppose that a candidate for attorney general claims that the incumbent attorney general seeking reelection has spent more tax dollars per capita operating the office than any other attorney general in the country. The press is trained to investigate the facts behind a charge like that one.

The press knows, or can discover, that every attorney general in the United States, for example, belongs to the National Association of Attorneys General (NAAG). This organization, like the organizations for other statewide elected officials, compiles information on the offices, budgets, staffs, and responsibilities of all attorneys general.

A reporter investigating the ad can call an organization like this one and gather information not easily available to the average voter. That information may support or dispute the charge made by the candidate. This press person is now in a position to determine the real facts behind the charges and the response. An investigation by the press helps you understand whether it's the charge or the response that's more credible and reliable.

Journalists don't review just the accuracy of the facts being claimed in an ad — they also make a judgment on the fairness of the conclusion that the ad reaches. If these journalists determine that the conclusion isn't fair, they may label the ad misleading or unfair.

Getting the media analysis you need

Some newspapers and television stations go beyond the he said/she said approach when political advertising is involved. They've begun evaluating political advertising for accuracy, an approach referred to as *media watch* or *truth in advertising*.

The newspapers and television stations that perform these services for voters research every charge and claim made in a commercial. As new television commercials appear for candidates, some journalists do independent analyses of the accuracy of the claims or attacks made. Thorough reporters examine the commercials word-for-word to see whether the claims or attacks in the ads have facts to back them up. If they do, the analysis concludes that they're truthful. If the claims or attacks can't be substantiated, they're labeled unfair. There are also Internet sites which fact check claims by politicians. Some of them that can help you understand what is true and what is not are:

>> www.politifact.com

>> www.npr.org.sections.politics.fact-check

>> www.factcheck.org

When truth-in-advertising or media-watch analysis is done well, the media spell out which points are supported by the facts and which are not. Make it a point to watch these analyses during the heat of a campaign. They can help you understand what's actually going on. When you know which facts are correct, you can decide for yourself whether the implication is fair or accurate.

The media analyze each new ad as it airs during the course of a campaign. If more than one television station or newspaper performs the media-watch or truth-in-advertising analysis, watch or read as many as you can. When you view or read more than one and each analysis makes the same points, you can be more confident that the analysis isn't just the result of the individual likes or dislikes of one reporter.

You can call your local television stations to find out whether they're reviewing the ads and when. The television stations may even promote the truth-in-advertising reviews in the teaser spots they use to drum up viewers for their nightly news shows. Newspapers may have a special box and location in the newspaper where you can always find the reviews of the advertisements.

If the media do their job well, their evaluations can help you decide whether you should pay attention to the advertising or ignore it completely. They can help you understand which candidate is playing by the rules and which isn't. The media can help you become an informed voter.

Hounding your news media: Review the ads and get on the stick!

When newspapers and television stations perform media-watch and truth-in-advertising services, they help to keep the excesses of campaigning in check. If campaigns don't have this type of analysis to fear, they will always push the envelope. That is, campaigns will always try to get away with overstating a claim or an attack. After all, they're trying to persuade you how to vote. They want to use the most powerful arguments they can to bring you over to their side. Campaigns that aren't afraid of press exposure and criticism will occasionally bend the truth to win you over. They probably won't lie — the risks are too great — but they may stretch the truth to make a point.

All newspapers and television stations should perform these fact-checking services. It should be a priority, and a proper amount of time and resources should be devoted to it. That's the only way you can know the truth in the commercials you see. If your television stations and newspapers aren't conducting automatic reviews of political ads, call them and demand that they do it.

SPEAKING UP

Call the League of Women Voters, the press associations, and the association of broadcasters in your state and tell them to get on the ball. Tell them that you need help and that they should provide it or help you put pressure on those who can. If these organizations are not listed in your phone book, call or write the national headquarters and ask for a name, address, and phone number or an email address to contact them.

Whose Side Are the Media On, Anyway?

When you're trying to figure out what's going on and which candidate to support, you may wonder whether the media reporting on candidates and issues is reliable. Does the media choose sides in elections? Is the reporting objective? Can you trust what you read in newspapers and see on the nightly news? Is the media there to assist you in making an informed choice on election day, or is it just another obstacle to making that informed choice?

The answer to each of these questions is a little of both. Since the Federal Communications repealed the Fairness Doctrine in 1987, stations are free to advocate more for one candidate or party or another. The Fairness Doctrine required stations to be honest, equitable, and balanced in reporting on controversial issues. Now some stations identify more with one party or another. For example, Fox News is seen as more favorable to Republicans, and MSNBC is viewed as more favorable to Democrats. The networks and public television news are seen as more objective.

Taking the good with the bad

In reality, journalism is no different from any other profession. Journalism has good and bad reporters, lazy reporters and energetic reporters. Some reporters are smart, and some aren't so smart. Some reporters like some candidates and dislike others. Some reporters can't help rooting for the underdog and bending over backward to help give that candidate coverage. (They call it *leveling the playing field.*) Some reporters like to be schmoozed by important people, including candidates and officeholders — if these reporters are treated right, they treat the candidates right.

REMEMBER

Most reporters try to cover campaigns fairly and to the best of their abilities. They try as much as possible to leave their own, personal prejudices at the newsroom door. Some reporters try harder than others, and some are more successful than others in achieving that goal. Nonetheless, an energetic and aggressive press is essential to a democracy. The Founding Fathers realized how essential reporting is to a democracy when they prohibited laws abridging the freedom of speech, or of the press in the Second Amendment to the Constitution. Despite all the recent accusations regarding media bias, fake news, and the media being the enemy of the people, most journalists take pride in being objective and seeking the truth. A democracy would be difficult to maintain without them.

Acknowledging that there's such a thing as being too objective

REMEMBER

A problem many journalists have is that they try to be too objective. "Hold on," you might say — "it isn't possible for a journalist to be too objective. It's like a judge being too fair or a minister being too religious." Actually, reporters may try too hard to present all sides of an argument. For example, if a thousand people march in favor of an issue, the reporter will report that fact. But if the reporter gives as much coverage to the handful of demonstrators who oppose the issue, the way the story is covered will make it seem as if the amount of support for and against the issue is equal. In other words, in trying to report both sides equally, the reporter is being too objective.

Perhaps you think that reporters should not filter the election news you receive — you want to get it all with no editing or commentary. You may be more satisfied with the reporter saying that a thousand people marched in favor of the issue and six people showed up in opposition. You feel that you're better equipped to make judgments about the candidates and the issues if you have just the facts, all the facts, and nothing but the facts. You may want the reporters to keep their judgments and opinions and ideas about equal coverage to themselves. If they have opinions or viewpoints, they should be columnists, not news reporters.

Sure, you have the main facts, but you weren't there

When reporters try to be too evenhanded in their campaign coverage, they give each candidate equal time. The ideas and responses of both candidates are given identical weight in the news story. The reporter writes a story saying that Candidate Anderson said the following about Candidate Baily. Candidate Baily responded by saying the following about Candidate Anderson. Sounds okay so far. Sounds as if the reporter is doing what you want — giving you the facts so that you can make a judgment for yourself. The reporter isn't filtering the information you're receiving. You're getting it just the way it happened. It's just as if you were there.

The problem is that you *weren't* there. You don't have the benefit of knowing the candidates personally. You probably aren't quite as familiar with the issue and the facts as the reporter covering the campaign. You may not know that Candidate Anderson's attack is completely bogus. You may not know that the charges have no merit and that Candidate Anderson is just a little bit flaky. A he said/she said story is merely a reporter's regurgitation of the charges and countercharges made by the candidates or the campaigns. The reporter doesn't evaluate the charges or tell you that the issues raised by one or both of the candidates are without merit and that voters should disregard them.

Independent evaluations: Do you have the time?

WARNING

Some reporters don't necessarily do an independent evaluation when a candidate makes an accusation. They feel a responsibility to report what the opposition says in answer to a charge or attack in a campaign, but that's the extent of their duty as they see it. They may not explain the context behind a claim. They may not perform an investigation of the underlying facts and charges to determine which have more merit. They may leave to the opponent the responsibility of providing the other side, who will seem a less trustworthy source.

The problem with reporters who maintain this kind of objectivity is that you, the voter, lose. If the reporters don't provide any independent evaluation of the facts, you're left to sort between the charges and countercharges to find out which is true. But you're handicapped; you may not have ready access to the information that's available to reporters. It's much more difficult for you to do an independent evaluation to determine the truth than it is for a trained professional reporter.

Knowing the truth allows you to make an informed choice. You don't want to be manipulated into voting for a candidate who doesn't share your views and values. You don't want your support going to a candidate who has suckered you into supporting them by making unfair attacks on the opposition. You want the candidate who is right for you. Knowing the facts allows you to vote for that candidate and have confidence in your decision.

If You're on Your Own

What if, despite your entreaties, the various media in your community don't perform a media-watch or truth-in-advertising service for the voters? How do you decide on your own which of two dueling commercials is accurate and which is not? If you don't know which facts to rely on, how can you decide whether the attack or the defense is more credible?

Here are some ways to guard against forming a false impression from campaign ads:

>> **Listen carefully to campaign advertisements.** Separate the objective facts from the conclusions drawn by the opponent in the campaign's presentation.

>> **Beware of any conclusions a campaign ad makes.** Don't accept anyone else's conclusions based on the facts given in the ad. The ad may be conveniently leaving out other facts that support a different conclusion. Reach your own conclusions.

>> **Be skeptical of simplistic arguments.** Things are seldom as simple as a campaign ad can make them appear. Because most ads are between 30 and 60 seconds long, they don't have time to show the complexities of the situation. It's much easier to present a complex problem as a simple indiscretion.

>> **Listen carefully to the explanation given by the candidate under fire.** If the candidate being attacked doesn't give an explanation, call their headquarters and ask for one.

>> **Pay close attention to the exact wording of each campaign's claims.** Often, both sides are telling the truth and you can figure out what's really happening by the differences in the language they have chosen.

If it takes 30 seconds to attack and 5 minutes to defend, the attacker wins — unless *you* fight back by seeking the truth.

Listening to neutral parties

One way that incumbents deal with an attack they think is unfair or misleading is to bring in third parties to dispute the attack. Perhaps the victim's sister is offended by having a loved one's death exploited for political advantage and is willing to inject herself into the controversy. She may appear in an advertisement for the incumbent or issue a statement to the press disputing the facts in a candidate's attack. She's in a position to know what did happen, and she isn't trying to win an election.

If a third party with knowledge of the issue comes forward, it's much easier for you to ascertain what happened and whether it should influence your choice on election day. You can judge for yourself whether a third party has a partisan interest in the outcome. If the third party is someone who isn't politically involved, the information they provide is more likely to be prompted by the facts and not by partisan loyalties. If the third party is a friend or colleague of one of the candidates, you should view the information provided with a grain or two of salt.

Learning the truth yourself

The media analysis isn't available, and no third party comes forward: How do you decide who's telling the truth? The answer is that it's not easy.

You must listen carefully to the charge and response and be certain of precisely what each side is claiming. Then you can compare the two versions and determine where there's a discrepancy in the facts that each side alleges. The discrepancy may be either of the following:

>> What happened?

>> What's the significance of what happened?

Go to the newspaper

If the disagreement is about what happened, you can go to your local newspaper and see whether the episode that's the basis for the ad was the subject of any independent investigation or was even reported by the press. If it was, the reports are probably the most reliable indicator of what transpired.

If you still have questions, call the newspaper and ask to speak with the reporter. Or try sending the reporter an email request. Ask the person directly what you want to know.

Approach the candidates directly

SPEAKING UP

If you're having trouble finding media reports of an incident that an ad is based on, call the office of the elected official in question and ask what the facts are. Ask the person you speak with for copies of the police reports or any written information that supports the claims of the elected official.

Call the candidate making the charge and ask any follow-up questions you may have. Ask the candidate who is making the accusation for written confirmation of the charges in the commercial. Don't hesitate to take the direct approach. Both these candidates are eager to earn your vote. Tell them that you have some questions that must be answered before you can commit yourself. Make them work for your vote by justifying their attacks. (See Chapter 5 for more about how to communicate with your elected officials.)

Don't let cleverness distract you from the truth

TIP

If the dispute between the two campaigns isn't about what happened but rather about what something that happened *means*, you still need to listen carefully to the charge and the response. Don't be distracted by the visuals or cleverness of the ad. Don't let the ad's appeal to hot-button issues prevent you from hearing exactly what the opponent is alleged to have done or failed to do. (See the later sidebar "Pushing your buttons" for more about hot-button issues.)

Call both campaigns and ask for transcripts of the ads you have questions about. Without the pictures and music, you'll be able to understand the charges and responses made in the course of each 30-second television spot. When you've done that, you can decide for yourself which side is telling the truth.

Analyze the results

After you hear the arguments both sides make in support of their positions, you need to weigh the facts presented to decide whether the attack or the response is more credible to you. Ask yourself these questions:

>> Was the incumbent derelict in their duty?

>> Is the failure sufficient reason to deny their reelection?

>> Does the attack omit important mitigating facts and create a false impression?

>> Is the attack fair or unfair?

These are questions you need to answer for yourself before you cast your vote.

The more time you spend analyzing the attack and the response, the closer you'll be to discovering the truth behind the charges and countercharges. After you decide which side is telling the truth, you can decide which candidate deserves your vote.

If you decide that one side was unfair . . .

If you decide that one side's attack is unfair and that the other side is telling a more truthful story, you may still decide to support the candidate who launched the unfair attack. On balance, that candidate may be the better choice. But they should be significantly better to overcome the liability of creating a false impression about their opponent in the minds of the voters.

Don't Let Either Side Manipulate You

When you're analyzing political advertisements, you should be on the lookout for certain red flags. A candidate who makes a blatant appeal to voters on a highly emotional issue is trying to manipulate you. The candidate is hoping that your emotional reaction will trigger a response in their favor without additional analysis.

Beware of straw men or appeals to emotion

A manipulative candidate has no interest in telling you why they want your vote. They don't want to discuss controversial solutions to complex problems. They're not interested in discussing the important issues in the campaign; they're looking for a diversion like raising a straw man. Raising a straw man would be attributing to a candidate a position that the candidate has never held when that position is so divorced from reality as to be ludicrous. For example, claiming that all Democratic candidates favor open borders or all Republican candidates support white supremacists because one left- or right-wing candidate of a party has done so.

PUSHING YOUR BUTTONS

WARNING

Hot-button or *wedge* issues are designed to arouse your emotions but not to promote a debate on the emotional issue. Rather, the candidate raising a hot-button or wedge issue hopes that the words and images they use will trigger an emotional response from you and other listeners.

For example, a candidate might say that English should be recognized as America's official language. A candidate using that as a hot-button issue isn't truly concerned about English as the universal language of this country. They're not in a policy debate with their opponent about English as the national language. No one is suggesting that the United States become a dual language country. The candidate is appealing to listeners' fear of immigrants. They're hoping that the bias many feel against foreigners who are different in appearance and language will translate into support for the candidate.

Hot-button issues emphasize those characteristics that divide rather than unite us as a nation. They are us-against-them issues that motivate voters to vote against a candidate.

Racism

Appeals to racial prejudice, no matter how subtle, are designed to manipulate you. Television ads that play on the fears or prejudices of White citizens are manipulative. Some campaigns use African American people in ads focusing on crime to engender fear in voters. Some campaigns use xenophobic rhetoric, like when they rail against illegal immigrants "invading" the United States. The appeal may be visual only, with no race-related words used. The subliminal message is that a vote for the opponent will result in more African Americans or illegal immigrants having the opportunity to commit serious crimes, which may victimize the voters or their families.

WARNING

Campaigns seldom make a racial appeal openly. That tactic is much too risky. If it's obvious what the campaign is doing, various public service groups hold press conferences and denounce the tactic. The media may condemn the practice in editorials and political columns. It could backfire big-time.

Campaigns can employ buzzwords or code words based on racial prejudice to trigger an emotional reaction in voters. The emphasis here is on the word *can*. Campaigns can also raise these issues to stimulate legitimate public policy debate.

If you hear candidates use any of the following terms, listen carefully to what they're saying:

» Affirmative action

» Racial quotas

» Immigration

» English as the official language

See whether the candidates using these terms have identified a problem that you think is legitimate. Has the candidate raising the issue made specific proposals to solve a real concern affecting the quality of your life? Or do you feel that the candidate's motive in raising the issue is to manipulate you and other voters?

REMEMBER

Don't accept at face value the candidate's declaration that these issues are causing problems where you live. Ask yourself, when you hear these appeals, whether any problems in your community or state stem from affirmative action, quotas, immigration, or the status of English as the official language.

SPEAKING UP

Demand to know precisely how these policies are hurting you and your neighbors. Demand to know what the candidate proposes to do instead. Tell the candidate at your next opportunity that you're concerned that they're trying to manipulate you instead of addressing important policy issues. Ask them whether you're justified in feeling that way and if not, why not. Obviously, the candidate won't admit to manipulation, but the explanation of why they brought up the issue will help you make a more informed decision. (See Chapter 5 for more about communicating with officials.)

POLITICAL STUFF

THE DOOMED DUKE CAMPAIGN

An example of a racial appeal made too openly was the campaign of David Duke for governor of Louisiana in 1991. David Duke was a Nazi sympathizer and had been a leader in the Ku Klux Klan. He had used racist and anti-Semitic rhetoric in earlier campaigns for public office but said he had changed his views.

Duke ran for governor as a Republican but was publicly repudiated by President George H. W. Bush and former Republican Governor Buddy Roemer. Duke's opponent, Democrat Edwin Edwards, was quite unpopular but won the election anyway because Duke's appeal to middle-income White voters was seen as too racial by the majority of Louisiana's voters, who turned out in record numbers in a nonpresidential year to give Edwards more than 61 percent of the vote.

Patriotism

Another red flag to watch out for is the use of patriotism in a campaign. Almost every candidate, like almost every voter, is a patriotic American. Each is committed to our political system and our country. No candidate has a corner on loving their country. Unless you have hard-and-fast evidence to the contrary, assume that every candidate is a patriotic American who is working to make our country a better place to live.

TIP

The issues to watch out for are

» Flag burning

» The Pledge of Allegiance

When a candidate talks about constitutional amendments to ban the burning of flags or to require the recitation of the Pledge of Allegiance, your antennae should go up. Is this candidate raising a legitimate problem and proposing a solution — or trying to manipulate the voters? No candidate wants to see the flag desecrated. Every candidate believes in the principles espoused in the Pledge of Allegiance. So why is this issue being discussed in the campaign?

When a candidate uses another candidate's opposition to quotas of minorities in hiring or admission to schools to charge that the candidate is a racist, you should also beware. Candidates can oppose these affirmative action ideas without being racist, and a candidate linking racism with opposition may be trying to push your hot button and manipulate you.

WARNING

When a candidate tries to corner the patriotism market, watch out. They're trying to avoid discussing the more difficult issues by making an emotional appeal. The candidate hopes that the emotional appeal will cause you to vote against their opponent. They think that wrapping the campaign in the American flag or patriotism will be sufficient reason for you to support them. The unstated argument is that they are patriotic and their opponent is not.

REMEMBER

Analyze carefully what the candidate is attempting to do. See whether there's any merit to the contention that the opponent isn't patriotic. A candidate with a different approach to a certain issue isn't necessarily the same as a candidate who's disloyal or unpatriotic. If you have no proof that the candidate is disloyal or unpatriotic, disregard the advertisement.

If you don't want to be manipulated . . .

Racism and patriotism are just two of the issues that candidates use to try to manipulate voters. Other us-versus-them issues include

>> Prayer in public schools

>> Appeals to class warfare, pitting the rich against the poor

TIP

Whenever a candidate raises one or more of these issues in a campaign, you should analyze what they're attempting to do. These are questions you should ask yourself:

>> Are these issues legitimate concerns?

>> Are there differences in approach between the candidates that merit debate?

>> Is the candidate using these issues as hot buttons to try to manipulate voters into an emotional response against an opponent?

If you answer *no, no,* and *yes,* the candidate is trying to manipulate you and the other voters. If these aren't legitimate issues for a candidate to raise in an election where you live, they're attempts to make subtle appeals for support based on racial, ethnic, class, or religious prejudice.

Campaigns that rely on straw men and wedge issue appeals to racism and patriotism are hoping that the manipulation will succeed because you won't analyze what you're seeing. The campaigns want you to simply react by voting against the target of the ad. After you know what to look for in the advertising campaigns, it's harder and harder for campaigns to manipulate you. The more you know about what campaigns do, or try to do, the less likely you are to fall for these kinds of emotional appeals.

TIP

Make it a point to listen carefully to every ad and watch the tactics that campaigns are using. You can learn to recognize the attempt to manipulate you, and then it won't succeed.

REMEMBER

In fact, you should think long and hard about supporting any candidate who would resort to such tactics in the first place. Ask yourself whether this type of person would make a trustworthy officeholder. And take a closer look at the candidate discussing the *real* issues in your local community or state or even country.

It's Go-Time: Demanding Answers to Your Questions from Candidates

SPEAKING UP

Make candidates talk about issues of importance to you and your fellow voters. Don't let them duck and weave. You have a right to know what type of officeholder you're being asked to support. Make them tell you. Don't take no for an answer; refuse to be sidetracked by issues that don't affect the quality of your life. Of course, a candidate who doesn't know the answer to your question should be permitted to say so.

Tell candidates that you have a right to this information. You do! You shouldn't be asked to vote for a pig in a poke. You want to know what the candidates will do if they're elected. It's not unreasonable for you to ask for that information before you cast your vote — the information doesn't do you much good after the candidate is elected.

Don't be nervous about holding candidates to account. After all, with your newfound political savvy, you're going to hold them accountable as officeholders. You may as well get them used to your demands early. Read Chapters 5 and 7 for more about communicating with candidates and officials and letting them know what's important to you. Read Chapter 16 for more about communicating the issues you want the candidates to discuss.

Chapter **13**

Casting That Vote!

You have only one vote to cast, and your choice is nonreturnable — at least until the next election. How do you decide which candidate you want to support? What do you look for in a candidate? How do you know who will make a good officeholder?

Odds are that you won't know every candidate intimately by election day. With a little effort and a little reading on your part, though, you can know *something* about all of them.

Reach Out and Ask Someone: Others Can Help You Decide

When people are confronted with big decisions, they often turn to close friends, colleagues, or authorities for help. It's just human nature. Even though your vote is your own, you shouldn't feel bad about consulting with others to make your decision.

Voting by party

If you haven't read or seen enough about some of the candidates to answer all your questions about them and comfortably make your selection, you have a couple of alternatives:

>> Decide not to vote in some of the races.

>> Rely on the party affiliation of the candidates as a guide in making your decision.

   If you think of yourself as a Republican and all things are otherwise equal, vote for the Republican you don't know rather than the Democrat you don't know. If you think of yourself as a Democrat — well, you know the drill.

REMEMBER

When you vote by party, you're trusting that the party label means that the candidate you have selected will be closer to you philosophically than their opponent. It's not a foolproof method of selection, but it beats throwing darts or relying on the political consulting firm of Eenie, Meenie, Minie, and Mo.

If you're truly an independent and don't register as a Democrat or Republican or vote by party in a primary, you're out of luck! Of course, you can always vote only for the candidates you know and leave the rest alone.

WARNING

If you decide not to vote, the election will still be held and someone will be elected. The system works much better when all eligible citizens participate.

If Frank likes this guy . . .

One way to make the decision of whom to vote for is to rely on the judgment of people you trust. If a candidate has the support of other individuals — particularly, nonpolitical people — whom you know and trust, that's a good sign. Friends and coworkers of yours and of the candidate can provide insight. So can individuals who have known a candidate in a different context. Maybe the candidate coached softball or was active in the PTA or a United Way campaign. Maybe people you know have children in the same school as the candidate's children. You can learn whether the candidate takes seriously their duties as a parent or member of the community.

TIP

The insight you can glean about a candidate's earlier experiences can be more valuable in understanding the candidate than anything you can learn while that candidate is running. During the campaign, you can be sure that the candidate will be on their best behavior. Learning how the candidate behaves when their guard is down can help you understand what a candidate is truly like.

WARNING

When you rely on the opinions of people you trust, you should discount the endorsements of other elected officials. Except in rare cases, the nominee of a political party enjoys the support of all elected officials in that party. It's the 11th commandment of politics that one Democrat or Republican does not speak ill — at least not publicly — of another Democrat or Republican.

If your local Republican mayor endorses the Republican nominee for governor, it's hardly newsworthy. However, if the local Republican mayor refuses to endorse the Republican nominee for governor, endorses with less-than-anticipated vigor, or — even more intriguingly — warmly endorses the *Democratic* candidate, that is an item worthy of note. In other words, don't simply pay attention to what they say; listen for what they *don't* say!

Checking out endorsements

You can also rely on the endorsements of groups to which you belong or are sympathetic. Various groups — from labor unions to chambers of commerce and from teacher and police organizations to individual businesses and environmental groups — have *political action committees (PACs)*. (See Chapter 9 for more discussion of PACs.) These committees interview the various candidates in races of interest to them and then decide which candidate to endorse and how much money to contribute.

Support of or opposition to a candidate by groups whose goals you share can provide insight into which candidate you will be comfortable supporting. Conversely, support or opposition by those groups whose objectives you oppose can help you decide whom not to support.

Making Up Your Own Mind

If you aren't content to rely on the opinions of others, you can form your own opinion of the candidates in a given race. When you're deciding which candidates should get your votes, think of the selection process as if you were interviewing and hiring the candidates for a job. After all, that's exactly what you're doing: You're hiring candidates to work for you by representing you. Think of each vote as a hiring decision. Consider the answers to these questions:

>> Which candidate would you enjoy working with?

>> Which candidate demonstrates a better work ethic?

>> Which candidate would fit in better at your workplace?

CANDIDATE SELECTION CHECKLIST

TIP

If you're deciding whether to vote for Carly Candidate, here are some things to look for:

- Does Carly Candidate appear intelligent, or does she give the impression that she's just filling the suit?

- Is Carly Candidate qualified by education and experience for the job?

- Do you like Carly Candidate's programs and ideas?

- Is there anything in Carly Candidate's background that causes you concern?

- Are you comfortable with the groups and individuals who support Carly Candidate?

- Can you trust Carly Candidate? Does she pass the elevator test? (If an elevator door opened in front of you and getting on board meant you would ride alone with the candidate, would you get on?)

Gathering information

The more information you seek before choosing a candidate, the more comfortable you'll be with your decision. Here are some suggestions for ways you can utilize the various sources available to get your interview questions answered:

- Attend any meetings scheduled by civic groups to provide voters opportunities to meet the candidates. Many times, when you go to these events, you have the opportunity to ask questions of the candidate directly.

- Watch debates between the candidates for a particular office.

- Request any position papers on issues that the candidates may have. (*Position papers* are writings that candidates release to give their stances on issues in much greater detail than news coverage provides.)

- Write to the candidates and inquire about their positions on issues of importance to you. You won't always get responses, but sometimes the failure to respond speaks volumes.

- Take a few minutes to read the pamphlets or direct mail messages you receive about the candidates' ideas and backgrounds. Save them, too, so that you can remember the candidates' names and the offices for which they're running.

- Take the time to watch the television news coverage of the campaigns as election day approaches.

» Be sure to read the candidate profiles that your newspaper puts together prior to election day.

TIP

» Read the questionnaires that newspapers submit to each candidate regarding popular issues. Prior to election day, the newspapers publish the candidates' responses or the lack thereof. These questionnaires can provide you with specific information on the candidates' backgrounds and positions.

None of this preparation takes long to complete, and it increases your comfort level in choosing which candidates to support.

Looking to the campaigns

One important factor to consider when you're deciding which candidate to support is the type of campaign the candidate is running. Consider the following questions:

» Do the printed materials and television and radio advertisements from the candidate give any indication of what that person will do if elected?

» Is all the information provided to voters warm and fuzzy or appealing to emotion, or do issues or specific ideas on the improvement of the office that is sought play a role in the campaign?

» Is the campaign largely, if not completely, an attack on the opponent?

» Do the attacks focus on matters that generate heat but very little light?

TIP

The type of campaign a candidate runs can provide you with valuable insight into the type of person that candidate is. After you know what type of person they are, you can predict the type of officeholder they will become. People are more comfortable when they know what they're getting.

Making your choice

When you're making voting decisions, don't be afraid to trust your instincts. Your gut feelings can be a valuable guide. (But having enough information can help you be sure that your gut feeling isn't just indigestion.)

WARNING

Ask yourself whether you're choosing the candidate based on looks. Remember what your mother always told you: You can't judge a book by its cover. That's true with a candidate, too. If you want your decision to be reliable, it has to be based on something more than a candidate's hairstyle, orthodontia, or fashion sense. (See Chapter 11 for more information on the image that a candidate presents.)

TIP

A MATCH MADE IN HEAVEN?

Here are some questions to consider when you're choosing a candidate:

- **Do you normally feel more comfortable supporting one particular political party?** If the answer to that question is yes, you should look to that party's candidates first when you're deciding whom to support.

- **Are you satisfied with the way a particular office is being run?** If the answer to that question is no, you should look to the outsider candidate (either the nonincumbent or the opposition party candidate) as a starting point in your decision-making. If you're satisfied, stay with the incumbent, or with the party of the incumbent if the incumbent isn't seeking reelection.

- **Which candidate is working harder to win your support?** Have you been contacted by one or both of the candidates in person or on the phone? If the district is too large for personal contacts, is the candidate trying to meet as many voters as possible? The candidate who wants the office enough to work at getting elected will probably work hard at being a good officeholder.

- **If you had an opportunity to meet or hear both candidates, did one of them impress you more than the other?** Your gut instincts on these situations are usually reliable.

- **If the candidates haven't debated each other or appeared together, is it because one of the candidates is reluctant to participate in such an event?** If a candidate is reluctant to appear, ask yourself whether you're willing to support a candidate with so little self-confidence that they won't give you a chance to compare the candidates for yourself. Candidates should debate (maybe not every day of the campaign, but once or twice) to give you ample opportunity to listen and make your comparisons.

TIP

Here are some important actions to watch out for if you want the type of candidate who will pay attention to you and the other voters and be a leader at the same time. Look for a candidate who

- » Makes specific proposals for solving problems

- » Admits that they don't have all the answers

- » Disagrees with you on some issues

- » Declines to promise quick, easy, and painless solutions to complex problems

- » Speaks up to tell you that you will have to sacrifice to do things that need to be done — like pay more in taxes to increase teachers' salaries

- » Expects you to have a role in solving problems

>> Gives you a convincing reason to vote for them

>> Tells you more about their finances than they're obligated by law to do

>> Promises not to accept free lunches, gifts, or trips from special interests who are trying to influence their official duties

>> Understands that public office is a public trust

>> Is willing to embrace new ways to improve the political system and make it more responsive to voters

TIP

When you find a candidate who can do most of these things, don't just vote for them — get involved in their campaign! Read Chapters 7 and 8 for ways to work in helping to elect this person to office. A candidate like this one is precisely the type of candidate the country needs. If this person wins the election, they will work to make the political system and government more responsive. With your newfound political savvy, you can help them be successful.

Knowing when to make your decision

The obvious and correct answer to the question of when to make up your mind on how to vote is *when you're ready.* You should decide when you have enough information to be comfortable with your decision. It's a personal decision that you need to make for yourself. If you're not completely sure about whom to support, you may consider waiting at least until you've

>> Received information — whether it's written or oral or consumed via the media — about the candidates and the issues from both sides, or from all sides if more than two candidates are in the race

>> Taken the opportunity to observe and/or listen to all candidates, preferably in person, but at least on television or radio

>> Evaluated the type of campaign each candidate is waging (See Chapter 18 for more on how to recognize negative campaign tactics)

>> Confirmed which groups or individuals you know (and do or don't respect) are supporting which candidate

>> Taken the opportunity to read in the newspapers any media interviews or questionnaires from the candidates

Many of these events don't take place until shortly before the election. Obviously, if you supported one candidate in the past or you know one of the candidates personally, you'll be comfortable making your decision earlier in the campaign. If not, you may want to keep an open mind until just before the election so that you'll have as much information as possible to make an informed choice.

5

Let the Campaigns Begin

Chapter **14**

Who Says Talk Is Cheap? (Where Your Contribution Goes)

You've decided to get involved. You've made up your mind to contribute to a campaign. You've even decided which candidate deserves your money. You're about to write out your check, but, before you do, you wonder how your candidate plans to spend your hard-earned dollars. Your question is not unreasonable. After all, you're new to this thing called politics. You have a right to know where your money goes.

Campaigning at the Local Level

For the most part, the level of the office you're supporting determines how your campaign contributions are spent. A campaign for a local officeholder, city councilperson, state legislator, or county commissioner is run pretty much on a personal level. Most of the individuals involved with campaigns at the local level are volunteers; paid political consultants are rare at this level of politics. This race is the type where the level of contact between the candidate and the voters is shaking hands or kissing the baby.

Going door-to-door

One of the best tactics a candidate can use on the local level is knocking on every door in the district and asking each voter personally for support. Of course, if the race involves hundreds of thousands of households, or even millions of them, this method isn't practical. Door-to-door campaigning works only when the number of votes cast is small enough for a candidate to get to all of the doors during the election season.

The downside

Although going door-to-door is quite an effective method of reaching and persuading voters, it's also time-consuming. It occupies weeks and months of the campaign. Day after day, through the heat of summer, despite the rain and the menacing dogs, candidates must be energized and interesting as well as interested in what the voters have to say. Door-to-door campaigning wears out numerous pairs of shoes in addition to the wear-and-tear it puts on the candidate.

REMEMBER

Keep in mind that going door-to-door may not be practical for a candidate who isn't physically able to do all that walking, because of either age or disability. It goes without saying that you shouldn't hold this against a candidate.

The upside

As difficult as it is, no method of communication is more effective with voters than person-to-person contact. Door-to-door campaigning has the additional virtue of being an inexpensive means of campaigning — it puts no strain on the campaign coffers. The only expenses likely to be incurred in a door-to-door effort are for literature about the candidate that the candidate personally distributes on visits to voters' homes and sends to the homes later for follow-up contact (and, perhaps, a new pair of shoes. The candidate can tell instantly whether the residence they are visiting contains registered voters, how frequently the people vote, and the party, if any, with which each voter identifies.

TIP

Because the voter list is at your fingertips, there's no confusion about whether the person being visited is registered. If you aren't on the list, you need to be registered. You can register on the spot, as part of the campaign's well-honed, to-your-door service, or you can always go online to Turbovote (https://turbovote.org) to verify whether you're registered. (If you're not, you can use the Turbovote site to register yourself.)

SPEAKING UP

When the candidate comes to your door, you can use the opportunity to tell the candidate what you want from an officeholder. Don't hold back! Specify which issues are important to you and ask what they can do about them.

Meeting face-to-face with a candidate is the best way to find out whether this is the type of person you want to support. If you have decided to become more involved, you can determine whether this campaign is worthy of your involvement. Do you think this is the type of candidate you would give your hard-earned money to? Is this the kind of candidate you would be willing to volunteer to help? Use this opportunity for conversation to see whether this is the candidate who meets your standards. Consider this a job interview — and you're the employer.

TIP

If you just want to be left alone, tell the candidate that you're supporting the opponent and that nothing they can say or do will change your mind. Chances are that the campaign will no longer knock on your door after that — and no doubt will take pains to avoid reminding you to vote.

Follow-up letters

Many candidates follow up their visits with personalized letters. The candidate or an assistant makes notes on issues you raise during the visit, and those notes are fed into the computer to generate a number of form letters. For example, Mr. Smith at 100 Pine Lane wants a stop sign at the next corner. Ms. Jones at 102 Pine Lane thinks property taxes are too high. The campaign sends personalized letters to Mr. Smith and Ms. Jones on the issues they raised. An efficient campaign makes certain that Mr. Smith and Ms. Jones receive letters from the candidate within a day or two following the personal contact, espousing their staunch support for more stop signs and lower property taxes.

If you aren't at home when the candidate comes to visit, you may still receive a personalized "Sorry I missed you" letter. Most people like receiving this personalized mail because it demonstrates that they're important enough for the campaign to contact them directly.

Thousands of other voters probably receive similar letters. On the other hand, the candidate is concerned enough about your views and your vote to go to this trouble to try to win you over.

Alternative contacts

In local races, your money may be used to buy literature about the candidate or the issues or even campaign tchotchkes like nail files, mini calendars, refrigerator magnets, cards listing emergency phone numbers — all with the candidate's name on them. Your money may also be used to pay for yard signs and newspaper, radio, and television ads that are designed to bring your candidate to the attention of the voters.

Television ads

Sometimes a local campaign produces cable television spots by itself, without professional help. Such spots can be filmed at many cable television studios using the workers at the cable stations. The quality of the commercial may leave something to be desired, but the message can still be effective.

These cable spots can cost as little as several hundred dollars — as opposed to thousands of dollars for a professional spot — to create. That leaves a limited-resources campaign with a lot more available cash to get its message out to you and other voters. Because cable television advertising is inexpensive, more and more local candidates are using campaign money to put their families on cable.

REMEMBER

As inexpensive as a cable TV ad or social media ad is, it's not free, and neither are the other kinds of advertisements. Your contributions can be used to pay for radio and television time and for the production costs associated with the advertisements your candidate is airing and for the direct mail about the candidate you receive in your mailbox.

Radio advertising

Depending on the office and the district, radio can be a much more effective tool for communicating than TV or even cable TV. Most radio spots are 60-second ads. Those ads can be produced in the radio studio for minimal cost. Knowing what to say in these ads is a function of the campaign's polling. Candidates or their volunteers often use a trial-and-error method to write their scripts.

Direct mail

If the district is too large for the candidate personally to contact all the necessary voters, your contribution can be used to send mail directly to the voters. Sometimes, a well-financed campaign sends direct mail in addition to the personal contact. Direct mail is quite an effective method for reaching the voters who need to be persuaded, but it's also expensive.

To have the desired impact, a campaign must send several pieces of direct mail to each household that the candidate is trying to persuade. If the candidate needs to persuade 10,000 voting households to vote her way, 40,000 to 50,000 pieces of mail may be needed to get that job done.

Campaigns send their mail at the bulk rate, but the postage and printing for that volume of mail can cost between $25,000 and $40,000! And that's just to say "Hello, how are ya?" and "Hey, look me over." You can see why campaigns need your money.

In recent years, many millions of dollars have been spent to put political ads targeted to certain audiences on social media like Facebook. These ads may be used to campaign for offices with large and small constituencies. Using data regarding age, median income, ethnicity, and political leanings, candidates can direct their messages directly to voters they want to persuade or motivate to vote. In the 2018 election cycle, Propublica.org, a non-profit news room, reports that the American Association of Retired Persons (AARP) spent more than $700,000,000 on social media in the 2018 midterm election cycle attempting to protect the Affordable Care Act. Propublica has also identified some social media ads which may not be what they seem. It identified a group called America Progress Now which urged liberals to vote for Green Party candidates. This group had no address or legal registration and was unknown to the Green Party candidates. With the margins in Wisconsin, Michigan, and Pennsylvania as close as they were in 2016, encouraging votes for third-party candidates may divert enough from the major candidates to change the outcome.

National and Statewide Campaigns

Campaigns for higher-level offices spend their money somewhat differently from campaigns for local candidates. Candidates for most congressional, senatorial, gubernatorial, and other statewide offices (those for which everyone in the state votes) have professional consultants in addition to volunteers helping with the campaigns. Your contribution may help pay the salaries of these professional consultants, who perform a variety of functions, all of which cost money. These consultants manage the campaign and determine what message the candidate should communicate, how the message is communicated, and the best strategy to win votes and support.

You have to see it (on TV) to believe it

For a statewide office, television and cable are the preferred methods of communicating with you and the other voters. TV and cable enable a candidate to deliver messages to the greatest number of people in the most cost-effective manner. Communicating by direct mail with numbers in the millions is too expensive for the average statewide campaign. Television and cable — and now social media — are the way most statewide candidates get their messages to you and the other voters.

REMEMBER

When voters don't see ads for a statewide candidate on television, they don't believe that there *is* a campaign. It doesn't matter how hard the candidate is working, how many miles the candidate has walked, or how many speeches a candidate has given — without television advertising, the candidate and campaign are invisible. With television, the candidate is recognized and has credibility. Television advertising helps reinforce everything else the campaign is doing.

A SAMPLE CAMPAIGN BUDGET

Let me give you an example of a campaign budget for a gubernatorial candidate in a midsize state. The population range for this state is 5.5 million to 6.5 million. States like New York and California with populations many times that size have gubernatorial campaign budgets many times as large. States with smaller populations . . . well, you get the idea.

Net income, $3.5 million: This figure is the fundraising total minus all expenses associated with raising the money in the first place (for example, the proceeds for direct mail soliciting minus the expense of creating the letters and mailing to potential contributors). All fundraising costs that aren't paid by the host or hostess of the fundraising event are paid by the campaign.

From the $3.5 million net fundraising income, the campaign must estimate all expenses that will be incurred in selling its candidate.

Here are the expenses for this example:

- **Staff:** A statewide campaign has a professional handler, a fundraiser, a press person, and a couple of support staff to answer phones, coordinate volunteers, and get things done.

  Total budget for staff: $300,000

- **Rent:** The candidate has to have a campaign headquarters unless the state party has enough room to provide a headquarters. The headquarters will likely remain open for one year. This figure includes the phone bill, which can be substantial in a statewide campaign.

  Total budget for rent: $100,000

- **Equipment:** The candidate tries to get as much equipment as possible by way of contributor donations but still needs desks, phones, computers, and copying machines.

  Total budget for equipment: $30,000

- **Travel:** This cost covers moving the candidate around the state with a car and a driver and then some airplane travel for the candidate.

  Total budget for travel: $30,000

- **Polling:** The candidate conducts focus groups and polls at the beginning of the campaign and at several other times during the course of the campaign. Right before the election, the candidate probably also tracks their own popularity and voters' familiarity with their message and their opponent's message. The candidate signs a contract with a professional polling company for this work.

Total budget for polling: $350,000

- **Direct mail:** The candidate wants to do some direct mail to segments of their *constituency* (the voters who vote in their election) where television is not an efficient method of communicating or where their message should particularly appeal to voters. If the candidate is an incumbent legislator, they mail all their constituents several times during their term in office using state funds if they're a state legislator or the franking privilege (free mail) if they're a US representative or senator. Using taxpayer-financed mail during a campaign is frowned on and in some cases an ethical violation, so incumbents complete their taxpayer-financed mailings before the campaign heats up.

Total budget for direct mail: $300,000

- **Printed materials:** Party workers want information on the candidate to hand out to voters at various times (door-to-door canvassing, county fairs, party events). They also want bumper stickers and buttons to give to supporters.

Total budget for printed materials: $25,000

- **Television production:** This amount covers the cost of filming and producing the TV commercials for the candidate. The media consultants hired by the candidate produce these commercials without too much of a markup. The media consultants make their money by receiving a percentage of the television buy — usually, 15 percent.

Total production costs: $200,000

- **Television time:** The candidate wants to be on the air from Labor Day until the election. This figure includes 11 or 12 weeks of television and the cost of buying the time. This is the most effective method of communication with the voters of this state; the vast majority of campaign resources are spent in marketing the candidate to you and the other voters.

Total television costs: $2.5 million

Your contribution and those of many others can help your candidate put a message on television among all the beer and deodorant commercials. If you and other contributors have been generous enough to permit it, a candidate hires another professional to produce the ads and buy the television time.

Buying the time

Producing professional ads for television and buying time are *expensive* propositions. How expensive depends on the location. Buying television time in New York City, Los Angeles, or Chicago requires deep pockets — pockets that contain millions of dollars. The pockets don't have to be quite as deep in Des Moines, Iowa, or Harrisburg, Pennsylvania. In less expensive television markets, hundreds of thousands of dollars for television may be sufficient.

Campaigns try to buy time as early as they can. Even if the ads won't run for weeks, campaigns buy time as soon as money is available. They buy time before they're ready to use it, for a couple of reasons. First, campaigns have definite ideas about which voters they want to persuade. The television stations provide information about what type of person watches what type of show. Often, more than one campaign may want ads on certain programs, and only so much ad time can be sold. A campaign with money will try to lock in its choices early, so the ads will appear when the campaign wants them to. Second, purchasing time early make also makes it more difficult for the opposing candidate to get all the time for ads they want — a double bonus!

CHEAP TV

Campaigns on a limited budget can avoid professional media buyers and buy their own time from the cable networks in the candidate's district. They tell the cable stations the type of person they're trying to persuade with their message and ask which programs they need to buy time on to reach that audience.

The candidate or campaign volunteers can write the commercial. They need to know what message they want to get across to voters — if they've polled, they should have ideas on what the most effective message is. (See Chapters 9 and 12.) Then they have to write a script to communicate the message in less than 30 seconds. That's the usual length of a campaign commercial on television. Sometimes ads can last 60 seconds, but buying time for a 60-second ad obviously is twice as expensive as for the normal 30-second spot.

If you've decided to volunteer for a campaign and end up trying to write a script that concisely (in 30 or 60 seconds) communicates a message, be aware that it's a tricky proposition. Don't despair if you aren't producing award-winning spots immediately. You'll get the hang of it with a little practice.

When a candidate goes on television with campaign advertising, being on once or twice or for a short period isn't enough. Every campaign's goal is to stay on television until the end of the campaign. But just airing its ads until the end of the campaign isn't enough, either. The campaign must try to buy more television time than its opponents so that it can respond to any attacks the opposition makes. Doing so can cost a campaign the vast majority of all the money it has raised, but it can't effectively reach millions of voters any other way.

Successful statewide campaigns pour the vast majority of every dollar raised into television advertising. If you're giving money to a statewide race and your candidate wants to have a good chance of winning, chances are that your contribution will be used for television advertising.

Getting Out the Vote: Just Do It!

Going into the election, a campaign has to worry about your mood and the mood of the other voters. Is there enough interest in the campaign to ensure a reasonable voter turnout? If you and the other voters couldn't care less about the election, does the campaign have sufficient funds to whisper sweet somethings and get you to come out and vote?

Campaigns spend significant resources encouraging you and other voters sympathetic to their campaigns to come out to vote. *Get out the vote*, or GOTV, is a vital part of any campaign. A candidate who convinces a majority of potential voters that they're the best candidate still loses if they fail to get these supporters to show up at the polls.

As a potential voter, you're reminded by mail, phone call, and advertisement to vote. All these reminders cost money. Mail sent in volume can cost 70 cents per letter. Phone contacts for GOTV can cost 50 cents to 70 cents per call. In races for higher office, these calls are made by professional vendors, not volunteers. The volume of necessary calls is too great for volunteers to complete them during the few days before an election. Calls in campaigns can come from anywhere in the country for higher profile races. In lower profile local races, volunteers may still make calls to help the candidate they are supporting.

Radio and television advertisements, targeted at you and different segments of the voting population, reminding you about the election and encouraging you to vote, are expensive. Millions of people vote in statewide elections, a couple of hundred thousand in a congressional election, tens of thousands in a state senate race, and several thousand in a state assembly race — all these people need reminders to get out and vote, and it takes a lot of increasingly expensive stamps and touch-tone pounding to get to the eyes, ears, and feet of the voting public. The time and cost of these contacts is one of the reasons online ads and reminders to vote are increasingly popular.

REMEMBER

Most of the public is motivated to vote in the greatest numbers in presidential election years and is less likely to vote in nonpresidential elections. Nonpresidential elections are wars of *turnout,* or numbers of voters. Whichever party or campaign is more successful in getting the public to turn out and vote will probably win. GOTV is a silent but important part of any successful candidate's strategy. It's designed to get voters to do something that they're not likely to remember to do if not reminded because of the demands of everyday living.

Where Your Money Won't Go

Hopefully, your money won't go to put disinformation or false attack ads on social media. Until the ground rules are established for advertising and posting on social media, that is always a risk. Campaigns may want to make vicious attack ads on the opposition but the risks of doing them publicly on TV and cable or direct mail where it is apparent which campaign is the source are too great. If a reporter uncovers that type of shenanigan, the campaign's plan backfires. They've suddenly earned the campaign the kind of extensive news coverage and publicity that money can't buy — or correct. Campaigns are required to disclose that they paid for and approved any ad they use. Independent expenditures which cannot be coordinated with a campaign can pay for attacks to benefit that campaign and use noble sounding names like Citizens for Good Government.

POLITICAL MYTH

Successful campaigns don't engage in unnecessary and risky shenanigans, despite what Hollywood may think. Some ground rules for acceptable campaign conduct are usually followed.

You can be confident that your contribution goes toward persuading other voters to support the candidate you've already backed with your hard-earned dollars. Your money isn't ordinarily used for some villainous purpose; indiscretions have an uncanny way of coming back to haunt the candidate.

Campaigns Never Say, "Enough!"

Campaigns have an almost insatiable need for money. Spending more is never a challenge. They want more money even when there's a substantial risk that they can't effectively spend what they have. Whether the campaign is for a local, state, or national office, the point never comes when the campaign staff says it has raised enough money.

Of course, the campaign must always be concerned about what will happen next. Given the secrecy that surrounds political strategy, a campaign can never be certain what its opposition has planned. It makes decisions about its own tactics in almost complete ignorance of what the opposition is doing — and how much the opposition is spending to do it.

Fundraising wars

In the battle for your vote, a campaign has to consider what its opponent will say or do. All these questions play a role in how much money a campaign needs to raise:

>> How successful is the opponent's fundraising?

>> Will the opponent start advertising on television first?

>> Is the opponent sending direct mail?

>> Will the opponent attack the campaign's candidate?

>> What information does the opponent have, and what form will the attack take?

>> Will you find the opposition's message more persuasive?

>> Will you believe the opponent's attack on the campaign's candidate?

>> Does the opponent have enough money to get their message out to you?

>> If you hear the message enough, will you change your vote?

Secrecy, spying, and surprise

Obviously, opposing campaigns don't share this type of information with each other. In fact, they often leak incorrect information (*disinformation*) to confuse their opponents. This disinformation may concern the success of fundraising, the results of polling, or the outcome of campaign tactics.

A campaign facing a credible opponent doesn't necessarily know what's coming, how it will come, or when it will come — which is why political campaigns are considered the leading cause of paranoia in even-numbered years.

The element of surprise can be crucial in the war for your vote. Each side wants to catch the other off guard. When a campaign is surprised, it may make a mistake.

If a campaign fails to respond or responds in the wrong way, you may question whether you're supporting the right candidate. All the secrecy, plotting, and campaign tactics are about getting your vote on election day.

REMEMBER

If a campaign resorts to military tactics, such as spying or paying for information, and those tactics are uncovered, its candidate is guaranteed to lose. Talk about flying blind!

Campaigns often may not know how much money the opposition has to launch the attack and make the charge stick in your mind. All campaigns must file campaign finance reports, but the timing of those reports may be critical. Many states require a report to be filed after the candidate becomes the nominee (after the primary or convention selects the party's nominee) and not again until just before the election in the fall. Some states are requiring campaigns to report large contributions (defined by state law) that are received after the last reporting period for filing a campaign report before the election. That requirement can make you aware of large contributions but not the total of cash on hand. If the attack comes shortly before the general election, the opposition campaign may not truly know just how much money the opposition has to launch an attack.

Despite this scarcity of information, a campaign must determine whether and how to respond. If the attack is effective, a campaign can't afford to let it go unanswered — voters may begin to believe the charge! The campaign must convince you that the charge is unfair, or at least distract you, if the campaign has any hope of keeping or winning your vote. A campaign has to figure on having the resources to let you know the candidate's side of the story. This extra caution is even more important if a campaign will play out over the airwaves, because advertising often must be purchased long before the candidate and the advisers know what claims and counterclaims they will need to make.

You can easily understand why no campaign is ever confident that it has raised enough money to meet every possible circumstance. A campaign is expected to fight a war when it doesn't know when the war will begin, what type of weapons the enemy has, or how large its army is.

Winning your vote

REMEMBER

Remember that this war is all about you and your vote. You, and others like you, are the prize each side is seeking to win. Money plays a vital role in this war. Without money, a campaign can't respond to an attack or distract the voters — it's merely adrift on the "ocean," being pounded by waves from all sides, without the power to reach the winning port, and no doubt rendered violently ill on election night.

When you see a candidate with enough money to go on television first, you can usually deduce that the candidate has won the fundraising war. Occasionally, though, campaigns will go on the air early and hope to raise enough money to stay on the air. That's a great strategy — if it works. If it doesn't and the candidate has to go off the air, the media will report that the candidate has run out of money, and the fundraising will dry up even faster.

When you receive direct mail from one candidate and not the other, you can be sure that it isn't because the candidate who didn't write you is taking your vote for granted. They probably don't have enough money to send direct mail at all or as much as their opponent. (See Chapter 17 for a discussion of direct mail.)

Looking beyond the money

TIP

If you aren't going to be persuaded by money alone, you need to view these overtures for your vote with a grain of salt. Listen to the arguments from the candidate with enough money to contact you, but try to find out what the candidate without the money would say to you if they had the dollars and stamps to contact you. In other words, spend some of your time and effort to discover what the other candidate's position or point of view may be before you decide whom to support. Think for yourself.

Because money *is* the single most important determinant in deciding who wins and loses elections, you may want to consider contributing to a candidate of your choice whose campaign appears to be underfunded. Your campaign contribution can

>> Defray the cost of creating and mailing letters

>> Help pay for the literature that the candidate distributes

>> Assist a candidate in getting input from real, live voters like you

>> Help to personalize campaigning, at least for local races

REMEMBER

The candidate with the most money doesn't *always* win, but does win much more often than not, which is why fundraising is an important part of any campaign. You won't know whether the losing candidate was the better candidate if the campaign lacked the money to get that message to you effectively. Perhaps incumbents win 90 percent of the time because it's easier for them as officeholders to raise money to retain their positions.

Chapter **15**

For Whom the Campaign Polls

One evening in the summer months before an election, you answer your telephone and the voice on the other end of the line asks if you're willing to answer a few questions. The person is working with XYZ Public Opinion and is taking a survey. You've been selected as a target for a polling firm for one of the candidates or parties in the upcoming election.

Why you? You were just minding your own business, watching *Jeopardy!* What did you do to deserve this type of treatment?

Pollsters are the marketing experts of a campaign. They get the information from you and other voters to focus their campaigns. The results of the campaign's polling decide when, how, and to whom the message gets out — as well as *what* that message is.

The campaign called you so that it can use your responses to shape its message and to determine the most effective way to communicate that message. Your responses help determine whether to use direct mail, what to say in it, and who receives it; what television shows to advertise on and how much time to buy; and whether the benefits of a last-minute phone drive overcome the wrath of voters like you who vigorously object to negative campaigning. The poll also might be serving an advertising purpose, with questions intended to persuade you how to vote along the way.

If money is no object, campaigns also sample voters by means of focus groups. These groups permit campaigns to conduct detailed interviews with a few specially selected representative voters in order to understand how these voters view the candidates and the issues. (See Chapter 10 for more about what focus groups are and how campaigns use them.)

The Role of Polls

A *poll* is a survey of a scientifically selected cross-section of the population of a district, state, or nation that's likely to vote in the next election. The people in this cross-section are asked a series of questions to obtain information and determine attitudes.

Most campaigns for high-profile offices employ professional pollsters. Many of the prominent polling firms that specialize in political campaigns are located in Washington, DC, and New York City, but polling firms exist in most large cities. They are hired to conduct polls that the *handler* (that is, the campaign consultant) and the candidate need and for which they can afford to pay. (See Chapter 10 for more on handlers.)

Like handlers, pollsters may, during the course of their careers, work for a variety of candidates running in many different states for many different offices, but they generally stay on one side or the other of the political fence — Republican or Democrat.

Who gets polled?

Scientifically conducted polls randomly select the voters who are interviewed. Randomness is the factor that permits a few hundred people to speak for all the voters (within a modest margin of error). In other words, you're as likely as any other voter in the district to be asked to participate in the poll. No sample is perfectly random, but pollsters try to make their surveys as close to random as possible because the sample is most reliable that way.

Methods to their madness

Random digit dialing is one technique used to ensure a sample's accuracy. In *random digit dialing*, telephone numbers are randomly connected to each working telephone exchange. This method is especially accurate and has the benefit of reaching voters with unlisted numbers, but it's expensive because the pollsters charge for the numbers they dial that either aren't working or don't belong to registered voters.

If the area being polled doesn't have clear exchange boundaries, like a city where different legislative districts represent people in the same exchange, random digit dialing may not be cost effective. That's because there's no way to separate out the phone numbers of people in the district of interest to the pollster. If the poll is for a primary race with low turnout, random digit dialing may not be cost effective then, either, because the pollster will reach many people who don't plan to vote in the primary.

When random digit dialing doesn't work, pollsters use voter file lists that have been *phone matched*. This method may not be as accurate as random digit dialing because some groups of voters don't have phones in proportion to the number of people in the group who vote. The following groups tend to be undersampled when this method is used:

>> Older voters in nursing homes

>> Voters who move frequently and use landlines

>> Wealthier voters with unlisted numbers

>> Young voters who are in college

In 2004, about 5% of the population used cell phones exclusively. In 2019, that percentage has risen to 13%. Pollsters disagree on the demographics of the 13%. Some pollsters believe the 13% is disproportionally young people and some do not. Pollsters are always concerned to poll the correct percentage of the population in each age group so they take different approaches. The pollsters who think that more young people use cell phones exclusively will use a sample with 13% of voters who use cell phones only. Pollsters who think all age groups use cell phones to the exclusion of land lines will make certain that the voters polled accurately reflect the population by age.

REMEMBER

No method of selecting the voters to be polled is perfect, but pollsters try hard to make the sample as representative as possible. After all, the candidate makes important decisions based on the answers you give.

Fitting a certain profile

If you get called for a poll, it's probably because your number came up at random. On the other hand, you may have been selected because you fit a certain profile. You may still have been selected at random, but from a small subgroup of the voting population.

Suppose that Harry Handler thinks that a position taken by the opponent will anger women under the age of 50. Harry may believe that publicizing this position will lose the opponent votes among that age-and-gender group. He wants to test this theory before spending any resources getting the word out to voters. He won't spend the money if the opponent won't lose votes.

Your name may have been selected from among those individuals who fit the profile of the interested subgroup — women under 50. The answers you give to the pollster's questions tell the handler whether to spend money getting the word out to other voters like you.

If you get that call . . .

Only a few hundred people are asked their opinions on these questions. Those few hundred people have a significant impact on the message and strategy for the campaign. Their responses help decide which programs a candidate supports or opposes during the campaign — in other words, the positions to which the candidate will be committed if victorious. The responses tell a candidate whether their message is getting through or needs to be refined.

As Chapter 3 discusses, no campaign will spend money finding out what you think if you aren't a registered voter. If you want an opportunity to shape political campaigns, make sure that you're registered to vote when that pollster calls you.

SPEAKING UP

If you're polled and take the time to respond, you can shape the approach and content of a campaign. You're one of only a few hundred people in your congressional district or state who get to speak about a broad range of issues while the candidate listens. You're in a position of influence. The candidate wants to know what you think. The candidate is paying the pollster good money, and lots of it, just to hear your views. You're a political pooh-bah. And all you did was register to vote and answer your phone! Of course, you also missed *Jeopardy!* — but now real folks, not just the television set, have had the benefit of your wise answers to questions.

Who polls?

Any campaign with sufficient money uses polls these days. The level of the office being sought doesn't matter — county and legislative candidates use polls, too. Polling is advisable whenever an office involves policy or a campaign is going to be anything more than "I'm Carly Candidate — vote for me!" A well-run, well-funded candidate tests the message before spending money communicating it.

Sometimes candidates for less visible offices pool their resources and poll together. Sometimes party organizations pay some or all of the costs. Occasionally, special interest groups use polling to convince candidates or officials of the wisdom of supporting the special interest position on an issue. (Refer to Chapter 8 if you're not sure what a special interest group is.) Special interest groups use polls to show candidates that their ideas are popular or that an idea the group opposes is unpopular.

Polls Are Expensive

One of the reasons campaigning for office costs more now than in the past is the increasing use of professional polls to find out what you and other voters want and think. (Flip to Chapter 14 for other reasons campaigning costs are on the rise.)

The candidate's *handler* — the campaign consultant who shapes and directs the entire campaign — knows how important polling is. Even though professional polls cost thousands of scarce campaign dollars, the Harry Handlers of the world spend that amount gladly in an attempt to contact you and find out what you're thinking.

Harry Handler uses polls throughout the campaign process:

>> He conducts a benchmark poll. (See the later section "Benchmark Polls.")

>> He goes back in the field with polls when he begins his television commercials to see whether you're responding to the message.

>> He also polls when the opponent begins their television advertising, to see whether you're persuaded by the opponent's message.

>> If Harry intends to attack the opponent or believes that the opponent will attack his candidate, he polls in advance to test your response to the attacks and the anticipated defenses.

>> Harry also polls you during the attacks to see whether you're inclined to change your vote.

Each of these polls costs tens of thousands of dollars! Why would a well-funded, professionally run campaign spend that kind of money on polling? Think of it as an investment to monitor your reaction to the campaign as it goes along. If your reaction is not what Harry Handler hoped, he adjusts the campaign strategy to win you over — wasting less money in the long run.

Size of the sample

The cost of polls, as well as the margin of error in polls, is determined primarily by the sample size: The greater the number surveyed, the more expensive the poll and the more reliable the results. But to get within a certain acceptable margin of error for their determinations, pollsters have to complete a given number of surveys. The *margin of error* is a statistic that represents the amount of random sampling error in a poll's results. Most pollsters release the margin-of-error calculation when the poll is released. If the margin of error is plus or minus 3 percentage points, that means about 95 percent of the time, the survey results should be within 3 percentage points of the true answer. So, if a candidate is supported by 52 percent of the people in the survey, the actual number may be as high as 55 percent or as low as 49 percent but is unlikely to be 57 percent support or only 46 percent. Some reports comparing polling with electoral results have shown the margins to be much greater and, thus, a less accurate predictor of election results.

In a statewide poll, the range of the sample is typically 600 to 800 completed calls. In a congressional district, the number of completed surveys may be in the 400 to 600 range.

But above a certain minimum size, bigger isn't always worth the price, in terms of statistical accuracy. For a particular survey question, the margin of error for a sample of 1,200 is only 1 percentage point less than the margin of error for a sample of 600.

REMEMBER

Suppose that 30 percent of the people responding to such a poll say that they dislike Opus Opponent. The campaign can feel fairly secure that 25 to 35 percent of voters dislike Opus, assuming that the survey questions were asked in an unbiased way — but anything more precise is impossible with such a small sample.

Pollsters need to contact more voters than the 600 to 800 sought in a statewide contest to complete that many surveys, because they have to make up for unanswered calls, calls to businesses, and calls to people who don't want to answer questions about politics The pollster tries to minimize the lack of completed calls and the hostility of the voter by calling after dinner (but not too late) on the days of the week when people are more likely to be home — Sunday through Thursday.

Length of the poll

The amount of time that the pollsters must spend on the telephone for each survey also affects the cost of polls. The longer the time spent asking questions, the more expensive the poll. Pollsters don't ask any extraneous questions, and they don't waste time asking questions when they already know the answers.

An example of a useless question that pollsters wouldn't waste their time on is whether convicted felons should serve prison time. Obviously, the answer to that question would be an overwhelming *yes*. The real question is whether voters are willing to spend $200 million to build the new prison necessary to make certain that all convicted felons do prison time.

It's not uncommon for pollsters to ask 60 to 80 questions after you agree to be interviewed. That number may seem like too many, but most of the questions are brief. The pollster tries not to take more than 20 to 30 minutes of your time. That's about how long it takes you to visit your polling place and vote on election day — and answering these questions can have a much more profound impact on the course of a campaign than your single vote can ever have.

Benchmark Polls

A *benchmark poll* is a lengthy, professional, public opinion survey taken very early in a campaign. It's the poll that determines campaign strategy and planning. Benchmark polls measure some important items, or *benchmarks,* to compare with measurements taken later in the campaign in order to chart the campaign's progress or lack of progress.

Before a campaign conducts a benchmark poll, it finishes its internal opposition research and its external opposition research. (For more discussion of internal and external opposition research, refer to Chapter 11.) In other words, Harry Handler now knows all that he needs to know about the opposition and his own candidate before taking a benchmark poll. Harry Handler first identifies matters in both the candidate's and opposition's backgrounds that may be persuasive to the voters. This poll tests how good, or bad, Harry's instincts were.

The object of the benchmark poll, taken so many weeks and perhaps months before the election, is to determine what the outcome of the election will be if the campaign unfolds as expected. If you listen carefully to the questions the pollster asks you, you can determine what message the campaign will use to persuade you to vote for the candidate. You can also guess what attacks the campaign may use to persuade you to vote against the opponent.

Knowing what to expect

Benchmark polls usually follow some variation on the following format:

Do you know the two candidates?

Do you feel favorably or unfavorably about the two candidates?

Answers to these first two questions tell Harry Handler how many voters he must persuade to win the election.

Answers to the following question tell Harry where the election stands now, before the campaign's message is delivered:

This November, there will be an election for governor between Democrat Carly Candidate and Republican Opus Opponent; for whom will you vote?

What do you feel is the most important issue in this campaign (for example: education, crime, taxes, immigration)?

How do you feel about specific programs Carly Candidate has proposed (for example: a road construction program, an educational program)?

Do you feel good about the direction your state is headed?

If you knew the following positive characteristics about Carly Candidate, would you be inclined to vote for her?

The answers to these questions tell Harry Handler which of Carly's many accomplishments should be used in the message to bring you around to supporting her.

Harry asks the following question to discover whether you find the positive info about Carly Candidate persuasive enough to support her:

Now that you have some information about Carly, for whom will you vote?

Answers to this question tell Harry Handler whether attacks on Opus Opponent will persuade you to vote for Carly Candidate:

If you knew the following negative information about Opus Opponent, would you be less inclined to support him?

Harry may ask the same question again later in the poll, to gauge the influence of information you've learned during the course of the survey.

Answers to the following question tell Harry Handler whether his responses to Opus Opponent's attacks will work and persuade you to vote for Carly Candidate:

Some people say that Carly Candidate is too liberal with taxpayer money. Her office budget has increased 40 percent during her six years as attorney general. Others say that Carly Candidate is a fiscal conservative who has refused a pay raise and that her office budget has increased only because her office is doing more for the taxpayers by not hiring outside attorneys, who charge large fees to represent the State in court. With whom do you agree?

Learning from the pollsters

If you listen carefully to the questions a pollster asks, you can tell who is taking the poll. The candidate taking the poll asks questions about their own characteristics and record in an attempt to determine what positive message to communicate to you and the other voters. The candidate taking the poll also spends a fair amount of time on questions testing the opponent's weaknesses to decide which attacks work.

TIP

You can also find out what facts in their own record concern the candidate conducting the poll. You can figure out what issues the candidate conducting the poll would be willing to use in the campaign, provided that you're persuaded by them. In fact, listening carefully to the pollster's questions can tell you much more about the records of both candidates than the campaign itself will ever disclose.

The candidate conducting the poll will use in the campaign only a few of the most persuasive positive factors in their own background and a few of the most persuasive negative factors in their opponent's record. (Flip to Chapter 11 for more information on how the message of a campaign is determined.) But if you listen to all the questions the pollster asks, you can tell what other issues are out there that the campaign decided not to use.

Telling pollsters which arguments persuade you

Polls ask you questions about the candidate as well as about their opponent. They test positive items in the candidate's background to see whether these items persuade you to support the candidate. They test anticipated attacks by the opposition and the candidate's rebuttal. Your responses to these questions help the handler decide which method to use to disguise whatever warts the candidate may have. (Alternative approaches are discussed in Chapter 11.) Your answers tell the handler which disguise for the warts will be most effective.

REMEMBER

When you answer a pollster's questions, you're determining the course of a campaign. If you're strongly opposed to negative attacks, your answers to poll questions should be consistent with that view. On the other hand, negative attacks may provide you with important information about a candidate that you want to take into account when comparing the alternatives. If you find out facts about a candidate that sound unacceptable in a potential public servant, you probably should communicate that message. You're in a bind: You can't oppose negative campaigns *and* allow yourself to be persuaded by them. If you tell the pollster that the attacks on Opus Opponent's record will persuade you to vote for Carly Candidate, Harry Handler will attack Opus Opponent — even if you tell the pollster that negative ads turn you off.

Is the Candidate's Message Getting Through?

Harry Handler must continually evaluate whether the campaign's message is getting through to you and then monitor the effect of the opponent's message on you. That message may be more persuasive than Harry bargained for. He may need to try another approach to disguising Carly Candidate's warts, or else her message may not be as persuasive as Harry hoped. Harry may need another message or another approach to the message that he's using to get through to you. Subsequent polls help Harry make the necessary midcourse corrections that keep Carly's campaign on target to victory. A campaign is fluid: It's all about moving the undecided voters into one or another candidate's corner. When the purpose of a campaign is to change minds, and the inflexible deadline of election day is looming, a handler had better be able to adapt and change course quickly. If a campaign has spent three weeks and hundreds of thousands of dollars on television telling voters what the candidate has done for them, and the poll reveals that the voters still don't know what the candidate has done, the message isn't penetrating and the campaign must go to Plan B.

Chapter **16**

Dodging the Issues: What You Can Do

When political ads appear during your favorite TV shows, they serve as examples of how important it is to gain your support in order for the various campaigns to be successful. But you may wonder about the messages contained in the advertisements. (Chapter 15 discusses how candidates poll voters to determine which items should be part of a candidate's message.)

The message and marketing are designed to grab your attention. All this research and scientific information-gathering costs campaigns a huge amount of time and money, but they do it because it's essential to the success of their campaigns. You know that already. What you don't know is *why* the campaigns decided on the message that you're seeing. Why are they talking about a trivial matter instead of something that you've identified as important?

TIP

The next time you hear an advertisement talking about an issue that you feel is unimportant, ask yourself why the candidate chose that message. What issue or issues is the candidate avoiding? Be wary of candidates who aren't willing to tackle discussions of complex problems when asking you for your vote. If they aren't willing to talk about these issues during the campaign, chances are that they won't want to deal with them when they're finally in office, either.

Tough-versus-Trivial Issues in a Campaign

If you observe election campaigns long enough, you notice that candidates avoid certain issues at all costs and spare no expense to harp on others. Unfortunately, the issues they avoid may be the ones you're interested in hearing about, and the issues they champion may seem petty.

Here are some tough issues that candidates try to avoid discussing:

>> Abortion

>> Gun control

>> Programs to cut to balance the federal budget

>> Steps to take to reduce the cost of spending on the elderly

>> Why schoolchildren perform poorly in schools and how to correct that problem

Instead, candidates of both parties talk about these issues:

>> Renouncing the perks and privileges of office

>> The need for campaign finance reform . . . at some point in the future

>> Term limits — under a definition that allows this candidate to spend their entire career as an officeholder

>> The moral decline of society and the need for prayer in schools to counter it

>> Cutting their office budget

To win, a candidate must build support

Say that you and a solid majority of the voters indicate in a poll that the most important issue in a legislative campaign is property taxes. Yet neither campaign is talking about the issue, or the challenger is attacking the increase in property taxes without offering any solutions. Why?

The reason is that there's no easy answer to this question. Proposals for changing the tax base of any community always work to the advantage of some groups and to the disadvantage of others. Communities need more, not less, money to repair their streets, pay their police, and finance their schools. Anytime a candidate makes a proposal to change taxes, people grow concerned that they'll pay more, even if the proposal is revenue neutral. For example, if property taxes are lowered, people with expensive homes will benefit to a greater extent than people who rent or have more modest housing. If you raise the sales tax in order to make up for lost revenue caused by property tax relief, lower income people will pay a relatively higher percentage of their disposable income in sales tax. People seldom accept at face value the argument that tax reform is sure to benefit them, because it may not — for some, tax reform ends up being just another tax increase in disguise.

REMEMBER

Whenever taxes are changed — even if the move is revenue neutral — people worry that they're paying more. A *revenue neutral* measure is one in which no more total money is raised through taxes but the way the money is raised may be changed. Governments may be willing to substitute revenue sources, but they're seldom willing to abolish a tax that provides a significant amount of revenue without replacing it with another. Property taxes in most states fund public education. They provide much of the money for local law enforcement, fire protection, and other essential government services. As burdensome and irritating as property taxes may be, political leaders who cut them may lose more popularity than they gain if the result is a significant decline in local services. Governments can't afford to abolish property taxes — or even lower them — without finding alternative sources of revenue.

As soon as candidates start talking about substituting one tax for another, they lose votes. Voters may agree that they want something done about property taxes, but they don't agree what that something is. They are fundamentally skeptical that any change will work to their advantage. Voters are just regular people, not eager to make tough choices. But they also have zero confidence that politicians will make the right tough choices *for* them.

YOU CAN'T HIDE FROM EVERYTHING

POLITICAL STUFF

Sometimes, issues that were successfully avoided for years come to dominate public discussion to such an extent that they're impossible for candidates to avoid. Candidates must take positions on them regardless of the potential for risk and controversy. For example, presidential candidates must make their positions clear regarding gun violence because of the incredible number of mass shootings in the United States.

Almost every day, the headlines in newspapers, on the Internet, and on television highlight the death toll and emotional impact of mass shootings. Until Congress takes some action, this issue will be discussed at every debate or town meeting during the 2020 presidential campaign. As much as candidates would like to avoid the subject, they will be required to articulate a position on gun regulation or the Second Amendment.

A candidate who wants to win builds support. They win by convincing as many people as possible to vote for them. When a candidate begins talking about something as complicated as property tax substitutes, they raise doubts in the minds of some voters. Those doubts can fracture the fragile coalition of support that a candidate has worked to build. Building support is difficult when doubts about a candidate's program or judgment surface in a campaign. Fractures can eventually break a candidate's winning majority.

Proposing change is risky: I'll take vanilla instead

Proposing any change is risky. Proposing significant and specific change may be foolhardy. Winning elections is all about avoiding as much risk as possible. A candidate hesitates to propose anything that doesn't already have the strong backing of a majority of the electorate. Anything new or — heaven forbid — radical is out of the question.

However, a candidate must have a platform or a message to communicate to the voters. A candidate has to say something besides "vote for me," after all. That means that, yes, a candidate does have to give you a reason to vote for them, but that also means their message or platform will be as uncontroversial as possible — as plain-vanilla as the electorate and media permit.

Sticking to symbolic issues

Almost all the time, a candidate who latches on to an issue that appeals to you and other voters yet isn't complex or controversial comes out ahead. An example may be a candidate's refusal to use the car paid for by the taxpayers, which has traditionally been a perk of the office. Taxpayer-provided cars symbolize all that voters dislike about politics. A vehicle paid for by tax dollars is a perk or privilege that few, if any, of the rest us receive. It's a symbol of how elected officials are out of touch with average citizens.

The symbol could just as easily be a taxpayer-provided credit card for official duties, taxpayer-provided travel to conferences, or a pay raise. Any of these issues can strike a chord with voters. Any of these issues can provide voters with a reason to choose one candidate over the other.

Issues such as these are particularly potent when a candidate refusing to take these perks or privileges runs against an officeholder who has taken their share and then some. The smart candidate uses the refusal to take the perks and privileges of the office as the reason you should elect them and retire the current officeholder.

Incumbents in this position find themselves playing defense and following the Ten Commandments of Modern Politics, laid down in Chapter 24, and they may need to attack their opponents on some other issue to protect themselves.

Voters pay attention to issues like these. These symbols — though unlikely to make a difference in the quality of their lives — are easy to understand. They may not have anything to do with the important issues in an election; they may say nothing about property taxes or other important issues or what government can do about these issues. But they do give voters insight into how much a candidate wants to represent them and why. They may tell you how the candidate will respond to other examples of unnecessary spending when they arise in the future. That, by itself, can be useful information.

Using Diversions to Avoid Risks

A creative candidate may take even further the symbolic issue of turning down a perk. They may argue that a serious attempt to reduce waste or fraud in government, of the sort represented by their rejection of office perks, could lower the cost of government sufficiently to reduce the need for more property taxes. That argument is an ingenious way to turn the property tax debate, an issue for which the candidate has no program, into a vague debate over perks and privileges — an issue for which the candidate does have a program.

A thinking voter knows that cutting all the perks and privileges won't affect property taxes one iota. A skeptical voter presumes that serious tax cuts require serious changes in government policy rather than just a bit of willpower. Taking this line does, however, give the candidate something to say when property taxes come up in debates or question-and-answer sessions. Here's a sample:

>> A candidate can't say that they haven't thought about property taxes when the overwhelming majority of voters has identified property taxes as the number-one issue in the campaign.

>> The candidate can always say that property taxes are too burdensome. Voters will agree with that gem of wisdom. But that answer exposes the candidate to the inevitable follow-up question: "What are you going to do about property taxes if you're elected?" It's easy for a candidate to respond by promising to cut needless and wasteful spending.

>> The last thing a candidate wants to admit is that they don't want to propose alternatives to property taxes, because they're afraid of losing votes. It may be true, and the political realities may give the candidate no choice, but the voters and the media will have no patience with the answer. The diversion permits the candidate to say something responsive to the question about high property taxes without much risk.

Dodging with diversions

By resorting to a diversion, the candidate can sympathize with the problem and propose an uncontroversial "solution" to help deal with it. They can say that taxes are too high and that an alternative fund source for local governments needs to be explored. They may even propose something uncontroversial that, on closer analysis, probably won't work.

For example, the candidate may propose providing property tax relief by using part of an existing source of revenue. The candidate may say that a percentage of the state's lottery revenue should be used to provide property tax relief. However, most states quickly spend every cent that their lotteries generate, leaving no large pot of lottery revenue sitting in a bank, waiting to be spent for property tax relief or anything else. If lottery money is spent to solve the property tax problem, then some other equally worthy cause may be left short of funds. In addition, lottery revenue is not the consistent, reliable source of revenue that governments need in order to provide teacher salaries or pay to heat or cool schools.

The candidate views that situation as someone else's problem. They can tell everybody that they're looking at the big picture and that they'll sort out the details if elected. They'll assure you that they've elegantly answered the property tax question — the solution may not work, but they get away with it without having to propose a real program that will provide property tax relief but also risk losing the candidate votes.

REMEMBER

The candidate will never propose new revenue sources, because increasing or adding new taxes is risky politically. The candidate can recognize the problem and give a mealy-mouthed suggestion for a solution — such as changing the issue to a perks-and-privileges debate. All these alternatives are designed to avoid taking positions that may solve real problems but that also may cost candidates elections.

A candidate talks about unimportant items instead of real issues to reduce the risks to themselves. A candidate wants to give you a risk-free reason for voting for them. They'll do that as long as you let them get away with that approach. If you aren't willing to let them have a risk-free campaign, keep on reading.

Diversions may not build support, but they don't jeopardize it, either

No voter ever refused to support a candidate for turning down the perks and privileges of an office. Voters are sick and tired of officeholders with lucrative salaries, who also have the ability to leave office and take a lucrative salary to lobby the very branch of government the officeholder just left. They're tired of officeholders who don't understand what it means to lose healthcare coverage or have the company you have worked for all your life go under and take with it the pension plan you were counting on for your retirement. Members of Congress don't have to worry about their pension plans. If members serve a certain length of time, they're guaranteed substantial pensions for life.

To put it another way, the diversion might work to diffuse a controversial issue, and to gain the candidate some votes. But if it doesn't work, it won't necessarily fracture the coalition that the candidate is building to win election. The candidate loses no ground if the strategy is unsuccessful. They simply have to find another approach to winning over enough voters like you in order to be successful.

Stick to Your Guns!

The candidates may not like it, but you still want them to talk about how they'll control the growth in property taxes. How do you find out what, if anything, they propose to do if they're elected? How do you make candidates talk about the issues you want to hear about? How do you make them take the very risks that they're trying so hard to avoid?

The answer is *persistence.*

Speaking up at local forums

SPEAKING UP

Candidates for local office often appear in forums sponsored by the League of Women Voters or neighborhood associations. These forums include a session for questions from the audience. Ask your questions, but do so artfully. Anticipate the diversion. Put it in your question, like this:

"Carly Candidate, you have said that you will refuse the car, the credit card, and the higher salary that come with the office you seek. I commend you for your stand, but we all know that those steps to hold down the cost of government, while good, don't affect the growth in property taxes we are facing. What else would you propose to do to bring property taxes under control?"

That question doesn't permit the candidate to use their stock, risk-free answer. It moves the discussion beyond the perks and into the tough choices that have to be made to bring property taxes under control.

If the candidate disagrees and tells you that refusing these perks will reduce property taxes, tell them publicly that that's hogwash! The entire amount involved in their proposal won't total a few thousand dollars annually. What will they do about the rest of the hundreds of millions of property taxes collected in your community each year?

Tell them that their unwillingness to give your question the attention it deserves must mean that they don't treat seriously the issue of rising property taxes or that they have no solution to offer. Tell them how difficult it is to treat seriously a candidate who hasn't thought enough about such an important issue to discuss it intelligently. After all, if this candidate wants your support, you have a right to know their positions before you give it.

REMEMBER

Although you should make candidates take stands on the issues you want to hear about, they may not have all the answers to your questions on the spot. Allow for the possibility that a candidate may not be trying to bob and weave. Ask them whether they or their associates can get back to you later with an answer. Then see whether the opposition has anything to say on the issue.

Getting help from the media

If you can't attend forums with questions and answers or if they aren't held where you live, ask the moderators of the forum to get the answers for you. You can also ask reporters who cover the candidate to ask your questions. Call the reporters who cover the races you're interested in, and voice your concerns. Ask the reporters to help you find out where the candidates stand on a particular issue. Tell them what the candidate's stock, risk-free answer is and ask them to power beyond it so that you can cast an informed vote. Go online to the candidate's website and ask your questions to see what answers you get.

SPEAKING UP

Don't wait until your local newspaper or television station calls you — call them and tell them what you want to know. Ask them to find out the answers to your questions so that you can make an informed and intelligent choice on election day.

TIP

You can also voice your concern by writing letters to the editor of your newspaper. If you provide a reasoned, thoughtful letter, you may provoke a response from the candidate. You may also interest the editors or news reporters for the newspaper to follow up on the points you've made. You can make comments on the candidate's website, even if only to highlight a lack of response to your questions.

Several television stations also encourage letters to the editor and read them in whole or in part on the air. Many of these stations also have email addresses, so you can use your computer to make contact. (See Chapter 5 for more information on using email to be heard.)

Completing candidate questionnaires

Another way to get the information you want is by reading *candidate questionnaires.* Many newspapers and special interest groups routinely send questionnaires to candidates for many offices. The questionnaires solicit background information from candidates as well as the candidate's views on important issues. Ask the newspaper, or any special interest group to which you belong, to include your question in its questionnaire. (See Chapter 8 for more on special interest groups.)

Newspapers publish the results of these questionnaires shortly before election day and, if you belong to a special interest group that has also been sending out questionnaires, you will have access to any results received. Read the results and determine how the candidates stand on the matters you care about. If the candidates don't answer the questions, consider that fact in deciding whom you can trust with your vote.

Many organizations also send candidates questionnaires that probe issues of importance to the organization. The results are sent to the organization's members. Neighborhood organizations, senior citizens' groups, the League of Women Voters, labor organizations, and chambers of commerce all use candidate questionnaires to obtain the type of information you're interested in having. Even if you aren't a member of the group, you can ask an organization or its members to give you copies of the candidates' answers so that you can read them for yourself. Also, many organizations post the results of their questionnaires on their home pages or websites.

REMEMBER

It never hurts to ask an organization for the information collected from questionnaires. All they can say is no.

You may already belong to a group that uses candidate questionnaires. If you do, you can volunteer to serve on the committee drafting the questionnaires, to make sure that your questions are included. If you don't belong already and don't want to join any of these organizations, you can still approach any of these groups about including your questions in their questionnaires.

TIP

The questionnaires are usually compiled by the political action committees (PACs). If you belong to such an organization and want to participate, ask the head of your organization who is in charge of questionnaires how you can participate.

When all else fails, don't forget the direct approach

Don't overlook the obvious. You can always use the direct approach to gathering information: Call the candidate and ask your question — what they propose to do about property taxes, for example. If you can't get the candidate on the telephone, write a letter asking for the candidate's views on steps that can be taken to control the growth of property taxes or whatever other issue you're interested in knowing about. (See Chapter 5 for more on how to contact elected officials.)

TIP

When you receive a letter back from a campaign spelling out the candidate's views, you have a right to rely on that information. Keep a copy of the letter. You may have to remind the candidate or the media of their position at a later date.

Remember that the shortest distance between two points is always a straight line. You may just get a response and the information you're seeking. Stranger things have happened in politics!

REMEMBER

Don't be shy. If you want to know something, ask and ask often. If you're polite and persistent, you will gather enough information to make reasonably informed decisions on which candidate you would rather see win. It's the squeaky wheel that gets the grease. Fortune, like informed politics, favors the brave, the curious, and the tenacious!

Chapter **17**

Campaigning for Your Vote

Republicans make up roughly one-third of the voting electorate. So do Democrats. Independents and undecided voters make up the final third that hangs in the balance and decides elections. The percentages may vary by state and by district, but thinking of the electorate in terms of thirds is a useful approach. Except in districts or states that are overwhelmingly one party or another, a candidate must appeal to a majority of the independent and undecided voters to win. This category of voters, by definition, is waiting to be convinced, by one campaign or the other, which candidate to vote for.

If a campaign isn't convincing the voters with one approach and message, it needs to try another one — quickly. As soon as a campaign really starts getting its message out, the time to an election is counted in days or, at most, weeks. A timetable like that doesn't permit much reflection or any indecision. When the election is just days away and it takes days for a message to get through, a campaign must act quickly if it's going to persuade you to vote for its candidate in time.

Launching a Direct Mail Campaign

Sometimes, sending good old-fashioned letters, called *direct mail,* can be a campaign's best approach. Campaigns use the information they've gathered by way of polls to target groups of receptive individuals and then send them literature about issues likely to persuade them to vote for a particular candidate.

You can tell a great deal about a candidate from the direct mail they send out, including which

>> Subgroups they want to target

>> Issues they want to discuss

>> Hot buttons they want to press

TIP

When you receive the direct mail, look at these items critically. See whether you think that the approach the candidate is using is fair to their position and that of their opponent. See whether this candidate is the type of person you're comfortable having in elected office. These considerations can help you decide how to vote.

Freedom from scrutiny

Direct mail is good for making more negative attacks on opponents than a campaign may be comfortable making on television. Some TV stations and newspapers have started analyzing the accuracy of the campaign advertising they carry. If a candidate has to justify every word they use in an attack, the candidate is more careful. Little if any monitoring of direct mail is done until after the fact. Candidates can hit their opponents harder and lower with direct mail attacks than they can on television or radio. Plus, the campaign can target the negative attacks to an audience who's likely to be receptive to the attacks.

Advantage of the delayed reaction

Candidates also use direct mail because it takes the opposition longer to respond. When a candidate makes an attack on TV, the opponent has instant access to the commercial. The opponent knows just what is being said and how often the commercial is on television. The opponent even knows the minimum duration that the advertisement will run — that is, if the candidate bought time for a week or more. By law, TV stations must allow access to records of political advertisement time purchased. Those records show anyone, including the campaign being attacked, how much money the campaign making the purchase spent, station by station, in a media market. In other words, when a campaign uses television, the opponent knows the current scope of the war and can decide how to respond.

A candidate using television to respond can produce and air a response advertisement in 24 to 48 hours, if the campaign has already purchased the broadcast time. If the candidate anticipated the attack, the response advertisement may already be produced. If it is, the response can be on the air as soon as the campaign gets the commercial and the payment to the TV stations or social media platform.

The televised rebuttal can be on the same day or the next morning, at the latest.

REMEMBER

A candidate *must* respond to an attack ad as soon as possible. When an ad goes unanswered, it's more likely to strike a chord with voters.

Direct mail, on the other hand, can torpedo a campaign. The candidate being attacked by direct mail may hear from someone who heard from someone else that direct mail is being sent to voters. They can't just turn on the television and hear what's being said. The candidate being attacked must take some time to get a copy of the material from someone who received it.

The victim of the attack doesn't know who else received the mail, so formulating a response can be tricky. A candidate doesn't want to publicize negative information about themselves to voters who may not have received the attack letter; they want to respond only to those voters who did. No candidate wants to spend time and resources repeating and responding to an attack unless it's necessary.

In addition, direct mail takes many days or weeks to arrive. The material must be drafted, printed, and mailed at bulk rate to thousands of voters. Responding by direct mail is much more time-consuming than responding by television. But direct mail does permit the candidate to restrict the scope of those receiving the response to only those voters who received the original attack, assuming that they can determine who they are.

Target the right voters

Campaigns give a great deal of thought to which groups of voters should receive a campaign's direct mail. The object is to mail to those voters who can be persuaded with a message that is so compelling that they'll vote for a candidate. Sometimes a campaign has a unique issue that appeals to only one group of voters.

Most direct mail campaigns are more general, though. In direct mail efforts that don't target subgroups, the handler decides which large groups of voters should receive the direct mail. Members of this group then receive three or four positive pieces on the campaign's candidate and one or two comparative or negative pieces that focus on the opponent.

AN ISSUE WITH LIMITED APPEAL

An example of an issue with limited but potent appeal is a proposal to increase the property tax exemptions of senior citizens. A candidate may propose to increase the exemption after they're elected to the state legislature, or one of the candidates may have voted against such a proposal in the state legislature. Either way, this issue has tremendous appeal to senior citizens.

The candidate proposing this exemption increase uses direct mail to communicate to property-taxpayers over 65 years of age in her district. The candidate feels that this issue alone will provide those voters with a reason for choosing the candidate over the opponent.

Or, if the case is that the candidate's opponent voted against this proposal, the candidate communicates the opponent's negative vote to senior property owners in the district as a reason for those senior property owners to vote against the opponent.

Obviously, if a candidate is proposing to lower the property tax burden for seniors, the property taxes of other citizens may need to increase to make up the difference. The candidate won't advertise that impact to the groups whose taxes may increase. The candidate's message to those groups may be about a topic other than property taxes.

Why is your mailbox full of political mail?

Why you? Why does your mail include one of these direct mail pieces every other day for a week or so? You've checked with your neighbors on both sides and they haven't received any. You, on the other hand, have received three or five or seven of these multicolored, self-folding, slick brochures. What list are you on to be so lucky?

The answer is simple: You're getting direct mail because a campaign has decided that it wants your vote and can get it — you're seen as a voter who can be persuaded. Here's the inside scoop on how it works:

>> First, you're registered to vote.

>> Second, your household probably consists of more than one voter. When a wife and her husband both fall into the persuadable category, the campaign can reach two voters with one copy of all the direct mail pieces. The campaign can kill two birds with one stone!

Any smart, computerized list generated to produce the mail will be sorted by household, not by voter. That permits the campaign to reach more voters without duplication. A campaign can get more bang for the precious campaign buck by mailing to the Jones Household on Pine Street rather than separate pieces to Mary Jones and Paul Jones. Check the label on your mailing and see for yourself.

Independence makes you popular

If you're receiving direct mail from one candidate for an office, chances are you'll receive it from the other candidate for that office, too. You have probably been identified by one campaign or both campaigns as an independent. If a campaign has money to contact the independents or persuadable voters, in addition to whatever is done on television or radio, it will do so.

You may be classified as an independent because you received a phone call during the campaign asking for whom you're likely to vote. If you indicated that you haven't decided, you were put in the category of persuadable voters and targeted to receive direct mail.

If the campaigns don't have the volunteers or money to call all voters and ask how they plan to vote, the campaign assumes that all nonprimary voters and those who switch their primary voting from one party to another are independents or persuadables. If the number of households in this category is too large and too costly to mail to, the campaign may cut down the number by making assumptions based on where you live.

For example, you don't vote in primaries and are an independent, but you live in a precinct that's 90 percent or better Republican. The campaign may eliminate you from the mailing by assuming that you're a Republican, even though you haven't declared yourself to be one by answering phone polls in that manner or voting Republican in primaries.

If the number is still too high, the handler may eliminate voters in precincts that are 80 percent Republican, and so on, until the number of households is manageable. Campaigns do the same in heavily Democratic precincts.

The method isn't foolproof, but it's rational. The campaign doesn't have enough money to do all the mailings it wants, so the number of households must be reduced. This method makes more sense than simply mailing the list in alphabetical order until the campaign runs out of money, or throwing darts at a map of the district and mailing wherever the darts hit.

Those voters who identify with the Republican or Democratic parties are important, too. But the campaigns assume that the vast majority — 80 to 90 percent — of the voters who identify themselves by party will support the candidates whom their parties have nominated. The campaigns spend some resources reminding these voters to vote on election day. But, unless they have a particular reason to do so, the campaigns don't send direct mail to persuade voters which candidate to support, because these voters will probably vote for their party's candidate anyway.

Still stumped?

The campaign may further reduce the number of households it mails to based on the likelihood of voting. For example, a household that votes every election has higher priority than one that votes sporadically. Persuading someone who will vote anyway to vote for a particular candidate is easier than motivating someone to vote in the first place. If money is tight in a campaign, and it almost always is, the campaign eliminates mailings to independent voters who aren't sure bets to vote on election day.

So why didn't your neighbors on either side of you get the same direct mail that you did? Well, maybe they voted in primaries, or maybe they don't vote regularly and, therefore, aren't a good target for the campaign, economically. Here's something that's even more shocking to consider: Your neighbors may not even be registered to vote! Shame on them! When you finish reading this book, you may want to lend it to them. (Better yet, tell them to buy their own copies.)

TIP

Carefully read the material that the campaigns send you. It may provide some insight into the types of elected officials that these candidates would be. The information can help you decide which candidate to support with your vote. After all, the campaigns spent a great deal of time and money getting this information into your hands. They must think that the information they're mailing you is persuasive. See if you think so, too.

And Now a Word from Our Sponsors . . .

Around the same time that your mailbox is stuffed with propaganda from both sides in a campaign, you're bombarded over the airwaves with the candidates' messages. In the weeks leading up to an election, candidate advertisements seem to fill up all the ad time on television. You see so much of it that you long to see the ads for your favorite beer or car, just for variety. You may hear the same commercials when you listen to morning radio on your drive to work. Why is the message coming at you from so many directions at once? What have you done to deserve the full-court press you're experiencing?

The answer is that you're paying attention. The total onslaught of news coverage, mail, and advertising has made you aware that an election is coming up. Most voters begin paying attention to an election only a few days or weeks before it's held. The campaigns try to make the most of your interest by timing their messages to arrive in your mailbox or on your television or radio or when you go online during the time you start thinking about the choice you have to make.

If congressional races are on the ballot, or a presidential race, you may also be bombarded by ads from lofty-sounding PACs trying to convince you to vote for or against a candidate. In the *Citizens United v. FEC* case, the US Supreme Court ruled that limits on spending by PACs was unconstitutional, so hundreds of millions of dollars are spent by these groups trying to influence the outcomes of elections. (See Chapter 8 for more on PACs.)

The timing of political advertising is also geared to cost. The Federal Communications Commission (FCC) requires TV stations to give political advertising the most favorable commercial rate for 60 days before a general election and 30 days before a primary election. Those rates represent a significant savings for campaigns. The lower rates enable a campaign to show you its ads a few extra times.

When and how candidates advertise on TV

After a campaign makes the decision to advertise on TV with a message (see Chapter 9 for more on the message), the campaign still needs to determine when and how to advertise. It hires the most effective media consultants to produce and film the commercials to win your support. (See Chapter 18 for more on television and campaigning.)

The candidate wants to reach the right people often enough to get their message through. The media consultant is responsible for determining which TV and cable shows the candidate's commercials must appear on to get that job done.

The media consultant is responsible for buying the TV and cable time. Polling for the campaigns has already told the media consultant whom the candidate needs to reach to be successful. The fundraiser has told the media consultant how much money has been allotted to get the candidate's message out on television or cable. The media consultant now has to decide how to spend the money available as wisely as possible to reach the maximum number of voters.

The media consultant decides which shows to buy advertisements on by who watches the shows. The consultant begins by finding out how many viewers a show has, but that's only part of the process. From a political campaign's perspective, the show with the highest ratings isn't always the smartest buy. For example, a show that appeals to those viewers under the age of 35 usually isn't a good buy for a campaign. The percentage of adults under the age of 35 who actually vote is very low.

On the other hand, the percentage of voters over the age of 50 who actually vote is high. A media consultant may decide that a show whose appeal is to a smaller number of older voters is a better buy. Most of those older voters already plan to vote. Because it's easier to persuade someone who's already going to the polls anyway to vote for your candidate than it is to motivate someone to turn out just so they can support that candidate, the older audience is a good one to target.

Older voters tend to watch the news, so you see many political commercials on news shows and shows that air adjacent to news shows. Campaigns with more limited budgets avoid prime-time shows because they're more expensive and they reach too many younger people who aren't likely to be voters.

REMEMBER

Political campaigns pay for advertising based on the number of *people* reached, not the number of *voters* reached. The media consultant is looking for voters, though, not viewers. The consultant isn't selling a product that will be purchased equally by all viewers, but one that will interest only a select group — in this case, older voters. That's why you see more political ads appearing with products that older voters would purchase, such as pain relievers and nutritional supplements, and fewer political ads on shows where trendy clothing brands and technology equipment advertise. Older, or more mature, voters are more likely to vote; younger ones are less likely to do so. The media consultant targets the more mature audience every time, hoping to reach the most citizens who take seriously their responsibility to vote.

Are you a target?

If political ads are appearing on your favorite shows, it probably demonstrates that you fit the profile. It's another piece of evidence that you're being targeted. You're not paranoid! They really are after you.

You are registered and are likely to vote, and you watch television shows that your peers also watch. Your tastes are typical. Because the campaign is trying to convince you and others like you to choose a particular candidate when you go to the polls, the campaign is spending its money wisely. Whether it's the news for you older voters or a popular music-streaming site for you younger ones, if you're seeing ads from candidates, they're targeting you.

REMEMBER

Finding advertising on the programs you like is just another example of how important you are to the electoral process. (Senior citizens need to realize that they're being targeted when they see political ads on the news and during their favorite programs. Also, when students see political ads in their social media feeds or on their streaming music sites, they should realize that the candidate placing the ad is specifically courting younger voters.) Campaigns are spending huge amounts of campaign resources trying to get your attention. The advertisements are designed to appeal to you and persuade you to vote for a particular candidate. Rather than view the ads as an annoyance, you should see them as examples of how much political clout you have if you're a registered voter.

Attack of the Killer Phone Calls!

Here's another tactic you should look for in the final days of a hard-fought campaign: If you're a persuadable voter, you may receive a "persuasion" call. This type of phone call delivers a message about the opponent that usually is very negative. It can be so nasty that the source of the message doesn't want any public scrutiny by the media.

These telephone attacks, also called *killer phone calls*, occur so late in the campaign — often, the weekend before the election — that the candidate being attacked can't possibly respond in time and set the record straight. The attack may be grossly unfair and easy to respond to, but the election will occur before the candidate can get the word out. By then, the damage has already been done.

WARNING

Sometimes, the caller in a killer phone call says that they represent an organization whose name you've never heard. That organization may not even exist. The group paying for the call doesn't want to risk the backlash that may come from sponsoring pointed, and perhaps vicious, attacks on the opposition. However, be careful about assuming that attacks on a candidate come from the campaign of the opponent. Sometimes, interest groups strongly opposed to a particular candidate will fund irresponsible attacks without asking the approval of the candidate they're trying to assist. (Technically speaking, they're not even allowed to coordinate their efforts with the candidate.)

WARNING

When campaigns fund these killer phone calls, they also may attach responsibility to an unknown group. They seek to not only avoid blame for the negativity but also increase the attack's credibility. The theory is that you expect attacks from the opposition and, therefore, discount those attacks. When third parties make charges about a candidate, they're more likely to be believed by the unsophisticated voter than an attack made by the candidate's opponent.

Be on the alert for any calls you receive immediately before an election if these calls do anything other than urge you to vote and vote for a particular candidate. Ask yourself, if this information is so good and so persuasive about the opponent, why is it being brought out only hours or days before the election? If the information is *that* solid, wouldn't the opponent have made it public early enough to ensure that every voter heard it? You'd better believe it. One explanation for the delay is that the information is not true or accurate. Another reason may be that the information *is* true and accurate but the candidate presenting it is trying to avoid a backlash from voters and the media for bringing it up in the campaign. Don't be persuaded to vote against a candidate by one of these last-minute, underhanded killer phone calls.

Chapter **18**

Negative Campaigning: The Dark Side of Politics

You hear it all the time (and probably say it yourself) as election day nears: "I'm sick and tired of negative campaigns. I don't want to turn on my television and see any more mudslinging ads. Why can't these candidates run positive campaigns?"

Understanding why campaigns resort to negative advertisements and being able to recognize when a negative one goes over the line are important steps to take if you want to discourage negative campaigning.

The More Things Change . . .

People tend to think of negative campaign tactics as a recent development. They believe that campaigns today are more vicious than they used to be. But you should realize that attacking an opponent in a political campaign in the United States is nothing new. Some of the most vicious, most highly personal attacks occurred in political campaigns of the 19th century.

Slinging mud in the 1800s

The election of 1800, between President John Adams and Thomas Jefferson, was a bitterly fought contest. Adams's supporters directly undermined democracy because they passed "sedition" laws that would let them lock up people who criticized their candidates. But Jefferson's supporters were not above predicting the ruin of the country if Adams remained president. Figure 18-1 shows a sample Jeffersonian poster used in the election of 1800.

Republicans

Turn out, turn out and save your country from ruin!

From an Emperor — from a King — from the iron grasp of a British Tory Faction —

an unprincipled banditti of British speculators. The hireling tools and emissaries of his majesty king George the III

have thronged our city and diffused the poison of principles among us.

DOWN WITH THE TORIES, DOWN WITH THE BRITISH FACTION,

Before they have it in their power to enslave you, and reduce your families to destress by heavy taxation.

Republicans want no Tribute-liars — they want no ship Ocean liars — they want no Rufus Kings for Lords — they want no Varick to lord it over them — they want no Jones for senator, who fought with the British against the Americans in time of the war —

But they want in their places such men as Jefferson & Clinton

(*The American Heritage History of the Presidency*, 1968, p. 139)

The election of 1828, between John Quincy Adams and Andrew Jackson, proved to be one of the most negative campaigns in US history. The Adams forces distributed handbills accusing Jackson of murdering six militiamen under his command. They also accused him of bigamy and adultery for having (unknowingly) married his wife, Rachel, before she was legally divorced from her first husband.

Andrew Jackson met Rachel in 1788 in Tennessee at Rachel's mother's home while she was married but separated from her husband, Lewis Robards. The Robards reconciled and returned to Kentucky. Sometime later, Rachel's mother told Jackson that Rachel wanted to leave her husband again. Jackson rode to Kentucky and escorted Rachel back to Tennessee. Robards petitioned the Virginia legislature for divorce, alleging misconduct by Jackson and Rachel on the trip. The legislature told Robards to take his case to court, but Robards circulated the rumor that a divorce was given. In reliance on that rumor, Jackson and Rachel were married in August 1791. However, the divorce was not actually final until two years later. In December 1793, Jackson learned that rather than being divorced in 1791 as Rachel had thought, the divorce was final in September 1793. In other words, Jackson and Rachel had been living together for more than two years without a valid marriage. They remarried in January 1794, but that didn't end the matter as far as his political opponents were concerned. Jackson's personal life was very much an issue in the 1828 election. One supporter of Henry Clay (another presidential candidate in that election) was Charles Hammond, editor of the Cincinnati *Gazette*. Mr. Hammond said in a pamphlet: "Ought a convicted adulteress and her paramour husband to be placed in the highest offices of this free and Christian land?"

The saddest part of this unpleasant campaign is the toll it took on Rachel Jackson's health. She died between the election and Andrew Jackson's inauguration and never had the opportunity to live in the White House with her grief-stricken husband. And people think that modern-day campaigns are negative!

For his part, Jackson gave as good as he got. He accused Adams of stealing the election of 1824, when Jackson received more votes than any candidate but lost to Adams in the decision by the House of Representatives.

In the 1884 election, Grover Cleveland's personal life became an issue. Cleveland was accused of fathering an illegitimate child. His Republican opponents thought that this accusation would kill the presidential campaign of the Democratic reformer. The negative campaign failed to work; Cleveland admitted the child might be his, and the sympathetic public elected him president.

The point is that negative campaigning is nothing new. It's been around for more than 200 years, and it's no more unpleasant now than it used to be. So why has it suddenly become an issue with voters and commentators?

JOHNSON VERSUS GOLDWATER: AN EXTREME CASE OF NEGATIVE ADVERTISING

One of the most famous negative ads, the "Daisy ad" was used against Republican presidential nominee Barry Goldwater in 1964.

The ad caused an uproar across the country. In fact, the public outcry about this ad was so huge that the Democratic Party pulled it off the air after only one day. The ad pictured a little girl picking daisies in a field. The screen then showed a nuclear explosion. The ad didn't even mention Barry Goldwater, Lyndon Johnson's opponent, by name, but the implication was that a vote for Barry Goldwater was a vote for nuclear war.

Barry Goldwater, Republican senator from Arizona, was from the more conservative wing of the Republican Party in that day. His anti-Communist rhetoric directed against the Soviet Union resulted in the attack, implying that his election would result in a nuclear war with the Soviets.

Joining the TV generation

The use of television in political campaigns has changed campaigning in many ways. One of the most noticeable changes is that television forces you to view more negative advertisements in political campaigns than you ever wanted to see. You can't miss the negative message of a well-funded campaign. Like it or not, it appears every time you watch your favorite network or cable show.

Campaigns no longer rely only on handbills and word of mouth to bring their attacks to your attention. You see the attacks whenever you turn on your television or use your browser. You hear them whenever you turn on the radio. You see them when you open your mailbox. Because information is communicated efficiently and effectively these days, you may feel as if you're drowning in a sea of negative campaign commercials and mail each time an election is near.

The percentage of money that presidential candidates spend on negative television ads hasn't really increased since television and the Internet have become factors in modern presidential races, but media advertising for other types of candidates — senator, governor, congressperson, mayor, secretary of state, and so on — has become more common. So, although viewers aren't seeing more negative presidential campaign ads, they may be seeing more negative political advertising in general. Therefore, when voters who are polled in presidential campaigns complain about negative political advertising, they may be reacting to all the advertising they're seeing and not just the presidential campaign.

Of course, the fact that the percentage of the negative presidential campaign ads hasn't increased is no consolation to you, the viewer. So many more campaigns are using television advertising that the total volume of negative advertising you're exposed to in a campaign cycle has increased dramatically over the years. Voters can change that volume by demanding that candidates refrain from negative advertising and holding the candidates to that pledge. When voters make candidates who run negative campaigns pay by voting against those candidates, the negative campaign ads will stop.

REMEMBER

You're tempted to throw up your hands and ask, "Why is politics consumed with mudslinging? Why can't campaigns give me positive reasons to vote for a candidate?" But before you wash your hands of politics and wonder whether the country is on the slippery slope to ruin, you should remember that the Founders engaged in a rough-and-tumble brand of politics. In many ways, the campaign tactics employed in earlier presidential campaigns make today's methods seem like a tea party!

Two Important Principles of Campaign Communications

In the midst of a heated political campaign, you can easily get bogged down in all the campaign ads, whether they're positive or negative. Keep in mind, though, that these campaigns have a method to all their madness. To recognize a political commercial for what it is, you need to remember the two important principles of campaign communications, which I discuss next.

Candidates try to make you like them

The first principle of campaign communications deals with what most people think of as a positive campaign. When a candidate tells you that they care about the same issues and ideals as you, they first tell you information about themselves that you'll like: their background, family, education, and qualifications, for example. The candidate also communicates on the two or three issues that polling and focus groups have identified as the most important issues in the campaign. (See Chapters 3 and 14 for more on polls and focus groups.)

All the communications under the first principle — whether television, radio, Internet, phone-based, or direct mail — are designed to make the candidate likable to you. Political consultants believe that you'll vote for the candidate with whom you feel most comfortable. If the communication under the first principle can reassure you that one candidate is qualified by education, experience, and ideas to hold the office and you identify with the candidate, you'll be more likely to vote for that candidate on election day.

That theory sounds reasonable. When a campaign is communicating in a vacuum, you're persuaded by a campaign following the first principle of campaign communications — as long as the opposition remains silent. A problem arises, though, when the opposition does the same thing. What happens when the opponent also follows the first principle of campaign communications? What happens when the opponent also appears likable to you and the other voters?

If both candidates have nearly equal campaign money to get their messages out, you're presented with two "likable" candidates. If both campaigns have done their jobs, the candidates and the issues they discuss in their advertisements are designed to appeal to you for your vote and are doing so effectively. You have two seemingly well-qualified, likable candidates on the ballot. How do you decide which one to choose? The answer to that question explains why campaigns turn negative. If all aspects are equal, voters tend to support the person already in office or support the candidate from their own party. Challengers to incumbents know that they can't win without shaking things up. Candidates from the minority party know *they* can't win unless they give voters a good reason to make an exception to their usual party preferences. That's where the second principle of campaign communications comes in.

Candidates try to make you dislike the opponent

After the candidate gives you reasons to vote for them in a competitive campaign, they give you reasons *not* to vote for the opponent. This area of campaign communications is the part that gives rise to charges of negative campaigning. (See the discussion, a little later in this chapter, of what makes an ad negative. For now, just look at *why* campaigns try to make voters dislike the opponent.)

If a campaign can give you a reason for choosing one candidate over the other — a reason that you'll find persuasive — it does so. After all, campaigns are in the business of winning elections. They're all about convincing you to vote for a certain candidate. If contrasting the two candidates gives you a convincing reason to choose one candidate over the other, campaigns do it in a heartbeat!

Just think about it for a minute. Campaigns would much rather provide you with a clear choice between two candidates. To do that, they look at all kinds of ways to contrast the two candidates. Most of the items campaigns explore to develop the contrast are fair game. The general rule about what is fair game is reasonably simple. For example, if a candidate is an incumbent with a record, anything in that record can be brought to the attention of the voters. Any part of that record can be compared and contrasted with the opponent to make clear the choice between the candidates. (For more specifics on what's fair game and what's not, see the later section "Separating the Good from the Bad.")

Candidates on the receiving end of this comparison and contrast may scream foul. They may protest to the media that the opposing campaign is engaging in dirty politics and label the opponent a negative campaigner. But with fair-game ads, that label is what's truly unfair.

What kind of system would the United States have if every candidate were free to create a picture of what they stand for and if that picture were never subjected to challenge by the opponent? All candidates should be forced to explain and justify their records. If the record of a candidate is different from the positions the candidate is taking in the campaign, shouldn't you know that before you vote?

Don't you have a right to know what a candidate has done, and not just what a candidate says they want to do? Comparing the record of a candidate with their positions in the campaign can help you understand what they're likely to do if elected again. So, any advertisement that makes this comparison for you can really help you decide which candidate you want to support.

REMEMBER

Campaigns use negative ads because they know something about opponents that they think you'd also like to know — information you'd want to consider if it were available to you. If they haven't been able to come up with anything bad about the opposition that would interest you, their negative advertising won't work. Negative ads succeed only when they help define the choice you face on election day. The process of comparing and contrasting the candidates is designed to make you feel better about the candidate you ultimately choose by making the opponent less acceptable. The campaigns hope that you'll no longer like both candidates the same; you'll like one candidate more.

Separating the Good from the Bad

The $64,000 question of modern campaigning may be, "What makes a campaign negative?" Campaigns are always quick to tell everyone that the opposition is running a negative campaign. Sometimes, people apply that label to the campaign that goes on the attack first. Sometimes, one particular ad or issue is so offensive that it overshadows the entire campaign and labels it a negative one. Sometimes, the amount of time and money spent communicating a negative or a contrast instead of a positive message makes you label a campaign negative.

Some of the more outrageous examples of negative campaigning are easy to recognize and condemn. Some others may be labeled negative by the person being attacked, but they aren't criticized as negative by analysts who are obviously more objective. How do you know which is which? Following some general principles can help you decide which commercials step over the line and which candidate to blame for mudslinging.

Above-the-belt ads

Many voters define as a negative ad any advertisement that mentions an opponent in a critical way. These voters think that candidates should talk only about themselves, not about the opponent. Even if you accept this definition of a negative ad, you should still be aware of the degrees of negative campaigning. Not every negative ad is, or should be, viewed by the public or the media in the same light.

In other words, not all negative ads are equally bad. How bad they're perceived to be depends on the nature of the material being used in the ad and the way that material is presented.

TIP

The general rule is that anything contained in a public record is fair game. Ads containing information that is readily available to any citizen who wants to look for it may be negative, but they're not below the belt.

Public records are just that — records available to any member of the public. These records require no influence or underhanded methods to obtain them. Examples include voting records, budgets, speeches, newspaper articles, comments from third parties who know the candidate, campaign finance reports, arrest records, lawsuits, property tax records, and financial disclosure statements required by law.

If a candidate has voted for or against tax increases, that's above-the-belt, fair-game material for ads. If a candidate has increased or reduced their office staff or office budget, that's fair game. If a candidate has taken positions on important issues like education funding, choice in reproductive rights, gun control, campaign finance reform, and so on, all these issues can be a productive source of contrast between two candidates. Candidates can air an ad mentioning an opponent's record based on any part of the public record and be assured that, even if the ad *is* considered negative, it won't be considered a below-the-belt attack — unless it distorts the record. (See the next section.)

NEGATIVE ADS CAN ACTUALLY HELP YOU CAST AN INFORMED VOTE

Sometimes, negative campaigning is necessary to give you critical information that you need in order to make an informed decision on which candidate to support. Suppose that a candidate for state treasurer discovers that his opponent was sued by clients in their private business for mishandling their money. Also suppose that those clients won the case because a jury found that the opponent was an incompetent money manager.

For the candidate to bring that information to your attention, they must air a negative advertisement. The ad could be considered negative because it mentions the opponent. It's also above the belt, though, because the jury verdict is a matter of public record. That ad would tell you that the jury had decided that the opponent was an incompetent money manager.

Are you opposed to the candidate running a negative advertisement such as this one? Wouldn't you like to know that one of the candidates was found by a jury to be incompetent as a money manager before you vote for a state treasurer to manage your tax dollars?

Below-the-belt ads

There are negative ads, and then there are *negative ads.* This type of ad can cross the line and become a below-the-belt blow in a number of ways. Here are some of the most common methods:

>> Using information obtained by underhanded methods

>> Distorting a candidate's record or background

>> Attacking an opponent anonymously

>> Using bogus groups to do the dirty work of attacking in a campaign

>> Altering a candidate's photo or using an old one

>> Exploiting *wedge issues* — emotional appeals designed to make you dislike a candidate

REMEMBER

If you determine for yourself that a candidate has engaged in below-the-belt negative campaigning, you should ask yourself whether you would be comfortable voting for that candidate. Do you really want an officeholder who either doesn't understand the difference between above-the-belt and below-the-belt punches or doesn't care?

Sneaking around

Any information that can't be obtained except by underhanded means is below the belt and not fair game. Any information obtained by private detectives, wiretaps, or any other secret means is subject to a charge of below-the-belt negative tactics.

Normally, confidential communications with any government agency should not be the subject of campaign advertisements or attacks. Any dealings that a candidate has with the Internal Revenue Service (IRS) or another government agency are not public information, unless they resulted in a lawsuit being filed. An opposing candidate should not use these dealings in a campaign unless they're willing to engage in a below-the-belt negative campaign.

Distorting the facts

Any charge that distorts the opponent's record or plays fast-and-loose with the facts is properly labeled negative and below the belt.

Consider the following scenario: Say that US Representative John Garcia is justly proud of his record on children's issues. Over a 10-year period, Garcia authored or sponsored a dozen pieces of important legislation to provide quality childcare, immunizations, and funding for at-risk children (children from homes where the household income is below the federal poverty level who are more likely to fail in school and life without outside intervention). His support for legislation improving the lives of children is a source of pride to him. In fact, Garcia voted against only one social welfare program during the course of his last term in office.

Garcia's opponent, Julio Fernandez, runs an ad telling voters about the one program intended to help children that Garcia opposed. The ad implies that Garcia is opposed to helping poor children. The ad is not, strictly speaking, false. Garcia did vote against one social welfare program for children. But it's designed to create a false impression — that Garcia regularly blocks pro-child legislation. This stretch of the truth would seem like an unfair distortion to anyone familiar with Garcia's overall record. For trying to take advantage of people's ignorance of the big picture, Fernandez has crossed the line. The fact is that the officeholder cast the vote in dispute, but the vote was on an irresponsible piece of legislation that would have busted the budget. The opposition introduced the measure to force the officeholder and others to vote against it so that they could use the issue in an upcoming election. The opposition had no hope of passing the legislation and no desire to have it pass. That vote did not reflect Garcia's support for at-risk children.

Lying blatantly

It goes without saying that lying about an opponent's record is a negative campaign tactic. However, because catching a candidate who does something as blatant as lying is so easy, this kind of campaigning seldom happens. A candidate's negative tactics must be subtler than that if they hope to succeed and win elections. When they *are* subtler, like the vote manipulation example mentioned in the previous section, they have a kernel of truth in them. That kernel of truth makes the charge much easier to launch and much more difficult to defend against.

Any candidate who wants to attack an opponent had better have documentation to support the attack. If a candidate can't document the attacks, the attacks are considered below-the-belt negative tactics, even if based on the public record.

Engaging in personal attacks

In a campaign, the public also considers certain areas of discussion to be below the belt, and it generally reacts unfavorably to them, even if they're based on public information. For instance, any discussion of a candidate's personal life is generally viewed by the public with extreme disfavor. You don't want to hear that a candidate was indiscreet in their personal life — that they smoked pot while in college, for example. You don't care how many times they inhaled or whether they inhaled at all. Anything that comes under the heading of a personal attack on the candidate or the candidate's family may backfire on the candidate making the accusation. This action is also likely to label the candidate making the attack a negative campaigner who hits below the belt.

Distributing anonymous literature

Attacking an opponent anonymously and using bogus groups to do the attacking are methods that occur late in campaigns. Unethical campaigns that don't want to be blamed for their actions permit or even encourage supporters to distribute leaflets attacking an opponent anonymously. These leaflets accuse the opponent of all sorts of scandals or wrongdoings, most or all of which may be baseless. These anonymous attacks occur so late in a campaign — usually within days of the election — that the person who's attacked has no time to get to the bottom of this tactic. By the time the victim discovers the attack and tries to rebut it, the election is over.

WARNING

Some campaigns produce the leaflets themselves, but most encourage others to do it, because doing it themselves and failing to put the disclaimer language on the flyer is a violation of election law. All written material is supposed to have a disclaimer that tells you who authorized and paid for the information you're reading. If you receive information without that disclaimer, throw it away. Better yet, bring the leaflet to the attention of the media or the candidate being attacked.

Making killer calls

A similar negative tactic involves the use of fictitious groups that make telephone attacks on the opponent. These groups have good-sounding names, like Citizens for the Environment or Neighbors against Crime, but they probably don't have an independent existence outside the campaign. The campaign or party uses these names in the telemarketing attacks on an opponent in the final days of the campaign, when they don't want people to know that they're actually the ones financing the attacks. (See "Attack of the Killer Phone Calls!" in Chapter 17 for more about these kinds of phone calls.)

The callers tell you that they represent these fictitious groups so that you'll give the attacks more credibility, or so that they can't be blamed for spreading the poison. They say they're calling because they're concerned about the opponent's record or positions on issues of concern to the group. The issues may be important to you, too.

WARNING

If you receive one of these calls, ask yourself why the group waited until 72 hours before the election to communicate this important information to you. The answer is that the group most likely doesn't exist. When a phony group attacks publicly in advance of an election, its credentials are questioned. The group may be exposed as a front. That's why the negative advertiser waits until days or hours before the election and uses telephones, emails, text messages, or anonymous flyers to communicate the message.

EVEN USING UNALTERED PHOTOS CAN SOMETIMES BE NEGATIVE

Sometimes, campaigns use a real photograph of the opponent to accomplish the goal of creating a negative impression with the voters. For example, in the 1994 campaign, the opponent of Republican representative JC Watts of Oklahoma used a photo of Watts that was more than ten years old. Most of us would be happy if an older photo were used, but Watts had a large Afro hairstyle in those days. That hairstyle presented a decidedly different appearance from the close-cut hair that Representative Watts sported in 1994.

As we all know, styles change. Hair and clothing styles that were once commonplace look ridiculous when we look at them years later, and may even take on a different cultural meaning. The image that the opponent wanted to put in the voters' minds was of Watts as a radical. By using the old photo, the Democratic candidate was trying to create a distorted and negative image of Watts for the voters to consider. The tactic failed to convince the voters to vote against Watts.

Altering the opponent's photo

Another technique that a negative campaign uses is altering the opponent's photograph for television commercials or direct mail. Sometimes, the alterations are subtle. The candidate may have a five-o'clock shadow added to an official photo. Or, the official photo's smile may be turned into a scowl when the opposition uses it. The object is to alter the photo so that the opponent looks sinister or untrustworthy but can still be recognized by the voters. Negative campaigns have also recently employed called *morphing*, where a candidate's photo is changed on-camera into the photo of another person. The new photo is of a person who's expected to create a negative image in the minds of voters, like you, who see the advertisement. The idea is to get you to associate the negative feelings you may have toward the person in the second photograph with the candidate who's being morphed.

Raising wedge issues

Wedge issues are emotionally charged issues that are used in campaigns to fracture an opponent's base of support. These issues, which produce a strong reaction among segments of the electorate, divide a candidate's traditional base of support into different groups, pitting those groups against each other. The candidate is forced to choose sides in an emotional conflict that will cost them votes — votes that they would normally be able to count on for support.

Wedge issues are most often used to appeal to emotions. A classic wedge issue is race, which has been used to divide the base support of Democratic candidates — particularly, in the South. Since Franklin Roosevelt's second election in 1936, African Americans have voted Democratic in overwhelming numbers. Working-class White voters are also an important part of the Democratic core vote. Appeals to racial prejudice are designed to pit African American Democrats against working-class White Democrats.

THE CASE OF WILLIE HORTON

The 1988 presidential campaign used race as a wedge issue very effectively. An ad ran blaming Governor Michael Dukakis, the Democratic candidate, for the release of Willie Horton from a Massachusetts prison. (Horton, a convicted murderer, had been released on a furlough program; rather than return at the prescribed time, he went on a crime spree that included robbery, assault, car theft, and rape.) The photo of Willie Horton showed that he was African American. The ad implied that Dukakis was soft on crime — even though many states had policies similar to that of Massachusetts, based on the theory that furloughs made sense as a way to ease convicted criminals back into society after their sentences were complete. Dukakis was the governor of Massachusetts at the time, so he was responsible for the policy. The ad distorted the situation by implying that Dukakis *alone* was responsible for Horton's release and subsequent criminal activity. The subtle message was that a President Dukakis would permit African American criminals to be released to rape and murder Whites.

This ad wasn't funded, though, by the campaign of the opponent, George H. W. Bush. When negative attacks, through ads, are made in campaigns, they're usually paid for by another group, like the national committee of a political party or a PAC. When another group pays for the ad, the campaign benefiting from the attack can say that it's not responsible for it. The goal is to prevent backlash from the voters and the media on the candidate whom the ad is attempting to help.

Although Bush's campaign didn't fund the ad, it worked in Bush's favor. White, working-class Democrats voted against Dukakis and for Bush. No one can say for certain whether this ad was the only reason, or even the primary reason, for the defection of a part of the Democratic core vote; however, it was clearly an example of a wedge issue, and defections in the Democratic base vote did occur.

THE CASE OF PAMELA CARTER

The Willie Horton wedge issue worked for George H. W. Bush. But wedge issues can backfire if groups use them too obviously. The 1992 Indiana attorney general's race serves as an example.

Democrats nominated Pamela Carter, a well-qualified, first-time candidate who happened to be African American. Republicans nominated a White male candidate named Timothy Bookwalter. Bookwalter challenged Carter to debate in all 92 Indiana counties, a time-consuming and ineffective campaign tactic. Carter refused to do 92 debates, so Bookwalter had two life-size cardboard images of Carter created, and he took them to as many of the 92 county courthouses as he could. He would then appear to debate the cardboard cutout, in the hope that the photograph of him and the cutout, which revealed Ms. Carter's race, would appear in the local newspaper.

Bookwalter claimed that Carter's refusal made the cutouts necessary. When asked by a reporter why two cutouts were necessary, Bookwalter replied: "In case one fades." The Bookwalter campaign achieved one goal: By election day, most voters realized that Carter was an African American. But the strategy backfired on Bookwalter. Voters saw the move as an overt appeal to racial prejudice and elected Carter.

Selling Negativity

Attacks are more likely to be viewed as negative when they *only* attack and then fail to compare and contrast the two candidates. These attack ads simply tear down the opponent. They're not designed to make you feel slightly better about the candidate who is doing the comparing or the contrasting; they're designed to make you dislike the candidate being attacked. They're so negative, in fact, that the candidate making the attack doesn't want to risk even being in them for comparison or contrast.

Even though these attack ads may deal with matters of public record, voters react more unfavorably to them because the way the information is presented to the voters is unpleasant. The tone of the advertisement is designed to shock and offend you into rejecting the candidate being attacked, making these ads generally unpleasant to watch. Even though they don't violate the simple rule that public matters are fair game, the tone of the ads may be enough by themselves to label a candidate a negative campaigner.

Product comparisons

Voters are much more likely to accept negative information if it's presented in comparison form, because all the commercial advertising they see every day comes in this format. Most people know the multitude of ads that compare different car companies, soft drinks, cereals, long distance telephone services, and so on, telling you to choose one over the other. Heaven knows that voters get enough of this kind of bombardment during the rest of year to be able to appreciate comparative campaign ads during election times.

Attack advertisements *without* comparisons, on the other hand, are used only in the political context. No commercial advertisement tells you not to buy a particular brand or product without offering an alternative. Companies don't pay for advertisements that only attack a competitor's product without promoting their own; they'd consider that to be a waste of time and money. Because these attack ads are used only in politics, you're probably more skeptical of them.

Laughter covers faults

When a candidate uses an attack ad, they sometimes try to soften the delivery of the attack by using humor to deliver a tough message. If voters laugh when they see the ad, they're more likely to feel a favorable attitude toward the ad (although not the victim of it).

Consultants are aware that you and other voters are tired of negative campaigning, so they try to vary the approach. They believe that making you laugh with an attack ad permits the campaign to get the attack message out without the risk that you'll be angry at the campaign doing the advertisements.

Humor can be a devastatingly powerful weapon. As soon as voters begin laughing at a candidate, that candidate is finished in an election. They won't be taken seriously again. Humor permits negative attacks with less potential for backlash from voters. Voters are less likely to view the attack as negative when humor is employed, and voters don't view candidates as serious contenders when they become the butt of entertaining jokes.

An example of humor as a weapon is Senator Mitch McConnell's campaign against Senator Dee Huddleston in Kentucky. McConnell ran for the US Senate in 1984 using a commercial that featured bloodhounds searching for incumbent Senator Huddleston in vacation spots, where he collected speaking fees while the Senate was in session. The use of bloodhounds tempered a negative attack on Huddleston with humor and permitted McConnell to make the attack successfully.

Why Use Negative Advertising?

If a campaign takes risks in going beyond comparison advertisements or stepping over the line in talking about matters that aren't public record, why do they do it? The answer is that they want to win your vote.

REMEMBER

The public may resent the negative ads, but negative ads still work. People are more prone to vote *against* something or someone than *for* something or someone. Hate is still a more potent force than love in politics.

Besides, despite the risks, it's easier for a campaign to give you a reason to vote *against* someone in 30 seconds than it is to give you a reason to vote *for* someone in the same time frame — especially if you belong to the opposite political party from the candidate running the ad.

Polling on the issues tests the strength of the attack in moving your support away from the enemy. The polls tell a campaign which facts about an opponent voters find the most troubling, and those are the issues that a campaign uses to attack the opponent.

REMEMBER

All negative campaigning is designed to persuade you to vote for one candidate — or at least dissuade you from voting for the other.

Countering Negative Campaigns

What can you do to eliminate or reduce negative campaign tactics? As an informed voter, you can have an impact on the types of campaigns candidates run. You can do several things to reduce the amount of negative campaigning and encourage candidates to take the high road:

>> Watch the marketing of the candidates carefully to determine whether anyone is engaged in negative campaign tactics.

>> Contact candidates who are running positive campaigns and compliment them.

>> Write letters to the editor of your local paper criticizing negative tactics of candidates and praising candidates who are positive.

>> Withhold your vote from a candidate who wages a campaign that's too negative.

REMEMBER

You can decide for yourself when a campaign for your vote has become too negative. Judge for yourself whether the comparison between the two candidates helps you make an informed decision or is unfair to the candidate being compared. Recognize a wedge issue for what it is — a subtle attempt to appeal to the worst in all of us. And use your voting power to punish those candidates who go over the line of fairness. After you understand what candidates are trying to do to win your vote, you know something about how far they're willing to go to achieve power. You can decide whether to give it to them or to their opponents. Remember that you're in control because you're the only one who can cast your vote on election day.

Preventing negative campaigning from discouraging good candidates

In many ways, holding elective office today is more difficult than at any time in US history. To many voters, the word *politician* is a completely negative word. Voters think that election campaigns are more and more negative, and they don't like it. A reasonable person looking at the election process and the attitude of many voters might well let the opportunity pass for serving in elective office.

Any person willing to put themselves forward for public office risks having every aspect of their lives made public in the press. Some people persist in finding conspiracies in the most innocent of events and then try to make a mountain out of a molehill to win a political advantage. A candidate may find themselves explaining that mistakes they made were just that and not something much more sinister.

SPEAKING UP

In this type of political climate, it's even more important that informed voters like you speak up and be heard. If you see good people running positive campaigns, help them. Volunteer your time. Make a contribution. Vote for them and try to persuade your neighbors, friends, and relatives to get involved, too. These candidates need all the help they can get. Tell them that they're precisely the type of people who should be running for office and that you're glad to see them doing it. Give them the encouragement they need to get through the election process successfully.

When you see a candidate who deserves to be the butt of the late night television jokes, work against them. Tell people who will listen to you why they shouldn't support them. Go to public meetings and speak out about the negative campaign tactics they're using in this campaign. Don't hesitate to call them to account for their actions. Don't let their negative campaign tactics attract your vote.

As long as voters are persuaded by negative campaign ads to change their votes, candidates will use negative tactics. Complaining about negative campaign tactics isn't enough. Voters like you must recognize a negative campaign for what it is and vote against it. As soon as negative campaign tactics cost candidates elections, candidates will stop using them. You're the key to increasing the positive nature of political campaigns.

Give 'em a pat on the back

Whatever the reason or the motive, the fact that many people are willing to take the risks that come with public service is a tribute to the strength of the US democratic system. When you see a public servant who is doing a good job, you can tell them so in different ways:

>> Walk up to the officeholder or write a note to say thank you for doing a job well for the average citizen.

>> When a good candidate for office asks you to volunteer or contribute, give the idea serious consideration.

>> Remember to vote!

REMEMBER

A little appreciation in this process can go a long way toward encouraging the type of public servants everyone wants to see run for and hold elective office. It can also go a long way toward keeping good officials running for the offices after they've been elected. Everyone likes approval; if the officeholder deserves your thanks, don't forget to give it now and again.

Chapter **19**

The Money Thing: Is Reform Possible?

S ome people may buy this book to understand politics just because they're interested in politics or because they're thinking about becoming politically involved. Some may buy this book because they're concerned about the political process. Something about politics is bothersome, and those concerned people are trying to determine what that is. They may want to explore ways to make the US political system more responsive to them. Is anything wrong? What is it? Can it be fixed, and how so? I think it's important to begin by discussing a big part of the problem with politics today — the cost of campaigns.

Campaigns Cost Too Much

You know that a huge amount of any candidate's time is spent raising money. In today's political climate, legislative races can cost tens of thousands of dollars. Competitive congressional races can cost millions. Races for the US Senate and state governorships that are competitive can cost tens of millions of dollars. What bothers most people is that in order to raise the necessary campaign finances, candidates must spend time with groups and individuals who can afford to give substantial campaign contributions.

Contributors get better access to politicians

The problem with the amount of time candidates spend fundraising is that, because they solicit from those who can afford to give, they spend time with the same set of contributors. That time gives contributors the opportunity to get to know the candidate and establish a relationship with them. The relationship that big contributors form with candidates provides access to the candidates when decisions are made that affect those big contributors and the rest of us.

REMEMBER

The fact that big contributors have access does not affect every decision an elected official makes or every vote they cast. (See Chapter 2 for more on the money-versus-vote analysis.) Most of those decisions are influenced by a variety of factors, including

>> **Party loyalties:** Often, it's party loyalties that determine how decisions are made. Party leaders ask elected officials to support the position taken by their political party to support a particular policy or to gain a public advantage.

>> **The bonds of friendship:** Elected officials have friendships with other elected officials — sometimes even across party lines. And, yes, sometimes those friendships have an effect on voting. If a colleague votes for a measure that an elected official friend wants one day, they may ask the friend to return the favor another day on another vote.

>> **The content of their character:** When officials are elected, they bring their own attitudes, points of view on issues, upbringing, friendships, and political promises with them to elected office. All those factors influence how an elected official behaves.

The access to elected officials that's available to large contributors may have a role to play in how officials make decisions, but it isn't the only factor. If money could be removed completely as a factor in campaigns, these other factors would still have an impact on how a candidate behaves when they're an elected official.

POLITICAL MYTH

If you think campaign contributions are the sole factors in determining who wins an election, think again. In fact, 8 of the 20 most successful fundraising candidates for Congress in 2018 lost their elections.

Voters end up paying

Although large contributions don't necessarily affect the way elected officials behave, the impact of money on politics is still of concern to people:

>> Some excellent candidates decide not to run, out of fear that they won't raise enough money to be competitive. When fewer good candidates seek elective office, you have fewer good candidates from which to choose on election day.

>> Candidates spend a great deal of time and effort on fundraising. The time spent fundraising is time not spent discussing issues and meeting voters.

The more time spent with individuals and groups that can afford substantial campaign contributions, the less time a candidate has to spend with average voters like you. Only so many hours are in a day and in a campaign. You want to see candidates spending more of those hours telling you why you should vote for them. You'd like more opportunities to hear the candidates speak and to get to know them. When so much of every candidate's time is spent fundraising, you won't have as many opportunities to get to know the candidates.

You can't remove money as a factor in politics, but you can take some steps to minimize the importance of money in political campaigns. You can urge politicians to support policies that encourage as many candidates for office as possible. You can also support measures to reduce the cost of campaigns, such as requiring states to donate time on television for candidates. The donated time would permit candidates to share ideas and platforms with voters, not with slick 30-second campaign ads, but in intervals long enough for all candidates for important offices to talk directly to voters. This approach would permit voters to develop a sense of who the candidates are as well as their positions on issues.

REMEMBER

If the cost of campaigns declines or rises more slowly than in the past, fundraising may not consume as large a portion of the candidate's time and energy, and candidates who have less experience with fundraising may be willing to run.

Campaign Finance Reform

Every so often, somebody starts a movement to reform the way campaigns and parties raise and spend money. Many ideas have been suggested to reduce the influence of money on the US political process. Sometimes, the debate centers on reducing the cost of campaigns themselves. At other times, the debate concerns who should be permitted to give money and how much. Will changing the way the campaigns raise money or spend money make any difference to you?

Federal campaigns

In the 1970s, significant changes were made in the way federal elections are financed. Congress imposed limits on individual contributions of $1,000 per election, imposed an aggregate limit of $25,000 for an individual to all federal candidates in an election cycle, and imposed a limit of $5,000 per election on PAC contributions. (For more on PACs, or political action committees, see Chapter 8.)

From the 1976 election until 2008, presidential campaigns were publicly financed. Since 2008, no nominee for president has accepted federal funding for their campaign. Accepting federal funding requires nominees to limit spending by state and not to raise any contributions themselves. The amount that would have been available for the 2016 campaign was $96.14 million. Instead, Donald Trump and Hillary Clinton spent a combined $2.4 *billion* in the 2016 campaign.

As you can see, the amounts raised by the two candidates are substantially more than the amount available by way of the public funding option, which makes accepting public funding far less attractive, even though the funding amount was adjusted for inflation. The cost of national campaigns has risen that much in the 32 years since the public funding option became law.

Recent changes

The original purpose of the Federal Election Campaign Act of 1971 was to get the candidates off fundraising and onto the issues and to level the playing field in terms of what the nominees would spend. The thought was that the candidates would spend more time telling you what they would do if they won and less time asking wealthy individuals and groups for money. It worked until the cost of campaigns so clearly outpaced the public funds available.

Candidates raise money, but outside groups raise and spend money in campaigns as well. The money that such groups spend in campaigns comes in two categories:

>> **Independent expenditures:** Individuals or PACs that support the election or defeat of one or more of the candidates may make independent expenditures. They can't make these expenditures in coordination with the campaigns that benefit from their activities, but they can make them on their own. The results of the *Citizens United v. FEC* decision (and other decisions by the courts) means that spending by individuals and PACs is no longer subject to limits. In other words, as long as they don't coordinate their activities with the campaigns they're assisting or give to the candidate directly, the PACs can spend as much money as they want and from any source that wants to contribute to the PAC — corporations and labor unions included. Some of these PACs take the position that they aren't required to disclose who contributes to them, either! Those groups, referred to as *dark money* groups, spent almost $181 million attempting to influence the outcome of the 2016 election.

>> **Soft money:** The political parties may spend *soft money* on behalf of a candidate instead of giving them hard cash. (See the "Soft money" sidebar in Chapter 8.) Soft money may be used to run issue-oriented ads in certain ways to benefit the campaign or to fund get-out-the-vote drives. Such "party-building expenditures" may not advertise a single candidate directly, but may help a particular campaign indirectly by concentrating in a district where the party's candidate faces a close race or even by criticizing the opposition in a fashion calculated to hurt the particular opponent in a close race.

Matching funds

Candidates for each party's presidential nomination also receive matching funds in the presidential election year, if they raise money in a certain way. Public funding of presidential primary campaigns is available to candidates who raise money in smaller contributions from many givers. When candidates who are competing for their parties' nominations want to be eligible for federal matching funds, they must

>> Establish functioning committees (committees that are doing something and not just existing on paper) in at least 20 states

>> Raise at least $5,000 in every state in contributions of no more than $250 each

>> Agree to limits on expenditures in primary states

>> Receive at least 10 percent of the vote in at least one of their two most recent primaries

State campaigns

States have experimented with many different types of campaign finance reform. All the experiments are designed to reduce the influence of money on the political process. The four basic categories of political contributors to state campaigns are

>> Corporations

>> Individuals

>> Political action committees (PACs)

>> Unions

As you can imagine, there are as many approaches to regulating political contributions as there are states. The fact that so many states have taken action indicates that most states recognize problems with campaign financing. Although most states see problems, they don't all see the same problem. Interestingly, some states take one approach, and others take the opposite. Fourteen states provide some form of public funding for candidates if they promise to limit what they spend or receive from any single group or individual.

Table 19-1 shows some of the approaches that states are taking.

TABLE 19-1: ## Public Financing for Candidates

Approach Taken	Some of the States For Providing Public Financing
Tax dollars available for gubernatorial candidates	Arizona, Connecticut, Florida, Hawaii, Maine, Massachusetts, Michigan, Minnesota, New Jersey, Rhode Island, Vermont
Tax dollars available for legislative candidates	Arizona, Connecticut, Hawaii, Maine, Minnesota
State tax checkoff for political parties	Alabama, Arizona, Iowa, Minnesota, New Mexico, North Carolina, Ohio, Rhode Island and Utah

States fund these campaigns in one of two ways: Clean Elections programs and Matching Funds programs. In Clean Elections in Arizona, Connecticut, and Maine, candidates must raise small contributions from a number of individuals to show public support. Candidates who do that are given a sum of money equal to the expenditure limit that's set for the election. The Matching Funds program in Hawaii gives 10 percent of the expenditure limit set by the legislature.

Candidates can and do opt out of these financing plans, much like they've done in recent presidential campaigns.

REMEMBER

If your state has adopted any campaign finance reform, you can judge for yourself whether the reforms have made a difference. Have they changed how campaigns are financed to any degree? Examine the reports of candidates for state and local office, or read the reports of the media or watchdog groups to see if the reforms have changed the sources for candidate funding or the size of the average gift.

You and other voters can urge your state representatives and state senators not to raise money from lobbyists while your state legislature is in session, and immediately before and after the session. Don't hesitate to tell them such fundraising makes voters like you uneasy about the access of the special interest lobbyists to the legislators and the influence they wield over legislative decisions. Tell your legislators that you aren't reassured when they raise money from lobbyists indirectly during these periods when legislation is being debated. Tell them that you won't feel any better about this practice if the money goes to their party's legislative caucus and not directly to them.

SPEAKING UP

When you see a fundraising practice you don't like, speak up. Tell the officeholder why you don't like it. Write a letter to the editor of your local paper. Call into your favorite radio talk show and condemn the practice. Let your elected officials know that you're paying attention and encourage your friends and coworkers to do the same. The best way to discourage elected officials from raising campaign contributions in ways that make you skeptical about politics is to convince them that such practices will cost them more votes than the money they raise is worth. The practices you don't like will change only when you make your displeasure known and convince the elected officials that you and many others are willing to act on that displeasure.

Getting More Good People Involved

Many times in US history, when barriers to voting have been removed, more citizens voted. The percentage of the eligible voting population that turned out to vote in 2016 nationally was 60.2 percent. In Nebraska, which has no registration requirement, 63 percent of eligible voters voted in 2016. Table 19-2 shows how the percentage of eligible voters voting in those states that permit election-day registration compares to the national average. In fact, the top seven states in terms of percentage turnout are all states with election-day registration or, in the case of Oregon, a vote-by-mail system. Also listed are the bottom performing states — all states with no election day registration.

If you think it's good to get more people involved, you should support laws that make it easier for citizens to do their duty and vote. And you should support candidates who agree with that goal. You should identify every potential barrier to participation and eliminate them, one by one.

WARNING

Working to expand political participation may seem like a virtuous cause. But, often, people don't vote because they have no interest in voting. You may receive little encouragement if you devote time, money, or other effort toward bringing more potential voters into the electorate. And, even if you beat the odds and help mobilize formerly silent voters, don't be surprised if you become disappointed with how they exercise their new political clout. Individuals who don't vote are typically less informed than those who do vote, so you can't really expect that expanding participation will automatically result in better democracy.

TABLE 19-2:

The Results of Making Voting Easier

States with Election Day Registration	% of voters	States without Election Day Registration	% of voters
Minnesota	74.8	Arkansas	43.1
Maine	72.8	Texas	51.6
New Hampshire	72.5	New Mexico	55.2
Colorado	72.1	Arizona	56.2
Wisconsin	70.5	South Carolina	57.3
Iowa	69	Nevada	57.3
Oregon	68.3	Utah	57.7

* Numbers represent the percentage of voting-age citizens who voted.

** The national average was 60.2 percent.

Registering and voting are two vital steps you can take to get more good people (namely, you) involved. Voting is the threshold test of political involvement, but it's not all you can do. You can also

>> Encourage your friends, family, and coworkers to register and vote, too.

>> Use your newfound political savvy to support good candidates by volunteering or contributing. (See Chapter 4 for more on how to do it.) And you can encourage good people to do the same.

>> Urge good people to run for office, and actively support them if they decide to do so. (Maybe you could run for an office yourself!)

TIP

When you notice an officeholder who is doing a good job, pat them on the back and thank them. Tell them their efforts have not gone unnoticed. If an officeholder has just made a tough decision that you think is the right decision, tell them so. One way you can encourage good people in politics is to make certain that those elected officials who meet that definition stay in public service. That's more likely to happen when they know their efforts are appreciated.

You Can Improve the System

The more you can encourage government to reduce the cost of campaigns and the more you can encourage good people to become involved in politics, the greater the number of good choices you'll have to select from on election day. The more you increase the good options available, the more likely you'll be to find a quality elected official to represent you. The more quality elected officials are representing you, the more responsive the government will be to you and other voters like you.

Making officials more responsive and reducing the impact of money on politics also increases your faith in the system. When you have more faith in the system, you'll feel better about being involved and encouraging others to be involved.

SPEAKING UP

The US system of government and politics isn't perfect, but it's the best in the world. You should recognize that it can be improved, but you should also recognize that it's your responsibility as a citizen to work to put those improvements in place. After all, this is a government of, by, and for the people. And you are one of the people. If you don't demand these improvements, who will see that they happen? If you're not willing to fight to make our system of politics and government better, do you really think someone else will do it for you?

6
Presidential Politics

Chapter **20**

Throwing Their Hats in the Ring

When Teddy Roosevelt was asked whether he would seek the Republican presidential nomination in 1912, he replied: "My hat is in the ring." Over the years, the expression "Throw your hat in the ring" has come to symbolize any candidate's announcement to run for office.

Running in the primaries is how today's presidential candidates throw their hats in the ring. To be nominated for president, a candidate has to receive a majority of votes cast by delegates to their party's national convention. (See Chapter 21 for more on national conventions and delegates.) And the most common way for presidential candidates to win national delegate votes is by winning presidential primaries in the many states that hold them between February and June of the presidential election year. (See Chapter 3 for more on primaries.) How well presidential candidates do in state presidential primaries determines the percentage of the state delegates to a party's national convention who are pledged to vote for that candidate.

Welcome to Iowa

Since 1972, Iowa has held the first Democratic presidential caucus. Since 1976, it has held the first Republican presidential caucus. *Caucuses* are neighborhood meetings that occur in the 1,700 precincts across the state. They are conducted by the political parties and not by the state. They are not elections. They are designed to show the level of support that candidates enjoy in that state.

At the Democratic caucuses, voters sign in and group together in their section of the room according to which candidate they support. Each candidate for president has their own area, and there may be an area for undecided voters. Everyone in the room knows which candidate the voter supports. Participants are permitted to speak and tell why they're supporting their candidate. Delegates to the county conventions are apportioned by the level of support that candidates have. To be viable, candidates must have the support of 15 percent of those present. If a candidate doesn't have that level of support, their group aligns with a viable alternative. In 2018, in an attempt to make caucus voting easier, the Democratic National Committee required all states holding caucuses to provide an absentee option for 2010. After votes are tallied, the results are announced and sent to the county party.

In the Republican caucuses, participants meet in similar groups and are permitted to speak in favor of their candidates. After speeches, paper ballots are distributed for participants to write down their choices for president. The ballot is secret. The results are announced and sent to the county party.

The caucus system can launch a campaign for a candidate who has been trailing in the polls. Even a showing that's better than expected can help jump-start a campaign. Donald Trump lost the Iowa caucuses in 2016 to Ted Cruz, but his second-place showing helped propel him to a win in the New Hampshire primary.

Welcome to New Hampshire

Ever since New Hampshire held its first primary in 1920, it has played an important role in the presidential selection process — a much more important role than its numbers would suggest.

New Hampshire has fewer than a million registered voters and only a couple dozen delegates to the national convention of either party. It has four electoral votes to cast for president; only seven states and the District of Columbia have fewer electoral votes. New Hampshire's size certainly doesn't make it a major player in the nominating process for president, but in politics, as in many areas, timing is everything.

Being the first

New Hampshire is a significant player in presidential politics because it's the first state to hold a presidential primary in every presidential election season. The only delegate-selection events before New Hampshire are the Iowa caucuses. The New Hampshire primary is the first opportunity for candidates of the major parties to win or lose delegate votes that will be cast at their parties' conventions. A candidate who does well in New Hampshire can gather momentum going into other primaries and win more votes than expected — perhaps the nomination itself.

New Hampshire also serves as the first step in the elimination of candidates leading up to the choice of the parties' nominees at their conventions. As the grueling selection process continues, the number of candidates for president in both parties dwindles. Weaker candidates are eliminated, and the voters and the parties are left to choose from the two or three strongest candidates. A candidate who can demonstrate surprising strength in New Hampshire can remain alive as a contender for the nomination when others are eliminated from contention.

During the New Hampshire primary, candidates can demonstrate their abilities and their appeal to voters while the national media is guaranteed to be paying attention. Voters and the press are watching with great interest. They want to know who the candidates are, what they stand for, where they come from, what they're discussing, and who will win.

REMEMBER

Because New Hampshire is the first presidential primary, it gets more attention than it would ordinarily receive, given its small number of delegates. The results of the New Hampshire primary may be good indicators to other voters around the country of which candidates have more appeal to average voters. If you see a candidate in New Hampshire who does better than expected, watch that person carefully to see what it was about them that appealed to New Hampshire voters. It may also appeal to you.

Who goes to Iowa and New Hampshire?

Iowa and New Hampshire spell opportunities for presidential wannabes. They have become steps on the journey to nomination. Anyone who thinks that they could or should be nominated and/or elected president of the United States (and who has the price of the carfare) goes early and often to Iowa and New Hampshire.

They begin going two years or more before the caucus and presidential primary. They appear at as many events as they can and speak as often as they can in order to raise their visibility among the party activists, journalists, and rank-and-file voters, hoping to make these groups see them as presidential. Remember that no candidate looks in the mirror and sees a loser — particularly if that candidate longs to sit in the Oval Office. Those wannabes who go to Iowa and New Hampshire have convinced themselves that they're intelligent enough, hardworking enough, and honest enough — just what you and I and the rest of the country need in a president.

Sometimes, candidates travel to Iowa and New Hampshire early in the presidential cycle to lay the groundwork for the presidential election in five or six years — not in the upcoming presidential election. They go, representing a candidate who's running in the upcoming election. Their travel helps the candidates they're supporting and helps their own ambitions. Many of the activists they meet will still be on the scene for the next presidential election cycle and will be in a position to help them later.

REMEMBER

For many politicians, travel to Iowa and New Hampshire is part of a carefully thought-out strategy to keep all options open and viable. No candidate can ever be sure that the time will be right to run for president, but all want to be sure that if the time does come, they're ready!

When an undeclared candidate visits Iowa or New Hampshire for the first time — maybe as early as two years before the presidential election — the wannabe gives another reason for going: to discuss foreign policy, to get input from voters on welfare reform, to speak to a party group — even just to see the scenery or take a vacation. Undeclared candidates give all kinds of different reasons to explain why they go. The real reason is for the exposure to voters. Iowa and New Hampshire provide candidates with their first opportunity to appeal to rank-and-file voters.

Getting off to a good start

Going to Iowa and New Hampshire is the way presidential candidates show that they're serious about seeking the nomination. It's the time-honored method of attracting attention and coverage from the national media.

Iowa and New Hampshire are small enough and have few enough registered voters who participate in the presidential caucuses and primaries to make it possible for each candidate seeking primary support to personally meet every voter. Think about it: Each and every candidate can shake hands with each and every caucus participant or primary voter. A candidate with the stamina and the time can make enough contacts to be a contender in the election without much more in the way of resources. For this reason, candidates, particularly long-shot candidates, go to Iowa and New Hampshire early and often.

Lesser-known candidates try to develop support among the voters in Iowa and New Hampshire before the better-known and better-funded candidates arrive. They want the voters to know them and remember their names when the pollsters and the media start taking surveys. The candidates know that if their names are mentioned often enough, the press will begin paying attention to their campaigns.

If a campaign draws media coverage and looks like it's gaining support, it will increase contributors. Many large contributors look on their contributions as investments in a candidate. They're not eager to contribute if the candidate isn't going to be around for the long haul. They want to back a winner. They particularly want to be one of the first to identify and back a long-shot winner.

The battleground after New Hampshire consists of states with many more delegate votes, where the emphasis must be on campaigning by television rather than on person-to-person contact. And many states, in different regions of the country, hold primaries on the same day, which makes personal contact impractical as a method of generating support. Candidates have to compensate with television, which requires money — money that they hope to get after a strong showing in New Hampshire, even if they don't actually win their primary.

POLITICAL STUFF

WHO PAYS FOR THE TRIPS?

The candidates have to raise the money to pay for the early trips by way of normal campaign contributions. The presidential matching funds (discussed in Chapter 19) don't become available until January of the election year. If these are undeclared candidates, without committees set up to receive presidential campaign contributions, they must use whatever means they have available to cover expenses. For example, a US senator can use their Senate campaign committee funds. A governor can use funds from their gubernatorial campaign committee. A non-officeholder must pay the expenses out of their own pocket or from a political action committee that may want to encourage their candidacy. See Chapter 4 for more about fundraising.

But because candidates hope to receive federal matching dollars in January of the election year, they try to raise small contributions to fund the early days of the presidential campaign. Getting many small contributions helps the candidates fund the campaign before federal matching funds are available and also qualifies them for federal matching money when the time comes. The federal government matches contributions of up to $250 for every individual contributor with an equal amount. Therefore, contributions of $50 from ten different individuals are worth more to a candidate than $500 from a single political action committee.

Candidates who think of themselves as presidential material go to Iowa and New Hampshire to earn their stripes, to build momentum in small states where they can compete on limited resources. The candidates hope that the momentum will bring them enough publicity, support, and money to enable them to compete in states where they'll need greater resources.

WARNING

When many states realized the impact that Iowa and New Hampshire were having on presidential selection, they began moving their primaries or caucuses earlier in the year. After the 2008 election, the national political parties established rules that largely dictated the order. In 2020, Iowa will be first, falling on February 3. New Hampshire comes next, on February 11. The Nevada caucus for Democrats is on February 22. Nevada Republicans will not hold a caucus in 2020. They are supporting Donald Trump. The South Carolina primary for Democrats is on February 29 and for Republicans it would have been on February 15, but the Republicans have cancelled their primary in South Carolina to support Donald Trump. It is important to note that not every state holds the parties' primaries or caucuses on the same day.

Iowa and New Hampshire are states with overwhelmingly white populations. Adding Nevada and South Carolina to the early selection states add some diversity to the voter mix for both parties.

Staying in the Spotlight

When a candidate runs in Iowa or New Hampshire, the opportunity for media coverage is there, win or lose. The media, particularly the national media, is obsessed with analyzing politics in terms of horse races. Who's winning? Who's losing? Did so-and-so do better than expected? Did they do worse than expected? A candidate who succeeds in diminishing the media's expectations for their performance in Iowa or New Hampshire before the fact and then exceeds those expectations may attract more media attention than the candidate who wins!

Getting a bounce

The media attention in Iowa and New Hampshire is vital to the future success of presidential wannabes. If a candidate does better than expected, they can get what's called a *bounce* out of either state. That means the media prints stories about them and begins speculation that this candidate has a real chance to win the nomination. A candidate who does particularly well in New Hampshire has the opportunity to gain many benefits in addition to a modest number of delegate votes at the national convention. A candidate can use the momentum gained in Iowa or New Hampshire to

» Raise additional money from campaign contributors

» Add new donors to their list of contributors

» Obtain endorsements from party officials in other states

» Gain national attention and receive more support in national polls

» Increase local media coverage in other states

Because New Hampshire is the first primary, it attracts the most serious contenders for the nomination. A strong showing in New Hampshire can even help candidates who lose in the primary — that is, as long as that strong showing is stronger than the media expected to see, in which case those results may be interpreted as a moral victory for the losing candidate.

In 2016, Bernie Sanders defeated Hillary Clinton in New Hampshire. The victory did not do him as much good as you'd expect, however, because New Hampshire was adjacent to his home state of Vermont and he was expected to win. In 2000, on the Republican side, John McCain beat George W. Bush handily (16 percent) in New Hampshire, and that victory helped his candidacy briefly, until primaries in southern states derailed his candidacy.

The media can also hurt

The media attention in Iowa and New Hampshire can also undermine a campaign if the publicity is unfavorable. The unfavorable publicity can occur if a candidate does poorer than expected. The key word here is *expected*.

Early in the process, the media makes predictions about who will win and the percentages each candidate will receive. If a candidate doesn't do as well as the media expects, the press prints a negative story. On the other hand, if a candidate does better than predicted, they get favorable publicity. A candidate who wants to win the media wars tries to manage the media's expectations. They and their spin doctors will talk about the stiffness of the competition, the candidate's late start in the race, and so on. The candidate and their spin doctors provide the media with reasons why the candidate's performances in Iowa and New Hampshire aren't a fair indicator of their ability to ultimately win the nomination. The goal is *expectations management* — to convince the media that the candidate's performance will be poorer than the candidate and the spin doctors really expect it to be. It doesn't always work, but it's usually better, in terms of future media coverage, to be seen as gaining, rather than losing, ground as the presidential primary season progresses. Doing better than expected shows that a candidate is a comer — someone to watch. (Refer to Chapter 1 for more about spin doctors and their roles in campaigns.)

A campaign can also be undermined if the media plays up the showing of the opposition. In other words, Carly Candidate wins the primary, but the next day's headlines and the lead stories on television are all about Michael Maverick's strong showing, speculating that the Maverick Express is coming on strong and that he could well have a real shot at winning the nomination. Michael Maverick may in fact be The One.

A day at the races

The media spends a substantial amount of time in any campaign speculating on who will win and who will lose the election. That speculation is called *the horse race question*. Who is winning a campaign and who is losing is news. A majority of voters know whom they will support very early in a presidential campaign, so they aren't interested in hearing about competing issue positions or well-reasoned speeches — they want to know how their team is doing. But too much speculation on the horse race question can harm the process. If the press reports early in the campaign that Carly Candidate is way behind and would have a tough time winning, that report can become a self-fulfilling prophecy. In other words, the report of Carly's slim chances can kill Carly's chances.

Contributors shy away from wasting their money on a candidate who can't win. Volunteers may look for another candidate who's in the running to work for. Voters and the press won't pay much attention to Carly's suggestions for change or ideas for improvement because she isn't truly in contention. No one wants to back a loser. As a result, you may not get all the information you might otherwise need to help you make your choice for a candidate in a closely contested race.

WARNING

When you see horse race stories reported early in the campaign process, keep an open mind. If you think the newspapers and television stations aren't giving you enough coverage of Carly's and her opponent's ideas, call them and complain. If you want more information on substance than you've been getting, go out and get it. See Chapters 5 and 6 for ideas about how to do that.

The media thoroughly cover the first events in the presidential election season. They help to create front-runners and raise the expectations for candidates' performances. The media emphasis on horse-race stories (which candidate is ahead and which candidate is gaining, in other words) can lead to early identification of a candidate as a front-runner — although front-runners sometimes finish last. (See the "Front-runners sometimes finish last" sidebar, later in this chapter.)

FRONT-RUNNERS SOMETIMES FINISH LAST

POLITICAL STUFF

Early identification as a front-runner used to be the key to winning the nomination. A *front-runner* is someone who's sufficiently ahead in the polls, making the election, therefore, theirs to lose. For another candidate to win, the front runner usually has to make a mistake.

From 1936 through 1968, candidates from either major party who were ahead in polls at the beginning of the election year went on to win their parties' nominations. Recently, this has not been as true for candidates from either party. In fact, being ahead in the polls going into the heat of the presidential nominating process when there's a contest (when an incumbent president isn't running for a second term) resulted in securing the nomination only about half the time.

Republican early front-runners in competitive races:

  2000 George W. Bush

  2008 Rudy Giuliani (John M. Cain, nominee)

  2012 Rick Perry (Mitt Romney, nominee)

  2016 Donald J. Trump

Democratic early front-runners in competitive races:

  2000 Al Gore

  2004 Wesley Clark (John Kerry, nominee)

  2008 Hillary Clinton (Barack Obama, nominee)

  2016 Hillary Clinton

Take the early polls with a grain of salt. They predict who's going to secure the nomination of their parties only half the time. The other half is determined by the ebbs and flows of the campaign. Who wins or loses or does better or worse than expected in early contests can move a winning candidate out of contention or put someone trailing in the polls into front-runner status.

The print, online, and television media can have a significant influence on which candidates are still in the hunt for the nomination after the early primaries and caucuses. Their positive or negative reporting on candidates can make or break fragile campaigns. In many ways, the media perform the function that used to be performed by the party — screening the candidates to reduce the number. From the huge number who may begin the presidential selection season, the process cuts out most for one reason or another, usually leaving the most able of the bunch to emerge as the favored nominee.

REMEMBER

Being the most "able" of the bunch doesn't necessarily mean having the kinds of qualities you may like to see in your friends or next-door neighbors. The ability to succeed in presidential politics means having characteristics that may not seem like positive attributes to most people. Candidates do have to be hardworking, intelligent, and articulate to varying degrees, but the process favors those who are intense, good at raising money, and thick-skinned. Remember that you're selecting the leader of one of the largest, most powerful nations in the world, not your next dinner companion, through this process.

Conducting Straw Polls

In addition to getting media coverage in New Hampshire, another way candidates gather momentum behind their campaigns is by winning straw polls, which are unofficial, unscientific surveys. *Straw polls* are informal, nonbinding trial votes taken at party functions in certain states. Anyone who pays a set amount, usually $25, can vote in a straw poll. Many times, voters don't even have to live in the state. Participants in a straw poll are asked which of their party's candidates for president they prefer from a list of candidates willing to compete in the straw poll.

State parties use straw polls in presidential years as a fundraising device because the party gets to keep the money that participants pay to vote. A straw poll isn't a scientific indication of the strength of the candidates in a state. In fact, presidential candidates, eager to win a straw poll, often bus or fly in supporters and sometimes even pay their fees to vote. If winning a straw poll has any significance, it shows that the winning candidate is the best-organized and -funded candidate in the state. It doesn't necessarily demonstrate that the winner is the most popular candidate with the voters.

REMEMBER

Winning straw polls gets candidates favorable stories in the media. The winning candidate then uses these favorable stories to motivate people to contribute to their campaign. If you read about a presidential candidate's victory in a straw poll, don't give that victory much thought. The winner may be better organized and funded than their opponents, but you want to know what they think about issues of importance to you.

Introducing the Nominees

Do political nominees have anything in common besides a good self-image and a healthy dose of ambition?

The answer is *yes*. Most of the nominees of both parties in the past 20 years have been current or former officeholders who generally come from one of three places: the presidency, the vice presidency, or a state governor's office. The US Senate was also a source of presidential nominees before 1976 and again 20 years later. The 1996 Republican candidates included four senators, including the eventual nominee, Senator Robert Dole.

Governors have been favored as nominees in recent years. Perhaps this favor comes from the fact that they have experience in running state governments and making the tough decisions on how to balance the budgets of their states. Or perhaps it comes from the fact that voters have more confidence these days in their state and local governments than they do in their national government. Yet another reason may be that such candidates aren't "tainted" by being part of the problem that many voters view Washington, DC, as being. Whatever the reason, a governor or former governor has been on the ballot for president in every election from 1976 to 2004.

Presidents and vice presidents continue to be key sources of nominees for both political parties. In fact, in the roughly 70 years from 1932 to 2004, an incumbent president or vice president was on the ballot for every election but one — 1952, when Harry Truman declined to run again, and his 75-year-old vice president, Alben Barkley, was denied the nomination at the convention.

Table 20-1 shows the presidential ballot from 1976 to 2016 and illustrates how the executive branch — at both the national and state levels — has been well represented.

TABLE 20-1: **Recent Presidential Nominees and Their Prenomination Occupations**

Year	Republican	Occupation	Democrat	Occupation
1976	Ford	President	Carter	Governor
1980	Reagan	Governor	Carter	President
1984	Reagan	President	Mondale	Vice president
1988	George H. W. Bush	Vice president	Dukakis	Governor
1992	George H. W. Bush	President	Clinton	Governor
1996	Dole	Senator	Bill Clinton	President
2000	George W. Bush	Governor	Gore	Vice president
2004	George W. Bush	President	Kerry	Senator
2008	McCain	Senator	Obama	Senator
2012	Romney	Governor	Obama	President
2016	Trump	No elective office	Hillary Clinton	Senator

Chapter **21**

Getting the Party Started: National Party Conventions

Both major parties hold conventions during the summer of a presidential election year. Delegates to each convention ratify the party's choice for president and nominate the choice for vice president.

Independent candidates for president don't undergo the nominating process; after all, independent candidates don't represent a party. Because they don't have to secure a party's nomination for president, they don't enter primaries or caucuses or hold conventions.

Sending Delegates to the National Convention

The national conventions are held every four years in the summer of the presidential election year. The party to which the current president belongs holds its convention in August; the other party, or *out party,* traditionally holds its convention in July. The national committee of each party decides where to hold its convention.

POLITICAL STUFF

The national committees of both parties consist of party officials from the 50 states and representatives of other groups within the party organizations. Each state party decides how it selects its representatives to the national committee, subject to national party rules. The rules for each party may differ in the same state. For example, in 2020, Democrats in Kentucky will hold a primary but Republicans in Kentucky will caucus. Conversely, Republicans in the state of Washington hold a primary; Democrats in Washington, a caucus. Each political party can decide how it wants its nominee chosen.

Democratic and Republican Party representatives, called *national delegates,* meet at the party's national convention to vote for the nominees for president and vice president. Each state has a number of delegates allocated to each party based on the population and the relative strength of each party in the state. The total number of delegates is different for each party, but each party's nominee must win a majority of those delegates in order to win.

Conventions don't choose presidential nominees

At one time, the national conventions chose presidential nominees — often requiring drawn-out fights with repeated ballots before settling on a choice. The results could be a genuine surprise. The national conventions no longer choose the nominees in most cases. Presidential primaries and caucus or conventions determine which candidates have enough votes to be the nominees. Generally speaking, the conventions simply ratify those choices. However, if there is no clear winner after the primary and caucus season, there is always the possibility of a *brokered* convention — one where the delegates choose the nominee.

The national conventions rubber-stamp the primary, caucus, and convention selections that occur in each state from February to June of the election year. The trend in the United States in the past 25 years has been toward primary selection for the national delegates based on the primary showings of the presidential candidates. In some states, voters express their preference for presidential candidates, and the delegates are selected later by way of a different selection process. In other states, voters directly select the delegates. The ballot may or may not indicate which candidate the delegate is supporting.

CONVENTIONS HISTORICALLY CHOSE THE NOMINEES

George Washington was elected US president twice with no process in place for nominating him. No one disputed him as a choice. Each member of the electoral college simply cast two votes for president, and Washington was chosen unanimously. That was the first and last time there was unanimity behind any choice for president.

A nominating process became important after George Washington's term ended, when alternative candidates for president sprang up. The nation experimented with a couple of methods of nominating national candidates before the parties began holding national conventions.

The national conventions gave party leaders control of the selection of presidential nominees. *Brokered conventions,* where party leaders traded support for a candidate for other considerations, were the norm.

Over time, particularly since 1968, the influence of the party leaders on the nomination process has diminished as primaries have increased in importance. The deals and compromises in the selection of nominees that were commonplace in the last century have ended. Because the primary is the key way to select nominees and delegates, more people participate in the selection process now than at any time in history.

The selection process varies from state to state, and from party to party within the same state. For example, in 2016, Democrats used the primary in states whereas the Republicans used a caucus or state convention to choose their delegates. In 1968, only 17 states chose their delegates by primary. In 2020, more than 40 states will use this method.

Because the national conventions ratify the choices of voters and party leaders, those voters participating in the primaries, conventions, and caucuses play a much more important role in the selection of the presidential nominees than ever before. By voting in your presidential primary or participating in your party's caucus or convention, you have an important role to play in who will be the next president of the United States.

These days, most delegates go to a convention committed to vote for a certain candidate on the first ballot. That's particularly important because all the nominees of both parties have been selected on the first ballot ever since the time Democrats required three ballots to nominate Governor Adlai Stevenson of Illinois for president.

WHAT IN HEAVEN'S NAME IS A CAUCUS?

The term *caucus* comes from a Native American word that means to speak or to counsel. It has several meanings in politics:

- A meeting of residents of a district who are of the same political party to elect state and national convention delegates and vote on party platforms and policies (for example, the Iowa caucuses)

- A meeting of individuals of the same party who share an interest in an issue or have ethnicity or race in common to promote policies favored by the caucus (for example, the Congressional Black Caucus)

- A group of elected officials of one party that meets behind closed doors to plan strategy and elect its own leaders (a legislative caucus)

- A meeting of party leaders of one political party to fill vacancies on the ballot or vacancies in office caused by the death or resignation of certain types of officeholders

That's a lot of meanings for one little word!

What happens at the national conventions?

The national conventions play a less important role than they once did in selecting nominees, but they still perform other useful functions. Here are some of the roles that national conventions fill:

- ❯❯ Approve the selection of the presidential nominees.
- ❯❯ Approve the selection of the vice-presidential nominees.
- ❯❯ Adopt party platforms.
- ❯❯ Adopt the rules that govern the parties for the coming four years.
- ❯❯ Showcase the candidates and future candidates of the parties.
- ❯❯ Rally the troops for the fall campaign.

Selecting the vice president

No method is in place for the general public to choose nominees for vice president. The choice of vice president is in the hands of the convention delegates. The conventions traditionally defer to the nominee for president to choose a running mate, who is then presented for nomination to the convention.

WHEN THE CONVENTION CHOSE THE RUNNING MATE

The last time that a real battle for the vice-presidential nomination in either party took place was the 1956 Democratic National Convention, when Adlai Stevenson, the Democratic nominee for president, left the choice of a running mate to the convention. He didn't ask the convention to ratify his choice; he let the convention choose. For two dramatic ballots, Senator John Kennedy of Massachusetts ran neck-and-neck with Senator Estes Kefauver of Tennessee before Kennedy lost the nomination on the third ballot.

The convention and the excitement of the balloting for vice president were carried on national television. The exposure that Kennedy received during the 1956 convention helped him to secure the presidential nomination itself in 1960.

Presidential nominees have to consider the wishes of the delegates because the delegates have the right to reject the presidential nominee's choice if it meets with disfavor. Occasionally, presidential candidates generate excitement and a spirited campaign by throwing the nomination of a vice presidential candidate to the delegates to choose. See the nearby sidebar, "When the convention chose the running mate," for details.

Sometimes, the choice of a running mate provides the only element of suspense in the convention proceedings. The delegates often don't know the nominee's choice for a running mate until the convention actually begins. George H. W. Bush made his surprise announcement of Indiana Senator Dan Quayle as his choice for vice president as the Republican National Convention began in New Orleans in 1988.

Adopting platforms

Conventions adopt *platforms*, which are declarations of principles and policies for the national parties, and thereby develop a consensus approach to important issues of the day. The platforms define who the parties are and what they stand for. Platforms can also serve as the framework for discussing the issues to be debated in the fall election campaign.

Unifying the party

Each party's convention adopts the rules for governing the party for the next four years and resolves questions about how to run the party. The convention serves to focus party members' attention on the opposing party and candidates rather than on rifts within the party itself.

The various factions of the parties that supported losing candidates during the nominating season are encouraged to focus on issues that unite them rather than on issues that divide them. The convention showcases the party nominees, calls attention to the party's rising stars, and unifies the party faithful.

National conventions serve to unite the Republicans or Democrats in a common cause: electing a national ticket. Parties spend a great deal of time and money organizing these conventions. After the 2012 national conventions, for which each party received $18.5 million from the federal government, Congress changed the law. The parties no longer receive federal money directly. Instead, the federal government gives $50 million to local law enforcement in the city where each convention is held to provide security at the conventions. Now each party raises millions from private sources to run their quadrennial conventions.

The Politics of the Conventions

At national conventions, everything is organized because the organizers want nothing left to chance. Even the placement of the state delegations is the subject of much debate and jockeying. Every delegation wants to be seen on television. Every delegation wants to be immediately in front of the stage to be able to see the nominees and other dignitaries up close and personal.

Who gets to address the conventions and what the speakers get to say are also rigidly controlled matters. With the possible exception of former presidents, speakers must submit their remarks in advance to those party leaders in charge of the convention and receive clearance for what they want to say.

POLITICAL MYTH

If you watch conventions on television, you see many floor demonstrations. Delegates march around the floor waving signs and chanting. These demonstrations appear to begin spontaneously in the crowd and spread through the hall, gathering force as they go. Those "spontaneous" demonstrations are actually carefully orchestrated. Delegates are told not only when to demonstrate but also which signs to wave.

The convention organizers distribute many signs of different shapes and colors during the convention. Delegates may be told to wave the red, square signs at one point and the blue, rectangular ones at another.

Creating the right effect

Campaigns leave nothing to chance at their national conventions because appearance is important when the national media is watching closely and where some cable networks are providing gavel-to-gavel coverage. If the event is staged properly, it can emphasize the unity of the party and its enthusiasm for its candidates. A successful convention can set the mood for the fall campaign and project an image of confidence.

A poorly executed convention can have a negative impact on a party's chances in November. In 1992, the Republican Party heavily emphasized family values and religion. The speeches at the convention struck many viewers as strident and extreme; the language Pat Buchanan used to appeal to "traditional family values," for example, was so extreme that many political observers have ever since referred to it as his "raw meat" speech. The strong language may have appealed to Republican delegates sitting in the audience, but it frightened the less partisan voters, particularly women, watching the convention at home. Many convention follow-up stories cited public opinion research that showed voters' uneasiness by what was viewed as the exclusionary message of the Republican convention.

Concentrating partisan energies

Although everything is carefully scripted, the conventions are great unifying and energizing forces for Democrats and Republicans alike. When the delegates leave the convention, they're part of something bigger than themselves. That something the delegates are part of has a clearly defined objective: victory in November.

The delegates leave eager to get home and accomplish the objective. The conclusions of the conventions unleash a flood of energy that flows across the country into every state in the union. The timing of the floodgate's opening is also important because the conclusion of the national conventions signifies the start of the fall campaign.

Playing Your Role as a Voter

Today, more people have the opportunity to participate in presidential selection because more states are using the primary selection method. Millions of Americans participated in selecting the nominees of both parties in 2016, but the overall percentage was still very low. This lack of participation has been true for a while — only 28.5 percent of the voting-age population in primary states bothers to vote for presidential candidates. The record primary turnout was 2008, when 30.4 percent of voting age citizens cast ballots.

More people have to participate in the selection process. Democracy works well only when people inform themselves about the issues and the candidates and make their wishes known. Reading this book is a great way to become informed about the process and prepare to participate on every level, including helping to choose the next president of the United States.

REMEMBER

If you don't like the alternatives, change them. Run for office yourself or persuade good people to do so. Work for their election. Tell your neighbors and friends to vote for them. Contribute to their campaigns. Get off your duff and make things better. (The chapters in Part 2 of this book tell what you can do.)

If you think that money plays too big of a role in politics, get campaign finance reform laws passed in your state. Start a movement to change the campaign finance laws on the federal level. Even constitutional amendments to change the consequences of the *Citizens United* Supreme Court decision are possible if there's enough momentum behind them. Every journey begins with a single step. If you take that step, you may start a movement to improve democracy in the United States, which would be a pretty good legacy to leave your children.

IN THIS CHAPTER

» Examining electoral college
controversies

» Finding out what the electoral college
means to you

» Deciding whether the electoral
college should be changed

Chapter **22**

The Electoral College and the 2000 and 2016 Presidential Elections

think it's fair to say that most people didn't spend a lot of time thinking about the electoral college and what it meant to their choice of president before the 2000 and 2016 elections. That has changed.

All of a sudden, political pundits are discussing the electoral college and whether it needs to be changed. In 2000, for the first time in more than a hundred years, the candidate with the higher popular vote count lost the presidential election — all because of the electoral college. Now the argument rages whether the electoral college should remain the official method by which the United States chooses its president and vice president every four years. (See Chapter 23 for more on electing a president.)

Explaining How the Electoral College Affected the 2000 and 2016 Elections

Before the 2000 election, most US residents hadn't thought about the electoral college since high school. A few people discussed changing the electoral college after the close election of 1960, but those discussions were short-lived. Al Gore won the popular vote in 2000 by about a half-million votes, but George W. Bush won in the electoral college 271 to 267. In 2016, Hillary Clinton won the popular vote by almost 3 million votes but lost the electoral college 304 to 227.

To understand what happened in these elections, you need to understand the way the system of electing a US president and vice president works. The following minitable lists the states that President George W. Bush won in 2000 and the electoral votes those states brought to his total:

State	Electoral Votes	State	Electoral Votes
Alabama	9	Nebraska	5
Alaska	3	Nevada	4
Arizona	8	New Hampshire	4
Arkansas	6	North Carolina	14
Colorado	8	North Dakota	3
Florida	25	Ohio	21
Georgia	13	Oklahoma	8
Idaho	4	South Carolina	8
Indiana	12	South Dakota	3
Kansas	6	Tennessee	11
Kentucky	8	Texas	32
Louisiana	9	Utah	5
Mississippi	7	Virginia	13
Missouri	11	West Virginia	5
Montana	3	Wyoming	3

Al Gore's populist campaign won the Northeast, except for New Hampshire. He also won the West Coast and split the Midwestern states with George W. Bush. Gore carried population centers, whereas Bush was more popular in rural areas. The following minitable lists the states that Al Gore won in 2000 and their electoral votes:

State	Electoral Votes	State	Electoral Votes
California	54	Minnesota	10
Connecticut	8	New Jersey	15
Delaware	3	New Mexico	5
D.C.	3	New York	33
Hawaii	4	Oregon	7
Illinois	22	Pennsylvania	23
Iowa	7	Rhode Island	4
Maine	4	Vermont	3
Maryland	10	Washington	11
Massachusetts	12	Wisconsin	11
Michigan	18		

If the 2000 election had been about who had greater support in the most square miles of the country, George Bush (and, in 2016, Donald Trump) would have been the winner by a long shot. (In the 2000 election, Bush won 2,463 counties, compared to Gore's 675.) If the election had been about who won the greatest number of votes, regardless of where they're located, Al Gore (and, in 2016, Hillary Clinton) would have been declared the winner.

Al Gore's margin of victory in the popular vote was 3 percent. That may not seem like much, but it's much larger than other presidential contests have had. In 1960, John Kennedy defeated Richard Nixon by 303 to 219 electoral votes. Even though the electoral votes weren't close in 1960, Kennedy defeated Nixon by only 112,881 popular votes. Kennedy's margin of victory was only one-tenth of 1 percent.

George W. Bush didn't win the popular vote, and his electoral vote margin was razor thin, but he did carry 30 of the 50 states. Part of the original justification for the creation of the electoral college was to guarantee that a successful presidential candidate must build a broad base of support around the country — and Bush did that.

In the 2016 presidential election, the margin of victory in the electoral college was much larger. Donald Trump received 33 more electoral votes than George W. Bush and carried one more state. What is remarkable is how much larger the popular vote was for the losing candidate. How did a candidate fail to be elected when she received almost 3 million more votes?

The answer is that the United States elects its president and vice president indirectly, by way of the electoral college.

Examining the Electoral College's Messy History

The Founding Fathers of the United States were the ones who set up the current electoral college (although it's had some changes since then). The electoral college was established to elect a president and vice president in a nation that, at the time:

>> **Was composed of 13 large and small states,** jealous of their own rights and powers and suspicious of a central government.

>> **Had a population of about 4 million people,** spread over more than a thousand miles along the east coast, with little or no communication or transportation.

>> **Had a population of approximately 700,000 slaves** — individuals who of course had no voting rights yet counted as three-fifths of a person when it came to determining electoral college votes. (This had the effect of ceding more political power to slaveholding states.)

In addition, the national mood discouraged the formation of political parties, and people believed that gentlemen didn't campaign for public office.

The Founding Fathers considered and rejected several other alternatives to electing the president and vice president, such as having Congress or — since they lacked confidence in Congress — even the state legislatures elect them. Direct popular election was rejected because the Founding Fathers feared that insufficient information would cause voters to choose *favorite sons* (favorite candidates from their home states), and no candidate would have a popular majority sufficient to govern the country.

Looking at other controversial elections

In the course of the 200 years of the electoral college's existence, several remarkable elections have taken place that people on either side of the debate regarding the fairness of the electoral college point to as support for their arguments.

Under the first design of the electoral college, electors could cast two distinct votes for president, and whoever emerged as the runner-up would become the vice president. The problem with this system became apparent in the election of 1800. The electors of the Democratic–Republican Party (the dominant party of the time) gave Thomas Jefferson and Aaron Burr (both members of that party) an equal number of electoral votes, even though the party had specified that they wanted Jefferson as president and Burr as vice president. The tie was decided for Jefferson by the House of Representatives, but only after 36 votes and many political deals. The Congress and the states adopted the 12th Amendment in 1804 to deal with any similar future occurrences — it requires that each elector cast one vote for president and a separate vote for vice president.

The next controversial election occurred in 1824. That year, John Quincy Adams, Andrew Jackson, William Crawford, and Henry Clay ran for president. Each of these men represented an important faction of the dominant Democratic–Republican Party. They divided the electoral vote, so no one received the necessary majority to become president.

The 12th Amendment requires that the House of Representatives select the president from the top three contenders, with each state casting one vote and an absolute majority being required to elect. The House narrowly chose John Quincy Adams over Andrew Jackson, although Jackson had received the greater popular vote. This election is often cited as the first example of the candidate with the larger popular vote (Jackson) not becoming president. This argument is a difficult one to make, though, because 6 of the 24 states in that election chose their electors in their state legislatures rather than by popular vote. New York, whose population was considerable even then, was one of those states. Therefore, the real popular vote was difficult to calculate. (By 1836, every state but South Carolina chose electors by direct popular vote of the whole state. South Carolina eventually came around to this method in 1860.)

It's well worth noting the significant parallels between the election of 1824 and the election of 2000. John Quincy Adams' father, John Adams, was a two-term vice president and a one-term president. George W. Bush's father, George H. W. Bush, was a two-term vice president and a one-term president. Andrew Jackson failed to carry his home state of Tennessee in the 1824 election, just as Al Gore failed to carry his home state of Tennessee in 2000! One other interesting note: When the contest between John Quincy Adams and Andrew Jackson was replayed in 1828, Andrew Jackson defeated John Quincy Adams.

The next dramatic election occurred in 1876. Much had happened since 1824, including a devastating civil war. *Reconstruction,* the process under which the federal army occupied the South after the Civil War, caused dramatic changes to traditional voting patterns, as did the economic depressions of 1867, 1869, and 1873. The Democratic Party nominated Samuel Tilden, governor of New York, as president and Thomas Hendricks of Indiana as vice president. The Republicans nominated Rutherford Hayes, governor of Ohio, and William Wheeler of New York. Third parties were also active. On election night, it appeared that Tilden had won, although South Carolina, Louisiana, and — you guessed it — Florida were undecided. Each of these states delivered *two* competing sets of electoral votes to Congress — one for Tilden and one for Hayes. Congress established a 15-member commission to decide which votes to count for each state. The upshot was that, after much political intrigue, Hayes was elected president, even though Tilden won the popular vote.

The dealmaking required to ensure the presidency for Hayes brought about an end of the US army's occupation of the South as well as the adoption of policies on the part of the federal government that removed all remaining barriers to the imposition of a system of brutal segregation in the South. In 1887, Congress enacted legislation making each state the final authority on the legality of its electors and requiring a concurrent majority of both houses of Congress to reject any electoral vote. The events of 1876 never happened again.

Benjamin Harrison's election in 1888 is the classic example of the majority in the electoral college being contrary to the outcome of the popular vote. The incumbent Democrat, Grover Cleveland, won by large majorities in the states that supported him. Benjamin Harrison carried his states with slender majorities. In consequence, Harrison was elected with an electoral majority, but with less popular support than the losing Cleveland. (Cleveland ended up with 48.6 percent of the vote, whereas Harrison had only 47.8 percent.)

Gauging the impact of the electoral college

As interesting as the history of the electoral college may be, you should remember that it isn't some dusty historical relic; it has a profound impact on the way campaigns are run today and on the messages that candidates present to voters. The history determines where candidates devote their time and money when it comes to state-by-state battlefields. Without the electoral college, candidates would concentrate on media markets where they could reach the maximum number of voters. The major megalopolises of America would receive far greater attention. An area like greater New York City, which has almost 24 million people, would receive considerably more attention than most entire states. Instead, New York is a center for fundraising but not campaigning because it is a state which votes for the Democratic candidate for president consistently.

The system forces candidates to appeal to those states which hold the balance of power in the electoral college. The balance of power is in the hands of those states which are not predictable in presidential elections —states which are trending one way or the other, in other words. In 2020 those states include: Pennsylvania, Ohio, Michigan, Minnesota, Wisconsin, Florida, Nevada, Virginia, North Carolina, and Arizona.

Arguing for the electoral college

Those individuals who support the status quo — the "it ain't broke, so don't fix it" group — argue the following points:

>> **The electoral college contributes to political stability in the United States by encouraging only a two-party system.**

The winner-takes-all nature of the state-by-state election encourages the parties to move toward the middle ground ideologically. It virtually forces political movements that could result in the formation of third parties into the main political parties in order to have any hope of electoral success. It also moderates the views of these third parties to make them acceptable to one of the major parties. In other words, political parties under a two-party, winner-takes-all system tend to become large tents embracing many different, and sometimes inconsistent, views. Accommodations to different positions are negotiated within the parties more than in the government.

>> **The electoral college increases the power of states.**

States and their boundaries play important roles in a national campaign. It's not enough for a candidate to run up huge margins of votes in metropolitan areas. To be elected president, a candidate must have a strategy to win 270 electoral votes. Winning California by 10 million votes doesn't do a candidate any more good than winning it by a single vote (except that it avoids a recount!). A candidate must build a national following to be successful. Having that national following makes it easier for a candidate to govern as president after the election. Regional appeals aren't sufficient for victory because no region of the country contains enough electoral votes alone to elect a president. Even a candidate who fails to win the popular vote must have obtained a good amount of the popular vote, and that vote is distributed across the country. Of course, some states vote repeatedly for one or another of the parties in presidential election. Because of their consistency in voting patterns, campaigns feel free to ignore these states, either because they are sure to win or because they are certain to lose those predictable states.

Arguing against the electoral college

Critics of the electoral college argue the following three main points:

> » **The electoral college hinders true democracy by limiting the numbers of parties that are able to compete effectively in presidential elections.**
>
> Many parties field candidates, but they seldom win any electoral votes and are more likely to be spoilers than to win outright. In 2016, Donald Trump won Michigan by fewer than 11,000 votes, whereas 275,851 votes were cast for third-party candidates and independents who had no chance of election.

> » **The electoral college allows candidates to take states for granted when the voters in those states vote consistently for one party in national elections.**
>
> *Winner-takes-all* means that 50 percent plus one vote is all a candidate needs in any state to win all of the state's electoral votes, with the exception of Maine and Nebraska. Because the margin of victory is irrelevant in the electoral college, neither candidate spends time courting votes in states where the outcome is certain.

> » **The winner-takes-all nature of state elections renders some votes for president essentially meaningless.**
>
> For instance, a Democratic voter in Indiana, a state that consistently votes Republican for president, or a Republican in Illinois, which consistently votes Democratic for president, essentially has no voice in the election of the president. Their state will give all its electoral votes to the other candidate, and the size of the nationwide popular vote doesn't affect the outcome of the election.

Critics of the electoral college don't end there, though. In addition to the main arguments in the previous list, critics argue that

> » **The electoral college depresses voter turnout in presidential elections because voter turnout is irrelevant to the number of electoral votes a state has.**
>
> For example, New Mexico has five electoral votes, even if only five citizens vote in the general election. (Of course, other elections take place at the same time — governor, senator, legislative, and county offices — and those can be turnout-dependent.)

> » ***Rogue electors* are always possible.**
>
> These are electors who are pledged to vote for one candidate but who actually vote for another. A number of states don't have laws requiring

electors to honor their pledges, and if only three electors had switched from Bush to Gore in 2000, Gore would have been elected. In 2016, ten electors voted for a candidate other than the one for whom they were pledged to vote, but the outcome was not changed.

>> **The distribution of electoral votes by state tends to overrepresent votes in rural states at the expense of voters in urban ones.**

For instance, the combined voting-age population of Vermont, Wyoming, Alaska, South Dakota, New Hampshire, Delaware and North Dakota is approximately 5.5 million. Each of these states is so scarcely populated that they have only one representative each. However, both have two senators. So, these states have three electoral votes apiece for a combined electoral vote of 21 electoral votes. In contrast, Wisconsin has a population roughly the same, and it has only 10 electoral votes. In fact, the 27 smallest states in terms of population have 98 electoral votes between them. Combined, these 27 states have a population approximately the size of California, which has 54 electoral votes. Obviously, votes cast in rural states for president have more weight in the electoral college.

Changing the Electoral College

Changing the electoral college requires either a constitutional amendment passed by a two-thirds vote of Congress and ratification by three-quarters of the state legislatures or action in all 50 states. Given that seven small states would see their electoral impact diminished by change, it would be difficult to pass. Approximately 700 bills have been introduced in Congress over the last 200 years to change the electoral college and none has succeeded.

The smaller states also realize that changing the electoral college could open discussion about the disproportional weight given to states with smaller populations in the Senate. For example, Wyoming routinely casts a little more than one-quarter of a million votes for presidential candidates in the general election, and New York casts more than 30 times that number. Both states have two, and only two, senators in the US Senate. In other words, the vote of a voter in New York for senator is worth $1/30$ of the vote of a voter from Wyoming — or North Dakota, Alaska, Montana. . . . You get the picture.

Despite the fact that smaller states are in a position to essentially block electoral college reform, you'll still find proposals put forward that are meant to change the way Americans elect their presidents. One proposal involves direct election with *instant-runoff voting*, or IRV. Voters would rank their choices in order of preference. Ballots are counted for each voter's first choice. If a candidate gains a majority, that candidate wins. If no candidate receives a majority, the candidate with the fewest votes is eliminated. The voters who selected the losing candidate as their first choice then have their votes added to the total of their next choice. This continues until a candidate has a majority. This system is used in several countries and in the state of Maine for congressional elections.

The other alternative to the electoral college is quite in line with the US system of democracy. Rather than use the electoral college, people simply vote for candidates, and whoever gains a majority wins. Sounds simple, right? Not quite. Because this system allows multiple candidates to run, one candidate may have a difficult time getting more than 50 percent of the national vote. If a majority were required for election, runoff elections would then have to be held between the top vote-getting candidates from the first race, or instant-runoff voting would need to be implemented because the cost and difficulty of having more than one national election every four years might be prohibitive.

All these proposals would require a constitutional amendment — a long row to hoe, practically speaking. One suggestion for reform that doesn't require a constitutional amendment is the National Popular Vote Interstate Compact, or NVIP.

Sixteen states have signed on to NVIP. This compact is an agreement by these states to cast their electoral votes for the candidate who wins the popular vote nationwide. This compact has one caveat: The total number of electoral votes belonging to states that join the compact must surpass 270 — the number needed for victory — if it is to take effect. With the addition of Oregon in June 2019, the total electoral votes for states signing is 196, or about 75 votes short of the total needed to activate the compact. All the states that have signed the compact are Democratic states that voted for the losing Democratic candidates in 2000 and 2016.

THE RUSSIANS AND US ELECTIONS

There has been much discussion of Russian attempts to infiltrate the US election system in the 2016 election and whether these attempts are continuing. The two issues that leaders of both parties agree on are the need to modernize our voting machines to provide better security and to create a paper trail of any ballots cast. Unfortunately, a great deal of money will have to be spent to accomplish both objectives.

IN THIS CHAPTER

» **Presidential campaigns**

» **Researching the candidates**

» **Graduating to the electoral college**

» **Does your state swing?**

» **Volunteering for the presidential campaign**

Chapter **23**

Filling Some Really Big Shoes: Electing a President

The conventions are over. The Democratic and Republican parties have their nominees for president and vice president. If a third-party or independent candidate is running for president, their name is on the ballot in at least some of the 50 states as well. The preliminaries are over. The campaign has begun. But you still have time to get involved in the process.

The presidential election campaign involves every corner of this country. Some corners are more important in the strategy than others. (See my discussion of strategy later in this chapter, in the section "The Electoral College and You.") But, because the election is national, you have plenty of opportunities to get involved, if you want to. You also have many ways to become more knowledgeable about the process. You'll cast an informed vote if you do, and you'll be able to impress your friends at with your political savvy.

Contributing to the Nominee

Since 2008, major party nominees for president have refused federal funds for their campaigns. Raising money is now more important than ever to presidential nominees, as evidenced by the $2.4 billion spent by Donald Trump and Hillary Clinton in 2016. Believe it or not, even with that amount of money, campaigns need to make choices on how and where to spend. (See Chapter 14 for more on the role money plays in politics.)

If you're so disposed, you can contribute directly to the candidate of your choice. The maximum amount you can give directly was established by Congress in 2002 but is adjusted for inflation at the start of each new election cycle. For the 2019–2020 cycle, the maximum amount you can give a presidential, senatorial, or congressional candidate is $2,800 for the primary and $2,800 for the general election.

You can give to national party committees in much larger amounts. The limits for individual contributions to national parties is $35,500, in case you have a lot of loose change you don't need! Those contributions help the parties raise additional *soft money*, which they use to fund the campaign in a presidential election year. In the 2016 election cycle, the Democratic National Committee (DNC) raised $344.6 million in soft money. The Republican National Committee (RNC) raised $320.1 million in soft money.

CHANGING THE TONE

If you're tired of the ultrapartisanship of US politics and US government, and if you think it's time for civility and compromise in both areas, good people have to become involved. At times in the country's history, men and women (mostly men) worked in Congress for laws that served the common good. They worked within a set of rules and customs. Elected officials in opposing parties were polite to each other, and they crafted legislation from facts that were generally accepted. Personal attacks and lies weren't tolerated. Much of that has changed in recent years. People demean their opponents' appearance and dispute what would be recognized by most people as fact. If you're discouraged by the political climate, ask yourself whether it's time for you to get involved. Sitting on the sidelines won't bring about the change you want.

Soft money is money contributed to state and national political parties that the parties can use for the election of their candidates. Parties aren't limited in the amount of soft money they can raise, but they are limited in how they can spend soft money. The Federal Election Commission (FEC) establishes rules for political parties about how they can spend it. Soft money can't be contributed directly to any federal candidate, because it's not federally qualified money. It may include corporate or labor union dues money or contributions from individuals or PACs in excess of the federal limit on contributions. Soft money cannot be used to promote a specific candidate, but it can be used for party-building activities like registration drives and get-out-the-vote efforts.

Shaping a Candidate's Message

Fundraising has become increasingly important as candidates have abandoned federal funding and the restraints that came with it, but the message of the candidate is every bit as important. By the time the conventions conclude, the candidates have polled and used focus groups extensively. (See Chapter 15 for more on polls and focus groups.) The nominees for president are just as eager to know which issues you care most about as the candidates for the House of Representatives, the Senate, and the state legislature are.

In 2016, Donald Trump adopted the slogan "Make America Great Again." He began using the slogan on November 7, 2012, the day after Barack Obama won reelection. Ronald Reagan used the phrase "Let's make America great again" in his 1980 campaign, but, as Trump observed, Ronald Reagan did not trademark the phrase. Also in 2012, Trump signed an application with the United States Patent and Trademark Office requesting exclusive rights to use the slogan for political purposes. He used the slogan in speeches and on social media using the hashtags #makeamericagreatagain and #maga. The slogan was also printed in white letters on red baseball caps. These caps became so important to the campaign that, at one point, the campaign spent more on making the caps, which were sold for $25 each, than on polling, consultants, or commercials. The hashtags were also quite successful in driving traffic to Trump's Twitter account, a platform he had already established back in 2009. In fact, Trump himself credits social media for his eventual victory in the 2016 election. In one of his more celebrated tweets after the election, he stated, "I won the 2016 election with interviews, speeches, and social media."

The MAGA slogan tapped into fears felt by many Americans that their country was changing in ways they could not understand and did not like. With the increasing diversity of the population in America and the amount of social change and economic inequality that had occurred in recent years, the phrase "Make America

Great Again" resonated with people who thought that a return to the "old" America was desirable.

Finding the right message and sticking with it are critical to a campaign's success. Candidates have to repeat their message over and over and over again until they almost gag when they speak it. Donald Trump repeated his slogan in every speech and continually on social media. Barack Obama used the slogan "Change we can believe in" and the chant "Yes we can." Only with constant repetition can a candidate's message penetrate the barrage of information that the voting public receives each and every day.

Identifying issues in your region

Much effort and energy is expended by campaigns in order to come up with a message that will resonate with the electorate. One strategy in deciding on such a message is based on determining which issues are uppermost in voters' minds. Here's where polls and focus groups come in, because both can alert the nominees to specific issues of importance in different regions around the United States. For example, grazing on federal land may be an important issue in Wyoming and Montana. If it is, any presidential nominee campaigning in those states had better be prepared to answer questions about it. Grazing on federal land isn't an issue in Florida, but immigration, federal disaster relief in hurricane season, or climate change may be.

Keeping candidates abreast of change

Candidates must continually evaluate their messages and whether they're getting through. If candidates aren't flexible enough to change their messages when such an action is warranted, they'll lose.

POLITICAL STUFF

An example of how key issues can reinforce an election strategy is the 2012 presidential election between Barack Obama and Mitt Romney. Early on, the Obama campaign began characterizing Mitt Romney as a superwealthy person who looked down on those with fewer resources. Rather than attempting to change the characterization of Romney as an elitist, the Romney campaign actually assisted the Obama campaign in making this case to the voters: His proposed tax plan would have lowered taxes on the wealthy and raised them on the middle class. Paul Ryan, Romney's choice as his vice president, was someone who wanted to reduce funding for food stamps, Medicaid, and Medicare. Perhaps the most dramatic mistake was Mitt Romney's own statement at a fundraiser saying that he didn't care about the 47 percent of Americans who didn't pay federal income tax and were supposedly government dependent to boot. "My job is not to worry about those people.

I'll never convince them they should take personal responsibility and care for their lives." he said. That statement was recorded on a cellphone by a worker at the event and posted on a website with devastating results.

Rather than refining his message to demonstrate he was a regular guy who cared about working people and those who need assistance, Romney 's refusal to change his message reinforced the Obama campaign to show Romney as out of touch with average citizens.

Acknowledging that the primary message may not be the final message

Just as leaves change color in autumn, the message that candidates for the party nomination communicate to primary voters or caucus participants in their own party may not be the same message they need to use in the fall campaign.

To win the nomination of either major party, a candidate has to give the party regulars something to be excited about. In each party, that attempt pushes the candidate to one end of the political spectrum or the other. The pressure on Democratic candidates pushes them to be more liberal; for Republicans, more conservative (that is, more liberal or more conservative than the voting population as a whole). They have to energize the true believers among the party faithful. They have to inspire these people to work for their nomination. The candidates have to respond to the party's pressure if they are to win the nomination, especially if they face opponents more extreme than they are. It's not surprising, therefore, that Mitt Romney selected a rather conservative message in the 2012 election. But the message that candidates use to win the nomination may not help them win the general election. In fact, the nomination message can actually hurt a candidate's chances for victory in November. A winning candidate in November has to be a consensus builder who inspires the confidence of a broad range of voters. These voters don't want candidates to take extreme stands on issues

POLITICAL STUFF

Campaign consultants urge candidates to say as little of substance as possible to win the nomination. The vaguer their positions on the issues they're asked about, the better. That way, the nominee isn't forced to explain an extreme position taken during the primary that may be received quite differently by a less partisan audience during the general election. After all, candidates can't be heard saying one thing to the party faithful during the nomination stage of the campaign and repudiating those same things later. Flip-flopping on an important issue can make a candidate seem indecisive to voters, at best, and a liar, at worst.

Neither do consultants want to be stuck in the general election with specific policy proposals offered to please the party faithful during the nomination fight. That's because specific proposals that may benefit one group of the population can have a negative effect on another. Suppose that the asphalt paving industry is a political contributor to one of the political parties. That industry may use its position as a party financial supporter to urge candidates to favor road construction in their platform. Road construction isn't unpopular with the voters, so that particular commitment doesn't present much of a risk. But suppose that the industry wants more. It wants support for construction of a specific road. The route for the road in question winds through an area that environmentalists argue would have explicitly negative environmental consequences. The environmental community strongly opposes building the road. It addition, the location of the proposed route itself is a source of controversy. Two communities are competing to have the road within their boundaries, but only one can win the competition. Obtaining the necessary funding for the road may mean that the state who wins the competition will have to raise gasoline taxes. Those gas taxes will affect all drivers, including those who care not a lick about whether the road at issue is ever built. You begin to see the dilemma. Although general support of road-building by a candidate is relatively risk-free, the more specific the proposal, the more the candidate risks alienating other groups of potential supporters. Environmentalists, voters in the city or town that fails to get the route, and voters who resent higher gas taxes may all take issue with the candidate's position. You get the picture. The more specificity, the greater the risk. So campaign consultants try to package the most plain-vanilla message they can on the issues and concentrate on other things.

When candidates discuss and define the issues, with input from voters, they can generate a national consensus about an issue or a problem. When a national consensus forms, it's easier to enact the necessary laws to deal with the issue or problem. Voters become aware of the problem and agree that something needs to be done. That attitude on the part of voters helps to shape the legislative agenda in the states and in Washington.

Acquiring the Information You Need to Vote for President

You can make it a point to follow what the presidential candidates are saying about important issues. See if you can distinguish the differences in approach to problems among the candidates.

One way to tell the differences among candidates is to watch the presidential and vice presidential debates. These events provide you with a unique way to view the nominees in an extended give-and-take format on important issues. Watching one or more of these debates gives you a good opportunity to see what you like and dislike about the candidates and helps you become a more informed voter.

The media loves a presidential campaign

It's easier for you to gain information about presidential candidates and their positions than about candidates for less-visible offices because everything presidential candidates do is reported. They can't sneeze in a campaign without making the national news. Reporters follow presidential candidates like flies follow honey. They hang on the candidate's every word, hoping for a mistake or misstatement that will make a good news story. Presidential nominees can compete successfully with train wrecks and hurricanes for time on the national news.

Candidates for local offices or for Congress can call press conferences or release position papers during a campaign and receive little or no response from the press. This lack of media response is particularly true when the candidates are explaining their ideas on programs or policies that are important but not controversial. A well-used adage for television reporting is this: "If it bleeds, it leads." In other words, an item has to be gory or sensational to warrant television coverage. Releasing position papers may provide insight on a local or state candidate's views, but it isn't sexy or exciting, so it doesn't make it to the television news. Fortunately for these candidates — and even presidential candidates — social media can provide an inexpensive way to get the campaign message out. (See Chapter 9 for more on social media.)

Presidential nominees have all the media access they want and even some they don't. Virtually everything they do makes news. That gives the presidential nominees a distinct advantage over other candidates in making their case directly to you and other voters. The nominees may not always like the coverage they attract from the media, but at least they can't complain that they don't receive enough coverage.

Turning to nontraditional media: Can we talk?

Lately, candidates have been dissatisfied with the way the press reports their messages. They feel that traditional network news, political talk shows, and newspapers interfere with their ability to speak directly to voters — that reporters are too cynical. The response from the press is that candidates are annoyed because they can't hoodwink professional reporters. Whatever the reason, candidates are abandoning the old ways of doing things and are reaching voters more directly through social media.

One major advantage of a social media approach is that the candidates can reach you directly, without subjecting themselves to the questions or analysis of reporters. When it comes to regular TV and radio, however, it gets trickier. A number of candidates for president have used free television and radio while avoiding those reporters who might upset the messaging apple cart with an undesired question or two. Candidates have done that by way of appearances on late night television talk shows that emphasize entertainment rather than close political analysis and by granting interviews to networks having a political slant that favors them. Because such interviewers tend to be less hostile and more conversational than the national media, this method of communication ends up being easier on the candidates.

REMEMBER

In addition to social media platforms like Facebook and Twitter, any campaign worth its salt has set up websites that potential voters may visit in order to find out more about the candidate. These resources not only give detailed information about each candidate's issue positions but may also offer a way for you to figure out what their proposals mean for you — such as a function to figure out the tax break you may receive from a candidate's proposed tax cuts or whether such a proposal would have a negative impact on you.

REMEMBER

Nowadays, you have even more new-and-different ways to find out which candidate you're comfortable supporting. You may also have additional ways to get your questions in front of these candidates: You can call in or apply to be in the audience for talk shows. You can even contact the Commission on Presidential Debates, which hosts presidential and vice presidential debates in each cycle. The commission was established in 1987 as a nonpartisan nonprofit organization to ensure that general election debates are held between the candidates for the highest offices in the country. The commission sets the location and rules for these debates, and audiences are permitted. You can contact them to see whether you can be in the audience. The commission has a recommended reading list for voters who want to increase their knowledge of presidential politics. You can contact the commission at

Commission on Presidential Debates
601 13th St. NW
Washington, DC 20005
202-872-1020
www.debates.org

The Electoral College and You

In most elections, the object is simply to draw more votes than any opponent. In fact, the object in most races is to attract 50 percent of the votes plus one more vote. A candidate who can do that wins the election. Every vote cast is equally important in coming up with that 50-percent-plus-one margin. This object under the US system is true in every election but one: the presidential election. The winner of a presidential election is almost always the person who receives the most votes — almost, but not always. That's because voters don't elect the president and vice president directly. Instead, the *electoral college* does the electing.

The Founding Fathers were leery of the passions of the populace — you and me. (Actually, the Founding Fathers weren't worried about women or minorities, because, at the time, women and minorities couldn't even vote.) The electoral college was created in part to make the presidential selection less direct than a simple popular vote. Voters are no longer concerned about why the electoral college was created. The fact is that it's there, and it has an impact on the way campaigns for the presidency are run. (See the "Large versus small states" sidebar, later in this chapter, for more information on the reasons behind the electoral college. For a more complete discussion of its place in history, the pros and cons of the system, and how it affected the 2000 and 2016 presidential election, see Chapter 22.)

The road to 270 electoral votes

To understand the fall election strategy, you need to understand exactly how you elect the president and vice president. Every four years, in the presidential election year, you vote for a slate of electors. The *electors* elect the president and the vice president by casting *electoral votes* for the presidential candidate who carries their state. (Nebraska and Maine are the exceptions that prove the rule here, in that they award their electoral votes proportionally.)

So, rather than hold one national election for president, the United States holds 51 separate presidential elections (the 50 states and the District of Columbia). A candidate must win enough of these 51 separate contests to supply the magical 270 electoral votes.

POLITICAL STUFF

A state's quantity of electoral votes is determined by how many seats it holds in Congress. Each state gets two electors to parallel its two senators, plus one for each member of the House of Representatives. The District of Columbia also gets three electors. Winning the election is all about getting a majority of the 538 electoral votes that are cast. In 2016, a candidate for president could lose 39 states and the District of Columbia and still win — that is, if the 11 states they won were the

11 most populous: California, New York, Texas, Florida, Pennsylvania, Illinois, Ohio, Michigan, New Jersey, North Carolina, and Georgia. Of course, the 11 most populous states don't all vote the same way. Some traditionally vote Republican and some traditionally vote Democratic and some are swing states and can go either way.

The states determine how their electors are assigned. Almost every state uses a winner-takes-all system in which the candidate with the most votes wins all the electors. (Again, the only exceptions are Maine and Nebraska.) In other words, whichever candidate receives the most votes, even if not a majority (as might be the case in a tight three-way race), wins all of that state's electoral votes. A candidate who comes in a very close second in most states wins no electoral votes. A candidate can receive 49.9 percent of the votes cast in a state and have nothing to show for it.

The winner-takes-all electoral college rules have a big impact on how the candidates conduct themselves in the fall campaign. They must always ask themselves where they can do the most good when it comes to gaining electoral votes. In states with strong competition between the candidates, the candidate may operate a grassroots campaign to register and turn out all possible voters who support the candidate.

POLITICAL MYTH

The idea that some votes cast are more important than others flies in the face of what voters believe a democracy is all about. But as things stand right now, the fact is that some votes are more and some votes are less important to the presidential candidates.

A vote cast to put a candidate over the top for a majority in one state is more important than a vote cast to give that same candidate 60 percent of the vote in another state or 40 percent of the vote in a third state. (Of course, in a three-person race, 40 percent of the vote might be enough to carry the state.) That's because the vote to put that candidate over the top for a majority also gives them that state's electoral votes. The vote to make their total more overwhelming is only icing on the cake. The vote to make their total 40 percent, but a losing 40 percent, doesn't matter in the larger scheme of things. The point is, a vote to give a candidate a majority is more important to that candidate than a vote to give him an overwhelming majority or a minority of the votes. Another way to say this is that, under the electoral system, some votes for president and vice president don't count. That may sound shocking, but it's true. If you're a Republican casting a vote for president in New York or a Democrat casting such a vote in Alabama, your votes for those offices are irrelevant to the outcome of the election.

The candidate versus the party

The need to develop winning margins in enough states to win an electoral majority drives the fall campaign. Candidates concentrate their resources and their campaigning in the states with large numbers of electoral votes — the swing states. A *swing state* is one that could go either way on election day. Candidates make only token appearances and devote only token resources to those states where they're sure to win or sure to lose.

Concentrating on swing states often puts the presidential campaigns at odds with state parties and with state and local candidates. When a presidential candidate is so popular in a state that they will carry it handily, the local candidates and the state party want that presidential candidate to come to their state often. A popular presidential candidate can energize the party workers and encourage some voters who might not vote to vote after all.

In states where a particular presidential candidate is almost certain to lose, the state party may still pressure the campaign to make appearances and to help in registering and turning out voters. The candidate may be unpopular with a majority of the voting population, but they will still have appeal to the party faithful.

POLITICAL STUFF

LARGE VERSUS SMALL STATES

The electoral college was a compromise between the large and small states and between the states and the federal government. Small states were guaranteed a minimum of three electoral votes to reflect their two senators and one congressperson. On the basis of population alone, some states would qualify for only one or two electors or perhaps none at all. Back then, state legislatures selected the electors in their states, according to their own rules, guaranteeing them a role in presidential selection. This method reassured the states that they were an important part of the national government.

Small states were given another advantage: If the electoral college doesn't award a majority of votes to any candidate, the election goes to the House of Representatives to be decided. Each state receives only a single vote at this stage of the process. That means California and Wyoming would have an equal say over the choice of a president, despite the fact that California has almost 40 million people and Wyoming has a little more than half a million. However, the House of Representatives never determined the president during the 20th or 21st centuries, so this source of inequality hasn't been a practical concern. That method was employed only twice in US history — in 1800 and again in 1824.

The candidate may not want to visit a state they can't win, but the local party people want them to visit. The size of the losing margin makes all the difference for victory or defeat for a party's statewide and local candidates. Their chances for victory are much better if the presidential candidate loses by a small rather than a large margin.

A Game of Strategy

When candidates decide where to spend their time and resources, they (and their campaign) look at two factors:

>> Where the electoral votes are

>> Which states are *one-party states* (that is, states whose electoral votes histori-cally are awarded only to Democrats or only to Republicans) and which are swing states (those whose historic voting records vary between Democratic and Republican)

For example, most Indiana voters vote for the Republican in virtually every presi-dential election. If a Democratic candidate for president carries Indiana, it's a landslide Democratic year. So Democratic nominees don't spend valuable time and resources trying to change history; they cede Indiana to their opponents. As for the Republican candidates, they have the luxury of taking Indiana for granted. They know they'll carry the state and win its 11 electoral votes, so they don't spend any money there, either.

Candidates put the most emphasis on some of the electoral-rich top 11 states. These states have demonstrated some ability to swing back and forth in their sup-port for the two parties in presidential elections. Exactly which states are swing states can change over time as the population of the states change. So many elec-toral votes are at stake in each of these states that candidates need to devote time and resources to them.

POLITICAL STUFF

Sometimes, the strength or message of a particular candidate causes a campaign to test whether historical trends will continue to hold true. Republican candidates for president enjoyed great support in the South in 1984 and 1988. No Southern state voted for the Democratic presidential candidate in 1984 or 1988. With the all-southern ticket of Bill Clinton and Al Gore, Democrats decided to take a run at the South in 1992. As a result of those efforts, Clinton carried five southern states. However, in the 2016 presidential election, history reasserted itself and the Republican's Trump–Pence ticket swept the southern states.

SWING STATES

After the campaigns in an election identify which states are swing states, they still have to decide which of these states to target. In 2020, several states may be swing states for the Republicans, and several others may be swing states for the Democrats:

- **For the Republicans:** New Hampshire, Minnesota, Nevada — all states that Hillary Clinton barely won

- **For the Democrats:** Wisconsin, Michigan, and Pennsylvania — all states that Donald Trump barely won

Each side analyzes a map of the country, state by state. After identifying the sure winners, the campaigns keep polling to make sure these states stay won. The sure losers are also listed. Candidates make no more appearances and spend no more resources in either of these categories than they absolutely must in order to keep the party from open rebellion. The states that are more difficult to predict are those whose populations are changing. Arizona, with increasing Hispanic populations, may be changing. Arizona elected a democratic US Senator in 2018. Donald Trump won Florida by a slight margin in 2016, but after hurricane Maria, tens of thousands of Puerto Ricans moved to Florida and are eligible to vote, which may have an impact on the election.

The game plan: Vote, and vote for me!

A campaign has to piece together a game plan to win 270 votes. The game plan must strive for a combination of electoral votes from one-party states and swing states. The candidate has to persuade swing state voters to take these two actions:

>> Turn out to vote on election day
>> Vote for them

When a candidate decides which swing states they can win and comes up with a game plan to do it, it's always a guess. Sure, polls and focus groups make those guesses educated ones, but they're guesses nonetheless. A campaign has to leave room for error.

A game plan can't target enough electoral votes to reach just 270 votes. It targets enough to reach, say, 300 or 325 votes. The extra votes can give the candidate a cushion if something happens in a target state, or if the candidate or the consultants guessed wrong about the ability to win one or more of the swing states.

You are the target

As soon as the campaign agrees on a game plan, the action begins. If you live in a swing state targeted by one or more of the candidates, you start to notice many visits by the candidates or their family members to your state. Presidential candidates give speeches and hold town meetings. Debates may be scheduled in your city. You see their commercials on your favorite television shows. You hear them on your radio programs. Ads appear on your tablet or cellphone.

You can be confident that the campaigns have set their sights on you. They'll do everything humanly and financially possible to convince you to vote and to vote a certain way. They're after you!

Candidates have decided that you hold the key to victory. The game plan has determined that you and others like you will decide the next presidential election. Rather than be bothered by all the attention, you should be flattered that you're so important. This opportunity presents the best chance for the citizens of your state to extract promises from the person who eventually will become president of the United States.

REMEMBER

The key is to remember that the strategy, the game plan, the trips, and the advertising are all designed to get your attention and your vote. The candidates are appealing to you — trying to win you over. You're a vital part of any presidential campaign. You can be even more important if you're willing to get involved, regardless of where you live.

Volunteer in a presidential campaign

Presidential campaigns offer ample opportunities for you to get involved as a volunteer. These campaigns use many volunteers because volunteers are free. The less a presidential campaign has to pay for staff, the more money it has to broadcast its message on television.

Volunteering in a swing state

If you have the time and the inclination to become more involved, and if you live in a swing state, you'll find almost endless ways to help out. Campaigns need

>> Hundreds of volunteers to build an enthusiastic crowd for cameras every time a presidential or vice presidential candidate visits

>> Volunteers to register voters so that they can vote on election day

>> Volunteers to call voters to persuade them to vote for your candidate

>> Volunteers to distribute literature

>> Volunteers to get the voters out to vote on election day

See Chapter 4 for more information on becoming a campaign volunteer.

Volunteering in a one-party state

If you're not in one of the key swing states targeted by a candidate's game plan, it's probably because your state's tradition of voting one way or another in presidential elections is too well established for campaigns to challenge.

TIP

If you want to help as a volunteer but don't live in a swing state, you can help circulate petitions to put your candidate on the ballot in the primary election (that is, if you live in one of the 41 states that has a primary for president). States require the signatures of a set number of registered voters before a candidate's name is placed on the ballot in the primary. Presidential campaigns are always hungry for volunteers willing to go door-to-door to obtain the necessary signatures in the early months of a presidential election year.

Qualifying in good order for the presidential primary in each affected state demonstrates how well organized a candidate is. On the other hand, if a candidate has to scramble to make the ballot, the media sees that as the mark of a disorganized or ineffective campaign. Bad news stories will be the result.

You can also volunteer to go to a swing state to work for a set period of time. Even a week or two can be a big help to overworked and understaffed campaign organizations in key swing states. If you have the time, energy, and inclination, go for it. It doesn't matter where you live — if you're willing to become involved, you can always find a place for yourself and the things you want to do.

REMEMBER

Just because your state isn't a swing state doesn't mean that you're less important as a voter. You'll still vote to elect all your state and local candidates. It's just that most of the voters in your state are too predictable in presidential elections — so much so that one side has written you off and the other side can afford to take you for granted.

7

The Part of Tens

Seeing what works — and what doesn't — in modern politics

Passing on the virtues of civic engagement to future generations

Figuring out where political campaigns go wrong

Relishing the political wisdom of the past

Chapter **24**

The Ten Commandments of Modern Politics

Politics, like many other areas of life, has ten commandments that people discover, periodically forget, and then (usually as the result of a scandal) spectacularly rediscover. These commandments are the tried-and-true realities of politics that apply wherever you are.

All Politics Is Local

Tip O'Neill, former Democratic speaker of the House of Representatives from Massachusetts, was famous for saying, "All politics is local." This quote aptly expresses the notion that all political campaigns are decided at the grassroots level by volunteers working with their neighbors and friends to encourage them to vote for a particular candidate.

You Can't Beat Somebody with Nobody

No matter how weak a well-known candidate is, that person still wins the election if their opponent is unknown and unfunded. It may not be fair, but a great candidate who is unknown is a nobody. A somebody candidate, no matter how unpopular, beats a nobody candidate every time.

Dance with the One That Brung Ya

After a candidate is elected, they must remember who helped them win. As soon as the candidate wins, many newfound friends want to become close to them to offer support and encouragement. They need to remember which individuals and groups were with them when they most needed them — before they were elected. They can't forget those people who were with them before being with them was popular. They need to dance with the ones that brung them.

Never Say Never

Candidates get into trouble all the time by taking absolute positions: The candidate won't run for a certain office. The candidate won't seek reelection. Read my lips: No new taxes. Over my dead body.

Politicians learn that situations change. Politicians learn to never say never.

The Three Most Important Ingredients in Politics: Money, Money, and Money

Robert Kennedy said it correctly: Money plays the most important role in modern politics. It's not only the most important factor but the second and third most important factors as well. Without money, any campaign is at a tremendous disadvantage. Money doesn't necessarily guarantee victory, but the absence of it certainly contributes to defeat. That's why the three most important ingredients in politics are money, money, and money.

It Ain't Over 'til It's Over

Politicians can win or lose elections in a matter of hours or days. Your mood and that of the other voters can change as the election approaches. A good candidate doesn't rest on poll results taken the week before the election, because their lead can evaporate. A good candidate campaigns hard right up until the time the polls close, not taking anything for granted. After all, it ain't over 'til it's over.

The Harder You Work, the Luckier You Get

Sometimes, people tell themselves that whether something happens is simply the luck of the draw. We say it's better to be lucky than smart. We're telling ourselves that our success or failure is the result of forces beyond our control. It doesn't matter what we do — luck or the lack of luck will determine the outcome.

Good politicians learn that luck, if there is such a thing, is a force over which you may have some control. The best way to ensure good luck in politics is to create it. The harder you work, the luckier you get.

The Best Defense Is a Good Offense

Attack ads are part of modern politics. If a candidate is sure that their opponent will attack them by way of the media, their usual approach is to attack the opponent first and put them on the defensive: The candidate goes negative on the opponent before the opponent can go negative on the candidate. After all, the best defense is always a good offense.

You're Never Too Far Ahead

Like the expression "You can never be too rich or too thin," you can never be too far ahead in a campaign. This statement fits with the commandment "It ain't over 'til it's over." A lead that looks insurmountable two weeks before an election can be overcome. Voters usually make their decisions early in the campaign, but with a scandal or a crisis, anything can happen. That's why no candidate can ever be too far ahead.

Most Political Wounds Are Self-Inflicted

If a candidate is wounded and begins receiving flak from the press or the electorate, they should look in the mirror before pointing a finger at an opponent or anyone else. If you have any doubt that most political wounds are self-inflicted, just ask one of these characters:

>> **Hillary Clinton** used the word *deplorables* to describe people not supporting her candidacy.

>> **Anthony Weiner,** who had been elected to Congress seven times before a sexually suggestive photo he sent to a woman was unearthed and publicized.

>> **Al Franken,** a former senator, groped several women and kissed them against their will, causing his resignation.

>> **Roy Moore,** a former chief justice of the Alabama Supreme Court and candidate of the US Senate, forgot that sex with a minor is unlawful.

Chapter **25**

Ten Things to Teach Your Children About Politics

You should tell your children some facts about politics. Who knows? Maybe some or all of it will sink in. Your kids may not look as though they're paying attention, but they'll probably remember. After all, someday, when you suddenly go from being the dumbest parent in the world to being okay (if only by comparison to the even dumber parents of your kids' friends), some of these points may have an impact on your children.

Voting Isn't Only Your Right — It's Your Duty

The first thing you need to know is that politics is not a sport for Monday morning quarterbacks. The very least that a democracy requires is for all responsible adults to familiarize themselves with the issues and the candidates and then cast informed votes in each election. Perhaps you've heard (or even said) some of the following statements:

» My vote doesn't make a difference.

» It doesn't matter who wins — the candidates are all the same.

>> I don't know the candidates.

>> Politicians are all corrupt.

>> I'm too busy.

>> I just don't want to get involved.

Excuses such as these just don't cut the mustard. Not one of them is a legitimate reason for not doing your duty, making your voice heard, and voting.

Public Service Is a Good and Honorable Profession

When you hear the talk show hosts and comedians complain about government bureaucrats, remember that many good people work for the government because they want to make the country a better place for us and our children. These people aren't paid much. Many people don't treat them well, either. When you meet a government employee who goes out of their way to help you or to be accommodating, don't forget to thank them and tell them that you appreciate their courtesy. Everyone likes to be appreciated, and government employees are no different from the rest of us.

Never Pin Your Future to the Outcome of the Next Election

If you decide to become active in politics yourself, that's fine and dandy. Just remember that politics is an uncertain profession. It's tough to know that your mortgage or rent payment is dependent on the outcome of an election. You need training and contacts outside politics to make certain that you can support yourself if the political tide goes against you or your candidate.

You also need some savings in the bank so that you don't have to call Mom and Dad to make the rent payment when you lose your job after you lose an election.

There's a relationship between financial security and political independence. This relationship doesn't mean that rich people always make better officeholders. It does mean that officeholders who don't fear temporary unemployment are more likely to do the right thing. That financial freedom permits officeholders to be true to their principles, even at the cost of reelection.

Never Trust Anyone Who Lies, Including a Politician

You've always been told to tell the truth. You've been told that little tiny lies are neither little nor tiny. You know that trust is a difficult thing to develop and an easy thing to lose. You expect people to trust you because they can count on you to be truthful. In turn, you should give your trust only to people who tell you the truth.

Don't trust anyone who lies to you. Politicians are no different from anyone else, so you should hold them to the same standard. If they lie about little things, they lie about big things, too. Also keep in mind that when someone lies, they aren't only disrespecting those to whom they lied, they're also revealing something about their character and about what you can expect from them in the future.

Democracy Is the Best System of Government

Democracy in the United States is *the* best example of representative government. Ever! People all over the world wish they had a system like the one in the States, where the majority rules with respect for the constitutional rights of a minority with whom they may disagree. That's why so many people want to immigrate to the States — they see a land of opportunity and safety and want those things for themselves and their families.

But someone is always complaining that the country is "falling off the wagon." When your grandfather was your age, people told him that the US experiment with democracy was going down the tubes. When your children are the age of your grandfather, people will tell them the same thing.

The system in the United States is the best, and it will continue to be the best as long as good people stay involved. That doesn't mean it can't be improved; it can and should be. For example, lawmakers need to restore the notion that representatives need to adopt laws that improve the country and not think only about their reelection campaign when voting. Lawmakers need to remember that the Founding Fathers thought that compromise was not a dirty word, but rather the key to a successful country. But it's still better than any other alternative. So don't listen to people who say that the country is on a slippery slope to decline and decay. Tell them that if they don't like how things are, they should stop wringing their hands and get busy making things what they could be.

Avoiding Politics Makes You More to Blame for Its Failures, Not Less

You can't refuse to participate in politics and then complain that politics is corrupt. If good people refuse to involve themselves in politics, who does that leave? If the situation needs to be improved, you have a responsibility to work to make it better. The system can be improved. No matter how tough a task reforming politics looks to be, the longest, toughest journey begins with a single step.

Learn the Facts and Form Your Own Opinions

Never trust anyone else to think for you. You owe it to yourself to find out the facts and draw your own conclusions. Don't let gimmicks and slogans prevent you from thinking an issue through and deciding what outcome is best for you and your community or country.

Just as you've learned not to accept at face value every advertisement you hear, don't accept at face value everything a candidate tells you. Ask for proof; ask what the other side says. Think for yourself. No one else can do it for you.

You Have to Wait 'til 18 to Vote, but You Don't Have to Wait 'til 18 to Help Others Vote Wisely

In the United States, generally the law recognizes that you have reached an awareness and maturity to be considered an adult at age 21. Intelligence, as we all know, isn't age related. Even though you may not be an adult legally, the 26th Amendment to the Constitution, authored by Birch Bayh, a Democrat from Indiana, permits you to vote at age 18. If you're not legally an adult, yet you can vote, what is magic about 18, you might ask? You have to wait until you're 18 to vote, because if you could vote earlier, the kid in your class who thinks William Henry Harrison played lead guitar for the Beatles could vote, too. (After that kid reaches 18, he still may think that, but *hopefully* he's reached a point in his life where he has enough awareness and maturity to make a sound decision in the voting booth.)

You don't have to wait until you're 18, though, to learn the facts, form your own opinions, and think for yourself. You can also use your energy and enthusiasm to work for the party or candidate of your choice. Find out what politics is all about by working on campaigns and gaining hands-on experience. If you're willing to work hard, you can make a difference before you're old enough to cast your first ballot.

Politicians Are Just Like the Rest of Us

The younger you are when you become involved in politics, the sooner you'll figure out that politicians are just people. Some of them are smart, and some of them are dumb. Some are honest; some aren't. Some may be brave, but others are simply cowards. Few, if any, are complete angels. They're people just like we are, with virtues and shortcomings. Many of them are worthy of your support, but some of them aren't and should be defeated. But just as you can't write off the whole human race because of a few bad people, you shouldn't write off politics because of a bunch of bad politicians.

When someone tries to tell you that all politicians are crooks, remind them that Thomas Jefferson, George Washington, Abraham Lincoln, Teddy Roosevelt, Harry S. Truman, Barbara Jordan, John Lewis, and Barack Obama were all politicians — good politicians. Sure, some others have come along who've dishonored the offices they've held. But many others have performed brilliantly and made us proud to be Americans. You shouldn't permit yourself to believe that all politicians are crooks because that may mean that only crooks will become politicians.

When Politicians Make You Promises, Make Sure You Want What They're Promising

Nikita Khrushchev, a famous politician in the former Soviet Union, once said, "Politicians are the same all over. They promise to build a bridge even where there is no river."

Listen when a politician makes promises. Ask yourself whether the person is promising to do what is right and good, not just for you but also for your community and country. Ask who has to give up something so that the politician can please those to whom they're making the promise.

One of the greatest things about the United States is that we're a country of many different backgrounds, religions, languages, and cultures united by our love for this nation of immigrants, this land of opportunity. We're all willing to make sacrifices to see this country grow and prosper. Be wary of politicians who promise that your government can constantly give you things without asking for anything in return. If something looks too good to be true, it generally is.

Chapter **26**

Ten Common Political Mistakes

I f politicians can do one thing for their own peace of mind — as well as for the good of the country — it's to learn from the mistakes of those who have come before them. Take a look at some of these common blunders, which seem to be repeated over and over again in the world of politics.

Believing That Anything Is Secret

In this day and age, nothing is secret. When tabloids pay money and publish the most sordid, intimate details of an official's private life, politicians had better start with the notion that everything about them is public information. When almost everyone has a cellphone with a camera and recorder, every eye roll, off-color remark, or grimace can become an item of record on the Internet.

Giving a Reporter an Interview "Off the Record"

A candidate should never give a reporter an interview that they aren't prepared to see on the front page of a newspaper. If the story is important enough, it'll be discussed. Sooner or later, other reporters or the candidate's opponents will figure out that the candidate is the source of the information. If they're not prepared to be associated with the story by name, they shouldn't talk at all.

Failing to Answer an Opponent's Attack

As much as a candidate wants their campaign to stay positive, the failure to answer an attack by their opponent can cause them to lose the election. Many voters who hear the attack without hearing the candidate's side will believe the attack. Voters may think the attack is true because of the lack of a response.

Promising Not to Run for Reelection

Candidates get ahead of themselves sometimes and make promises that later they don't want to keep. Take Teddy Roosevelt, for example. He became president when William McKinley was assassinated in 1901. After Roosevelt became the first vice president to succeed to the presidency and be elected in his own right, in 1904, he said that he wouldn't run again. In reliance on Roosevelt's announcement, William Howard Taft ran and won the election. When 1912 came around, Taft decided to run for reelection. He received commitments from Republicans to support him. After Taft had the Republican nomination for reelection sewed up, Roosevelt changed his mind and decided to run. Roosevelt's earlier promise, and subsequent change of heart, set in motion a series of events that cost the Republicans the White House. His change of heart meant that to run, Roosevelt had to run as a third-party candidate. So in 1912, Roosevelt ran on the Bull Moose ticket and split the Republican vote, permitting Democrat Woodrow Wilson to be elected and causing Republicans to lose the presidency.

Not Taking a Poll

In modern political campaigning, not taking a poll is political malpractice. The candidate must poll to see what's on the voters' minds, to know what issues voters want discussed. The candidate must know how the voters see them and their opponent.

Taking a Poll and Ignoring the Results

Even worse than not polling at all is polling and ignoring the results. If a poll tells the candidate that voters want them to discuss a particular topic and they don't do so, they're making a big political mistake. They have spent the money to take a professional political poll but aren't following the advice that the poll provides.

Not Knowing When to Retire

Perhaps the most common political mistake is not knowing when to bow out. Sometimes, politicians take polls that tell them they've been in office too long, and then they still run in one more election. It's much more fun to go out on a positive note by knowing when to say when.

Believing That Public Officials Can Have a Private Life

As Bill Clinton, Donald Trump, and countless others can attest, there's no such thing as a totally private life for any visible public official. Even activities that don't directly affect their public service will be the subject of press scrutiny and television talk-show speculation for visible elected officials.

Thinking That the Federal Treasury Is Your Piggy Bank

Just when you think you've heard it all, something happens to make you scratch your head and wonder what gets into people. You might think that people selected for cabinet positions would always have good judgment, but you would be wrong. Ben Carson was appointed to the Cabinet as secretary of Housing and Urban Development (HUD) by President Trump. Once in office, he spent $45,000 refitting his office, including $32,000 for a dining room table and $8,000 for a dishwasher. When the General Accounting Office (GAO) found that most of the expenditures violated the law, Secretary Carson, a multimillionaire, blamed his wife!

Failing to Follow the Strict Letter of the Law

As several would-be high-level Clinton appointees can testify, a potential appointee who submits their name for confirmation to the US Senate had better be sure that every *i* is dotted and every *t* is crossed in terms of compliance with federal employment and tax laws. Many high-level appointees of the federal government require a vote of the Senate to confirm their presidential appointment. Failing to pay Social Security taxes for domestic employees or hiring illegal aliens in a household can be a big political embarrassment, not to mention a good way to jeopardize the appointment, as has been the case for a number of nominees.

Failing to comply strictly with the law can also be an embarrassing problem for candidates. Ask Governor Pete Wilson of California, who made immigration a key issue in his campaign for the Republican presidential nomination, only to be embarrassed when it was revealed that someone employed by him and his former wife was an undocumented alien.

Chapter **27**

Ten (or so) Quotable Quotes

Over the years, politicians have given hundreds of thousands of speeches. Some of their most memorable quotes have survived long beyond their tenure in elected office. Here's some political rhetoric worthy of note.

On Politics

"It has been said that politics is the second oldest profession. I have learned that it bears a striking resemblance to the first." —Ronald Reagan

"Mothers all want their sons to grow up to be president, but they didn't want them to become politicians in the process." —John F. Kennedy

On Being President

"In America, any boy may become president, and I suppose that's just the risk he takes." —Adlai Stevenson

"When I take action, I'm not going to fire a $2 million missile at a $10 empty tent and hit a camel in the butt. It's going to be decisive." —George W. Bush

"My esteem in this country has gone up substantially. It is very nice now when people wave at me, they use all their fingers." —Jimmy Carter

"If I had to name my greatest strength, I guess it would be my humility. Greatest weakness, it's possible that I'm a little too awesome." —Barack Obama

"Being president is like being a jackass in a hailstorm: There's nothing to do but stand there and take it." —Lyndon Johnson

"Being president is like running a cemetery: You've got a lot of people under you and nobody's listening." —Bill Clinton

"I loved my previous life. I had so many things going. This is more work than in my previous life. I thought it would be easier." —Donald Trump

Did I Really Say That?

"I don't know whether it's the finest public housing in American or the crown jewel of the American penal system." —Bill Clinton on the White House

On Participation

"Yesterday is not ours to recover but tomorrow is ours to win or lose." —Lyndon Johnson

"The ballot is stronger than the bullet." —Abraham Lincoln

"One of the penalties for refusing to participate in politics is that you end up being governed by your inferiors." —Plato

"There are those who look at things the way they are, and ask why . . . I dream of things that never were, and ask why not?" —Robert Kennedy

On the Press

"I won't say the papers misquote me, but I sometimes wonder where Christianity would be today if some of those reporters had been Matthew, Mark, Luke, and John." —Barry Goldwater

"The media is, really, the word — I think one of the greatest of all terms I've come up with — is fake." —Donald Trump

Appendix

State ID Voting Requirements

Because federal law doesn't dictate voting requirements, each state has its own. This appendix offers an alphabetical list of what each state requires its citizens to take to the polls in order to prove identity and cast a ballot.

TIP

If you're unsure whether you're registered to vote, go to the Turbovote website at www.turbovote.org, which connects you to the portal for your state election authority. When you do that, you can see whether you're already registered, register online, or even change your address for your registration if you have moved. After you sign up with Turbovote, you'll get reminders of the dates of elections. When you use Turbovote to access your state portal, you can see any state-specific requirements to vote.

Some requirements are standard for all states. For example, you must be a citizen of the United States and a resident of the state where you're voting. You must be 18 years of age or older by the general election. (You can vote in a primary if you will be 18 by the time of a general election in November.)

Other requirements, such as the length of residency in the state, if any, or the proof you must show in order to prove your residency change from state to state.

Convicted felons are also treated in different ways for voting purposes. Some states require voting rights to be restored before convicted felons can have voting eligibility. In other states, it depends on the nature of the felony. Florida now permits voting by all ex-felons who have repaid fines and fees to the court. (Florida voters had approved Amendment 4 to permit all ex-felons to vote, but the legislature later passed a law requiring payment of back fines and fees for eligibility.) Ex-felons can ask a judge to waive financial obligations or convert them to community service. Florida has the highest number of people disenfranchised because of their criminal records. Virginia has a similar law, but permits the governor to restore the voting rights of ex-felons in individual cases, which has happened in more than 150,000 cases.

Most states also require that voters be of sound mind or, at least, not to have been deemed incompetent by a court of law.

The most recent changes in voting laws deal with the issue of voter identification. Thirty-five states now require some form of identification. Half that number require photo identification. Since these changes to voter identifications laws have led to significant changes in the voting process, it's useful to describe the requirements by state. The changes are in these categories:

>> **Strict voter ID requirements:** These require a voter to present an identification document that has a photo on it, such as a driver's license, state-issued identification card, military ID, or tribal IDs. A voter who doesn't have such an ID must vote on a provisional ballot and take steps after election day for it to be counted. For example, the voter may have to go to an election office within a few days after the election and present the required ID, or else the vote won't be counted.

>> **Non-strict voter ID requirements:** These states permit voters to cast a ballot that can be counted without further action by the voter. For example, the voter can sign an affidavit of identity, or a poll worker can vouch for the voter. In Colorado, Florida, Montana, Oklahoma, Rhode Island, Utah, and Vermont, voters without photo ID can vote a provisional ballot, which election officials will later review for validity. In New Hampshire, a letter is sent to anyone who signed a challenged voter affidavit, and the recipient must confirm that they live at the address indicated on the affidavit. Sometimes, these categories can overlap.

REMEMBER

Each state's requirements for identification in order to vote are different, as are the consequences of not presenting a valid form of identification. Some states don't require registered voters to present proof of ID at the polls. Some states recognize religious exemptions to photo ID requirements. Those states are

Arkansas, Indiana, Kansas, Mississippi, South Carolina, Tennessee, Texas, and Wisconsin. Indiana and Tennessee have an exemption for being indigent. If you have a reasonable impediment to obtaining an ID, you're exempt in South Carolina, North Carolina, and Texas. Voters who are victims of domestic abuse, sexual assault, or stalking and have a confidential listing are exempt in Wisconsin.

I've listed here the requirements by state for identification at the polls.

Alabama: Non-strict photo ID

>> Current Alabama driver's license or Alabama ID card

>> Current photo ID issued by another state or the federal government

>> Current US passport

>> Current government employee ID with photo

>> Current student or employee ID issued by a college or university in the state

>> US military ID

>> Current tribal ID with photo

>> If no acceptable ID is presented, the voter must cast a provisional ballot and then bring required ID to an election office by 5 p.m. on the Friday after the election. Note the exception, however: If two election officials sign affidavits that they know the voter, the ballot is counted.

Alaska: Non-photo

>> Official voter registration card

>> Birth certificate

>> Passport

>> Hunting or fishing license

>> Current utility bill, bank statement, paycheck, government check, or another government document with the voter's name and address

>> Without ID, the voter casts a provisional ballot unless an election official waives the requirement because the official knows the voter.

Arizona: Non-photo

>> Valid Arizona driver's license

>> Valid Arizona ID card

>> Tribal enrollment card or another form of tribal ID

>> Utility bill dated within 90 days of the election

>> Valid Arizona vehicle registration

>> Indian census card

>> Property tax statement

>> Vehicle insurance card

>> Recorder's certificate

>> Without ID, a voter must vote a provisional ballot, which is counted only if the voter provides the ID to the county recorder by 5 p.m. on the fifth business day after a general election with a federal office on the ballot or by 5 p.m. on the third business day after any other election.

Arkansas: Non-strict photo ID

>> Driver's license

>> Photo identification card

>> Concealed handgun carry license

>> Employee badge or ID issued by an accredited postsecondary educational institution in Arkansas

>> US military ID

>> Public assistance ID card if containing photo

>> Voter ID card

>> If no acceptable ID is presented, the voter must cast a provisional ballot accompanied by a sworn statement of eligibility. The ballot is counted unless the county board of election commissioners determines that it's invalid. The voter can also take ID to the commissioners or the county clerk by noon on the Monday following the election.

California: Non-photo

>> If you have voted before and your name is on the roster of voters, you're asked for your name and address; the poll worker repeats it back to you and you sign. Nothing else is required.

>> If it's your first time voting and you registered by mail without giving your California driver's license or state ID number or the last four digits of your Social Security number, you may need to show a photo ID — driver's license or state ID — or a paycheck, utility bill, or government document that shows your name.

Colorado: Non-strict photo ID

>> Colorado driver's license

>> Colorado Department of Revenue ID card

>> Employee card with photo issued by the US government or Colorado state government or subdivision

>> Pilot's license

>> US military ID with photo

>> Current utility bill, bank statement, government check, paycheck, or another government document showing the name and address of the voter

>> Medicare or Medicaid card

>> Certified copy of birth certificate

>> Certified documentation of naturalization

>> Without ID, the voter can cast a provisional ballot. An election official shall attempt to verify that the voter is eligible.

Connecticut: No Photo

>> Social Security card

>> Any other preprinted form of ID that shows the voter's name and one of the following: the voter's address, signature, or photo

>> If no acceptable ID is presented, the voter can sign a state form and provide name, residence, and date of birth and sign under penalty of false statement that the voter is the person whose name appears on the official list.

Delaware: Non-Photo ID

» Delaware driver's License or state ID

» US passport

» Signed polling place or Social Security card

» Signed vehicle registration

» A similar document which identifies the person by photo or signature

District of Columbia: No Photo

» If you have voted before, you don't have to present ID.

» If you're a first-time voter, you need to provide a current driver's license or the last four digits of your Social Security number or a state-assigned unique number.

Florida: Non-strict photo ID

» Florida driver's license or Florida ID

» US passport

» Debit or credit card

» Military, student, neighborhood association, or retirement center ID

» Public assistance ID

» License to carry a concealed weapon or firearm

» Employee ID issued by the federal, state, county, or municipal government

» If a picture ID doesn't contain the signature of the voter, an additional ID that provides the signature is required.

» If no acceptable ID is presented, a provisional ballot is issued. The canvassing board determines the validity of the ballot.

Georgia: Strict photo ID

>> Georgia driver's license, even if expired

>> ID issued by Georgia or the federal government

>> Voter ID card issued by the state or county

>> Valid employee ID with photo from the federal, state, county, municipality, board, authority, or another entity in Georgia

>> Valid US military ID

>> Valid tribal ID

>> If no acceptable ID is presented, voters cast a provisional ballot and have three days after the election to present appropriate photo ID at the county registrar's office for the vote to be counted.

Hawaii: Non-strict photo ID

>> Valid driver's license of state ID

>> Current utility bill, bank statement, paycheck, or another government-issued document showing name and address

>> If no acceptable ID is presented, the voter is asked for their date of birth and address, to corroborate the information in the poll book.

Idaho: Non-strict photo ID

>> Idaho driver's license or ID card

>> Passport

>> ID card, with photo, issued by the US government

>> Tribal ID with photo

>> Student ID, with photo, issued by a high school or an accredited institution of higher education in Idaho

>> Concealed carry license

>> If no acceptable ID is presented, the voter completes an affidavit under penalty of perjury, providing name, address, and signature.

Illinois: No photo

>> If you have voted before, no ID is necessary.

>> If you're a new voter who didn't have to provide proof of ID to register, you may be required to present ID at the polls.

>> Acceptable ID for new voters includes

- Current and valid photo ID
- Utility bill, bank statement, government check, or paycheck
- Lease or contract for residence
- Student ID and mail addressed to voter's residence
- Government document

>> If no acceptable ID is presented, a provisional ballot is cast if the voter declares that they're registered and eligible to vote.

Indiana: Strict photo ID

>> ID must be issued by the state of Indiana or the US government and must show the name of the individual to whom it was issued and must conform to the individual's registration record.

>> ID must contain a photo of the person to whom it was issued.

>> ID must have an expiration date and, if it has expired, it must have an expiration date after the most recent general election (military ID exempted).

>> If no acceptable ID is presented, voters can execute a provisional ballot, which is counted only if the voter returns to the election board by the Monday following the election and provides ID or executes an affidavit stating that the voter cannot obtain ID because the voter is indigent or has a religious objection to being photographed and the voter hasn't been challenged or required to vote a provisional ballot for any other reason.

Iowa: Non-strict ID

>> Iowa driver's license or ID card

>> US passport

- >> US military card

- >> Veteran's ID card

- >> A current signed voter ID card

- >> If no acceptable ID is presented, as of 2019, voters are offered a provisional ballot and can provide ID until the Monday after the election. Iowa requires the secretary of state's office to provide voter identification cards to existing active registered voters who have none of the valid types of ID.

- >> Other forms of ID current within 45 days prior to presentation include: a residential property lease, property tax statement, utility bill, bank statement, paycheck, government check, or government document. A written oath by another voter registered in the precinct attesting to the identity and residency of the voter will also suffice.

Kansas: Strict photo ID

- >> Driver's license issued by Kansas or another state

- >> State ID card

- >> Government-issued concealed-carry handgun or weapon license

- >> US passport

- >> Employee ID issued by a government office or agency

- >> Military ID

- >> Student ID issued by an accredited postsecondary institution in Kansas

- >> Government-issued public assistance ID card

- >> If no acceptable ID is presented, a provisional ballot is offered. To have the vote counted, the voter must provide a valid form of ID to the county election officer in person or provide a copy by mail or electronic means before the meeting of the county board of canvassers.

Kentucky: Non-strict photo ID

- >> Driver's license

- >> Social Security card

- Credit card

- When officers of an election disagree about the qualifications of a voter or the right to vote is disputed by a challenger, the voter shall sign a written oath as to their qualifications before being permitted to vote.

Louisiana: Non-strict

- Louisiana driver's license or special ID card

- Other generally recognized picture ID

- If no acceptable ID is presented, the voter signs an affidavit and provides further ID by presenting a current registration certificate, giving their date of birth or providing other information stated in the precinct register that is requested by the commissioners.

Maine: Non-strict

- If you're registered to vote in Maine and have voted before, you don't need to show ID to vote.

- If you're a first-time voter, you need either a current driver's license number, the last four digits of your Social Security number, or a state-assigned unique number.

- If you have no acceptable ID, you can show a current photo ID, copy of a utility bill, bank statement, paycheck, or government document that shows your address.

Maryland: Non-strict

- If you're registered to vote in Maryland and have voted before, you don't need to show ID to obtain a ballot.

- If you're a first-time voter, you need either a current driver's license, the last four digits of your Social Security number, or a state-assigned unique number.

- If you have no acceptable ID, you can show a current photo ID, copy of a utility bill, bank statement, paycheck, or government document that shows your address.

Massachusetts: Non-strict

>> If you're registered to vote in Massachusetts and you have voted before, you don't need to show ID to obtain a ballot.

>> If you're a first-time voter, you need either a current driver's license, the last four digits of your Social Security, or a state-assigned unique number.

>> If you have no acceptable ID, you can show a current photo ID, copy of a utility bill, bank statement, paycheck, or government document that shows your address.

Michigan: Non-strict

>> Michigan driver's license or personal ID card

>> If you have no acceptable ID, you can use a current driver's license or personal ID issued by another state, a federal or state government-issued ID, US passport, military ID with photo, student ID with photo from a high school or accredited institution of higher education, or tribal ID with photo.

>> Individuals without ID can sign an affidavit and vote a regular ballot.

Minnesota: Non-strict

>> If your voter registration is current and active and you registered at least 21 days before election day and you haven't moved or changed your name, you don't need any ID to obtain a ballot.

>> If you need to register or update your registration or haven't voted in four years or more, you need to show proof of residence before voting.

>> Acceptable ID includes valid Minnesota driver's license, learner's permit or ID or a receipt for any of these items, or tribal ID with name, address, photo, and signature.

>> If you have no acceptable ID, you can show a driver's license, state ID, or learner's permit issued by any state; US passport; US military or veteran ID; Minnesota university, college, or technical college ID; or Minnesota high school ID.

Mississippi: Strict photo ID

>> Driver's license

>> Photo ID issued by a branch, department, or entity of Mississippi

>> US passport

>> Government employee ID

>> Firearms license

>> Student photo ID issued by an accredited Mississippi university, college, or community or junior college

>> US military ID

>> Tribal photo ID

>> Any other photo ID issued by any branch, department, agency, or entity of the United States or any state government

Mississippi voter ID card

>> If no acceptable ID is presented, voters can cast an affidavit ballot, which will be counted if the individual returns to the appropriate circuit clerk within five days after the election and shows government-issued photo ID. Voters with religious objections to being photographed can vote an affidavit ballot, which will be counted if the voter returns to the appropriate circuit clerk within five days after the election and executes an affidavit.

Missouri: Non-strict

>> ID issued by the federal government, the state of Missouri, or an agency of the state or local election authority

>> ID issued by a Missouri institution of higher education, including a university, college, vocational, or technical school

>> Copy of a current utility bill, bank statement, paycheck, government check, or another government document that contains the name and address of the voter

>> Driver's license or state identification card issued by another state

>> If no acceptable ID is presented, the voter can still cast a ballot if two supervising election judges — one from each major political party — attest that they know the person.

Montana: Non-strict

>> Driver's license

>> School district or postsecondary photo ID

>> Tribal photo ID

>> Current utility bill, bank statement, paycheck, notice of confirmation of voter registration, government check, or another government document that shows the voter's name and current address

>> If no acceptable ID is presented or if the voter's name doesn't appear in the precinct register, the voter can sign the register and cast a provisional ballot. If the voter's signature on the provisional ballot affirmation matches the signature on the voter's registration record, the ballot is counted.

Nebraska: Non-strict

>> Only first-time voters who have registered by mail are asked to show ID before voting.

Nevada: Non-strict

>> Voter registration card

>> Driver's license

>> ID card issued by the Department of Motor Vehicles

>> Military ID card

>> Sheriff's work ID card

>> Student ID card

>> Tribal ID card

>> US passport

>> Any other form of ID issued by a governmental agency that contains the voter's signature and physical description or picture

New Hampshire: Non-strict

>> Driver's license from New Hampshire or any other state, regardless of expiration date

>> Photo ID card issued by the New Hampshire director of motor vehicles

>> Voter ID card

>> US armed services photo ID

>> US passport, regardless of expiration date

>> Valid student ID

>> Any other valid photo ID issued by federal, state, county, or municipal government

>> Any other photo ID that is determined to be legitimate by election officials. If one of the election official objects to the photo ID, the voter shall be required to execute a qualified voter affidavit.

>> If no acceptable ID is presented, the voter can execute a challenged voter affidavit. Unless the voter has a religious objection to having their photo taken, the moderator affixes the photo to the affidavit. The voter can then cast a regular ballot. The secretary of state later sends a nonforwardable letter to each voter who executed a challenged voter affidavit. If the letter isn't returned with a written confirmation that the person voted, the matter is referred to the attorney general for fraud.

New Jersey: Non-photo ID

>> If you didn't provide ID when you registered to vote, you must show some form of identification at the polling place.

>> Acceptable ID includes — but is not limited to — any current and valid photo ID, such as a New Jersey driver's license, military or government ID, student or job ID, store membership card, US passport, copy of a current utility bill, bank statement, car registration, government check, rent receipt, or another document that contains the name and address of the voter.

>> If no acceptable ID is presented, the voter can still cast a provisional ballot but must submit a copy of their ID to the county election office before the close of business on the second day after the election for the vote to be counted.

New Mexico: Non-strict

>> If you have voted before, you don't have to present ID.

>> If you're a first-time voter who registered by mail and didn't include ID with the application, you must produce ID in order to vote.

>> Acceptable ID includes a current and valid photo ID or a current utility bill, bank statement, government check, paycheck, student ID, or other government document, including ID issued by an Indian nation that shows your name and current address.

New York: Non-strict

>> If you have voted before, you don't have to show ID at the polls.

>> If you're a first-time voter, acceptable ID includes a current driver's license number or the last four digits of your Social Security number or state-assigned unique number or photo ID or copy of a utility bill, bank statement, paycheck, or government check that shows the voter's name and address.

North Carolina: Strict photo ID

>> Beginning in 2020, voters must show a photo ID because voters passed a constitutional amendment to require photo ID for voting.

>> Acceptable forms of photo ID include a valid and unexpired driver's license or non-operator ID from North Carolina; if expired, it must be for one year or less or else the voter must be over 65 and the ID was unexpired on the 65th birthday. Voters can use a driver's license or non-operator ID from another state only if the voter registered within 90 days of the election and the same rules on expiration are met. Acceptable photo ID also includes a North Carolina voter ID card, approved employee ID, and approved student ID with the same expiration rules. Acceptable ID also include an approved state or federal tribal ID as well as a military or veteran's ID, which can be used if expired or without expiration date.

>> If no acceptable ID is presented, a provisional ballot is required. It's counted only if the voter brings an acceptable ID to the county board of elections no

later than the day before the canvass, which usually occurs the Monday following an election. Exceptions to the ID requirement are allowed for persons with religious objections, the occurrence of a natural disaster, or a reasonable impediment to obtaining a photo ID. A declaration form and affidavit are required. The ballot is counted unless the county board has grounds to believe it's false.

North Dakota: Strict photo ID

» In 2017, North Dakota began requiring voters to present ID or have their ballots set aside until the voters present valid ID at the election office before the canvass six days after the election.

» Acceptable forms of identification are driver's license, ID issued by the North Dakota Department of Transportation, or ID issued by the tribal government to a tribal member residing in the state. If the valid form doesn't include a legal name, current residential street address in North Dakota, and date of birth, it can be supplemented by a current utility bill, current bank statement, check issued by a federal state or local government, paycheck, or document issued by a federal state or local government.

Ohio: Strict ID

» Current and valid photo ID that shows name, current address, and photo that includes an expiration date that has not passed and is issued by the US government or the state of Ohio

» Current utility bill or bank statement or current government check, paycheck, or another government document

» A voter who declines to provide ID can cast a provisional ballot by providing the last four digits of their Social Security number. A voter without ID or Social Security number can execute an affidavit and vote a provisional ballot. A voter who casts a provisional ballot because they didn't provide ID must appear at the board of elections within ten days of the election for the vote to be counted. A provisional ballot cast by a voter who declines or is unable to produce proof of identity shall be counted only if the voter's name, residence address, date of birth, and driver's license number or last four digits of the Social Security number as provided on the affidavit match the registration database.

Oklahoma: Non-strict

>> Document that shows a name that substantially conforms to the name on the precinct registry, shows a photo, includes an expiration date after the election, and was issued by the United States, the state of Oklahoma, or a federally recognized tribe or nation

>> If no acceptable ID is presented, a provisional ballot is cast with an affidavit. The vote is counted if the name, residence address, date of birth, and driver's license number or last four digits of the voter's Social Security number match the one in the registration database.

Oregon: Non-strict

>> Oregon automatically registers all eligible Oregonians to vote when they obtain or renew a driver's license or state ID card. Those registered are notified by mail and have three weeks to take themselves off the voting rolls. If they don't opt out, the secretary of state mails them a ballot 20 days before any election.

Pennsylvania: Non-strict

>> In 2014, a court overturned a 2012 Pennsylvania law requiring all voters to produce ID. Unless you're a first-time voter, you don't have to provide ID to vote.

>> Acceptable ID for a first-time voter is either a Pennsylvania driver's license or PennDOT ID card number or the last four digits of your Social Security number.

Rhode Island: Non-strict Photo

>> A valid and current document showing the photo of the person to whom it was issued, including Rhode Island driver's license, voter ID card, US passport, ID issued by an US educational institution, US military ID, ID issued by the US government of the state of Rhode Island, or government-issued medical card.

>> If no acceptable ID is presented, the person votes a provisional ballot. The local board determines the validity of the provisional ballot by comparing signatures on the application to the signature on the voter's registration.

South Carolina: Non-strict Photo

>> South Carolina driver's license or photo ID issued by the South Carolina Department of Motor Vehicles, passport, military ID with photo issued by the federal government, or South Carolina voter registration card with photo

>> If no acceptable ID is presented and there's a reasonable impediment to obtaining a photo ID, you can vote a provisional ballot after showing your non-photo voter registration card and signing an affidavit. A reasonable impediment is any valid reason, beyond your control, that created an obstacle to obtaining photo ID. Examples of a reasonable impediment are disability or illness, work schedule, lack of transportation, lack of birth certificate, religious objections to being photographed, or any other obstacle you find reasonable. The provisional ballot is counted unless the county election commission has reason to believe it's false.

South Dakota: Non-strict

>> South Dakota driver's license or ID card, US passport, photo ID issued by an agency of the US government, tribal ID with photo, or student ID issued by an accredited South Dakota school

>> A voter who doesn't provide acceptable ID can provide an affidavit under the penalty of perjury with the voter's name and address.

Tennessee: Strict photo ID

>> Valid Tennessee driver's license or ID card, valid photo-ID issued by the Tennessee Department of Safety, valid US passport, valid military ID with photo, or Tennessee handgun-carry permit with photo.

>> If no acceptable ID is presented, the voter can execute a provisional ballot. The ballot will be counted only if the voter provides the proper evidence of identification to the administrator of elections or a designee by the close of business on the second business day after the election. If the voter is indigent or has a religious objection and completes an affidavit to that effect, the voter's ballot will be counted.

Texas: Non-strict

>> ***Note:*** The original Texas voter ID law was struck down in federal court. These rules apply as of May 2017.

>> Texas driver's license or personal ID issued by the Department of Public Safety

>> Texas Election ID issued by the Department of Public Safety (DPS)

>> Texas license, issued by DPS, to carry a handgun

>> US military ID containing photo

>> US citizenship certificate containing photo

>> US passport

>> With the exception of the US citizenship certificate, the ID must be current or expired no longer than four years.

>> If no acceptable photo ID is presented due to a reasonable impediment, a voter can present a supporting form of ID and execute a Reasonable Impediment Declaration. Supporting forms of ID are a valid voter registration certificate, certified birth certificate, copy of or original utility bill, bank statement, government check, paycheck, or government document with name and address. (If the original government document contains a photo, it must be the original.)

>> If the voter has acceptable ID but doesn't present it at the polling place, a provisional ballot is provided. The voter has six days to present an acceptable form of ID at the county voter registrar for the vote to be counted.

>> Special provisions are made for persons with religious objections, the occurrence of natural disasters, and persons with disabilities.

Utah: Non-strict

>> Current valid Utah driver's license

>> Current valid ID card issued by the state or federal government

>> Utah concealed carry permit

>> US passport

>> Bureau of Indian Affairs card, tribal treaty card, or tribal ID card

>> Two forms of ID that bear the name of the voter and provide evidence that the voter resides in the precinct

>> If no acceptable ID is presented, the voter can cast a provisional ballot, and the county clerk can verify the identity and residence of the voter via another means.

Vermont: Non-strict

>> After January 1, 2017, any citizen can register to vote in Vermont up to and including election day.

>> If you have voted before, you don't need identification.

>> If you're a first-time voter, acceptable ID includes a driver's license or utility or bank statement.

Virginia: Strict photo

>> Valid US passport

>> Valid Virginia driver's license or ID card

>> Valid Virginia DMV-issued veteran's ID card

>> Valid tribal enrollment or another tribal ID issued by one of 11 tribes recognized by the Commonwealth of Virginia

>> Valid student ID card from within Virginia if it includes a photo

>> Any other ID card issued by a government agency of the Commonwealth, one of its political subdivisions, or the US

>> Employee ID card containing a photo and issued by the employer in the ordinary course of business

>> If no acceptable ID is presented, a provisional ballot marked ID-ONLY is executed. The voter must submit acceptable ID no later than noon on the third day after the election for the vote to be counted.

Washington: Non-strict Photo

>> Driver's license or state ID card

>> Student ID with photo

>> Tribal ID with photo

>> Employer ID with photo

>> If no acceptable ID is presented, the voter completes a provisional ballot, which shall be accepted if the signature on the declaration matches the signature on the voter's registration record.

West Virginia: Non-strict Photo

>> West Virginia driver's license or ID card

>> Valid driver's license from another state

>> US passport

>> Valid employee ID card with photo issued by the US government or West Virginia

>> Valid student ID card issued by a high school or an institution of higher education in West Virginia

>> Valid military ID with photo

>> Valid concealed carry permit with photo

>> Valid Medicare or Social Security card

>> Valid birth certificate

>> Valid voter registration card issued by a county clerk

>> Valid hunting or fishing license issued by West Virginia

>> Valid ID card issued by the West Virginia Supplemental Nutrition Assistance Program

>> Valid ID card issued by the West Virginia Temporary Assistance for Needy Families Program

>> Valid West Virginia Medicaid card, bank, or debit card

>> Valid utility bill or bank statement issued within six months of the election

>> Valid health insurance card

>> If the voter is accompanied to the polling place by an adult who has known the voter for six months and is willing to sign an affidavit attesting to the voter's identity or if a poll worker has known the voter for six months, the voter can vote without ID.

>> If no acceptable ID is presented, the voter can vote a provisional ballot, which will be counted if the election authority verifies the identity of the voter by comparing the voter's signature to the current signature on file with the election authority.

Wisconsin: Strict photo ID

>> Wisconsin driver's license or non-driver ID

>> ID card issued by a US uniformed service

>> US passport

>> Certificate of naturalization issued not more than 2 years before the election

>> ID card issued by a federally recognized Indian tribe in Wisconsin

>> Student ID with signature, an issue date, and an expiration date no later than 2 years after the election

>> Photo ID provided by the Veteran's Health Administration

>> If no acceptable ID is presented, the voter will be given a provisional ballot, which won't be counted unless the voters furnishes acceptable ID before the polls close or to the municipal clerk no later than 4 p.m. on the Friday following election day.

>> *Note:* In July 2016, a federal court ruled that Wisconsin's strict photo voter law was unconstitutional. In August 2016, an appeals court ruled the law could be implemented as long as the state keeps it pledge to provide temporary free IDs to those in need and to publicize the law.

Wyoming: Non-strict

>> In Wyoming, you can register to vote up to and including election day.

>> If you have voted before, you don't need any ID to vote.

>> If you're a first-time voter, acceptable ID must be presented.

>> Acceptable ID for first-time voters includes current driver's license number or last 4 digits of Social Security number or state assigned unique number or photo ID or copy of utility bill, bank statement, paycheck or government document that shows the voter's name and address.

Index

A

AARP (American Association of Retired Persons), 195
above-the-belt advertising, 241–242
access, 114, 115, 254
Adams, John, 236
Adams, John Quincy, 236, 237, 289
advertising. *See also* negative advertising
  above-the-belt, 241–242
  anonymous literature and, 245
  attack, 200, 238, 248–249, 315, 324
  below-the-belt, 243–248
  Daisy ad, 237
  evaluating, 172–175
  Facebook, 128
  fact distortion and, 243–244
  false conclusions and, 164–165
  humorous, 249
  lying and, 244
  manipulation and, 175–179
  media and, 167–172
  personal attacks and, 244
  photography and, 246
  racism and, 176–177
  radio, 194
  set-up legislation and, 165–166
  telephones and, 233–234, 245
  television and, 194, 195, 197, 198–199, 226–227, 238
  timing of, 231–232
  truth *versus* fact, 163–166
  underhanded information and, 243
  use of, 126, 194
Affordable Care Act, 195
African Americans, 247–248
Alabama, voting requirements within, 333
Alaska, voting requirements within, 333
Amazon, 126
America Progress Now, 195
American Association of Retired Persons (AARP), 195

anonymous literature, distribution of, 245
Arizona, elections and, 258, 307, 334
Arkansas, voting requirements within, 334
attack ads, 200, 238, 248–249, 315, 324
attorneys, candidacy of, 154–155

B

ballots, counting process of, 80–81
Banks, Jim, 124
Bayh, Birch, 320
below-the-belt advertising, 243–248
benchmark poll, 143–144, 211–213
benchmarks, 211
big-tent theory, 70–71
blanket primary, 71
Bookwalter, Timothy, 248
bounce, 270–271
brokered convention, 278, 279
Buchanan, Pat, 283
Burr, Aaron, 289
Bush, George H. W., 139, 140, 247, 281
Bush, George W., 70, 84, 271, 273, 286–288, 328

C

Cabinet, 10–11
California, voting requirements within, 335
campaigns. *See also* advertising; contributors/
    contributions
  benchmark poll and, 143
  budget for, 196–197
  challenges of, 201–202
  communication of, 239–241
  contact types of, 193–195
  contrasting, 240–241
  contributions to, 203
  contributor types for, 50–54
  cost of, 24, 76–77, 253–255

registering and, 93

states holding, 88

census, 11–12

change, proposing, 218

Citizens United vs. FEC, 15, 112, 231, 256

Civil Rights Act, 18

civil service employees, 11

Civil War, 290

Clark, Wesley, 273

Clay, Henry, 237, 289

Clean Elections programs, 258

Cleveland, Grover, 151, 237, 290

Clinton, Bill, 152, 306, 328

Clinton, Hillary

  campaign costs of, 256

  candidacy of, 70, 84, 271, 273

  downfall of, 316

  electoral college and, 286–288

closed primaries, 37, 71, 87

Collins, Chris, 23

Colorado, voting requirements within, 335

Commission on Presidential Debates, 302

Common Cause, 27

communication

  campaigns and, 239–241

  Congress and, 56, 57–58

  elected officials and, 55–58

  hotlines and, 56

  local officials and, 55, 60

  media and, 63–65

  mobilization of, 60–62

  national officials and, 55–56

  online, 124–130

  organizations and, 63

  questionnaires, 57

  state officials and, 55

  talk radio, 59

  teamwork and, 62–65

  town meetings, 58–59

compromise, 319

Congress, 10, 56, 57–58

Congressional Black Caucus, 280

Congressional Quarterly (directory), 57

Connecticut, elections within, 258, 335

constituency, 55, 75, 197

Constitution, 11, 16, 22

contributors/contributions

  candidates and, 127, 203

  dark money groups and, 256

  disclosure of, 200

  federal campaigns and, 255–257

  federal government and, 118

  guidelines for, 47–50

  labor unions and, 53

  levels of, 47

  local campaigning and, 191–195

  local government and, 117

  matching funds, 257

  momentum for, 269

  nominees and, 296–297

  nonlegislative candidates and, 113

  political action committees (PACs) and, 110–111, 116, 256

  role of, 76–77

  soft money, 119, 257, 296, 297

  special interest groups and, 109–114, 115–119

  state campaigns and, 257–259

  state government and, 117

  types of, 50–54

conventions, national, 88, 277–283

cookies, use of, 126

corporate tax rate, 23

counterattack, 158–159

Crawford, William, 289

criminal defense attorneys, candidacy of, 155

Cruz, Ted, 266

D

Daisy ad, 237

dark money groups, 256

debates, 302

deficit, 15

Delaware, elections and, 24, 336

delegates, national conventions and, 94, 277–282

democracy, importance of, 319

Democratic National Committee (DNC), 100, 130, 266, 296

time, donating, 43–47
voter turnout and, 259–260
youth and, 320–321
Iowa, 266, 267–271, 280, 338–339
IP (Internet protocol) address, 126
IRV (instant-runoff voting), 293–294
issues, avoidance of, 216
Italy, government of, 72

J

Jackson, Andrew, 97, 151, 236–237, 289
Jackson, Rachel, 151, 236–237
Jefferson, Thomas, 236, 289
Jeffords, James, 102
Johnson, Andrew, 152
Johnson, Gary, 70
Johnson, Lyndon, 237, 328
journalism. *See* media
judges, 10, 12
judicial branch, 10, 12
jungle primary, 71
jury duty, 35
Justice Department, 11

K

Kansas, voting requirements within, 339
Kefauver, Estes, 281
Kennedy, John F., 84, 281, 287, 327
Kennedy, Robert, 314, 328
Kentucky, voting requirements within, 339–340
Khrushchev, Nikita, 321
killer phone calls, 233–234, 245
kingmaker, 48, 53–54

L

Labor Department, 11
labor unions, contributions of, 53
large states, electoral college and, 305
legislation
  alliances within, 27
  analysis of, 27

consideration of, 26–28
cooperation and, 74–75
elected officials and, 326
lobbying and, 106
sedition laws, 236
set-up, 165–166
legislative branch, 10, 12–13
legislative caucus, 280
leveling the playing field, 170
leverage, money and, 23–24
Lewinsky, Monica, 152
Libertarian Party, 70
Lincoln, Abraham, 22, 328
litmus-test issue, 89
lobbyists, 105–109
local forums, 221–222
local government, contributions and, 117
local officials
  campaigning by, 191–195
  communication with, 55, 60
  contributions to, 113, 117
  election of, 13
  term limits and, 86
Long, Gillis W., 18
Louisiana, elections within, 37–38, 340
lower house, 13
lying, 244, 319

M

MAGA (Make America Great Again), 297–298
mail, direct, 226–230
Maine, elections within, 258, 340
majority rule, 16
Make America Great Again (MAGA), 297–298
margin of error, 210
marketing, 138–141
Maryland, voting requirements within, 340
Massachusetts, voting requirements within, 341
Matalin, Mary, 136
matching funds, 257
Matching Funds programs, 258
McCain, John, 271
McConnell, Mitch, 249

nomination of, 265, 275–276
quotes regarding, 327–328
role of, 10
press. *See also* television
advertising and, 167–172
benefits of, 167
bias of, 169–170
bounce from, 270–271
campaign issues and, 222–223, 230–233
disadvantages of, 271–272
independent evaluations and, 171–172
nontraditional, 301–302
objectivity of, 170–172
polling and, 40
presidential campaigns and, 301
quotes regarding, 329
role of, 14
social, 127–130, 302
speculation of, 272, 274
teamwork and, 63–65
press release, 122
press secretary, 14
primaries
blanket, 71
closed, 37, 71, 87
cost of, 88
importance of, 279
New Hampshire and, 266–270
open, 37, 71, 87
overview of, 87–88
purpose of, 265
registering and, 93
semi-closed, 71
types of, 71
voting in, 36–38
Pritzker, J. B., 124
property taxes, 217, 219–220, 228
proportional representation systems, 71, 72
proposing change, risks of, 218
prosecutors, candidacy of, 154–155
public opinion, 20–21
public records, 242
public service, importance of, 318

public spokesperson, 14
publicity, disadvantages of, 271–272

Q

Quayle, Dan, 281
questionnaires, 57, 223

R

racism, 176–177, 248
radio, advertising on, 194
random digital dialing, 206–207
Rather, Dan, 137
Reagan, Ronald, 297, 327
reconstruction, effects of, 290
recycled candidate, 85–87
Reform Party, 72
registering to vote, 32–36, 81, 93–95, 260
representatives, election of, 11–12
Republican National Committee (RNC), 100, 130, 296
Republican Party
beliefs of, 96, 97, 98
caucuses and, 266
characteristics of, 98
differences within, 102
history of, 92, 96, 97
national delegates for, 278
national symbol of, 97
Republicans, 93–95, 225
resources
Commission on Presidential Debates, 302
communication through, 125–126
Congress, 125
Democratic National Committee, 100, 130
Donald Trump, 122
FactCheck, 168
Federal Election Commission, 112, 116
Follow the Money, 117
government *versus* campaign, 122–124
legislation analysis, 27
National Association of State Legislators, 106
NPR, 168
Open Secrets, 112

teamwork, 62

telephones, 206–208, 233–234, 245

television

    advertising on, 194, 195, 197, 198–199

    campaigns and, 76–77, 226–227, 230–233, 238

    candidates and, 138

    Federal Communications Commission (FCC) and, 231

    role of, 76

    talk shows, 302

    teamwork and, 63–65

Tennessee, voting requirements within, 348

term limits, 86

Texas, voting requirements within, 349

third parties, 69–70, 72–73, 95–96

ticket splitting, 78–79

Tilden, Samuel, 290

time, donation of, 43–47

town meetings, 58–59

travel, candidates and, 269

Treasury Department, 11

Truman, Harry, 18

Trump, Donald

    campaign costs of, 256

    candidacy of, 273

    caucuses and, 266

    corporate tax rate and, 23

    election of, 70, 84

    electoral college and, 286–288

    quote of, 328, 329

    sexual conduct of, 151–152

    slogan of, 297–298

    social media use by, 122, 124, 130, 297

    Twitter and, 122, 130

    website of, 122, 130

truth-in-advertising analysis, 168

Turbovote, 57, 192, 331

turnout, 34, 200, 259, 260

Twitter, 122, 129–130

U

underhanded information, obtaining, 243

unions, political action committees (PACs) and, 116

upper house, 12–13

US Constitution, 11, 16, 22

Utah, voting requirements within, 349–350

V

verified checkmark, 128

Vermont, elections within, 13, 350

veto, 10, 13

vice president, 11, 275–276, 280–281

Virginia, elections within, 13, 332, 350

volunteering

    appreciation and, 252

    campaign finance reform and, 260–261

    election day and, 79, 81

    get-out-the-vote, 93

    grassroots political activity and, 81–82

    importance of, 46

    local level, 191–195

    negative campaigning and, 251

    political party identification and, 93–94

    presidential campaign and, 308–309

    time, donating, 43–47

    voter turnout and, 259–260

    youth and, 320–321

voters

    independent, 229–230

    influence of, 31–32

    motivating factors of, 25–26

    national conventions and, 283–284

    political action committees (PACs) and, 33, 113

    political voice of, 84

    registering, 32–36, 81, 93–95, 260

    senior citizens as, 231–232, 233

    swing states and, 307

    targeting, 227–228, 231–233, 308

    turnout improvement of, 34, 200, 259, 260

    whims of, 40–42

voting. *See also* primaries

    benefits of, 32–33

    decisions regarding, 182–187

    duty of, 317–318

    get-out-the-vote (GOTV), 199–200

    ID requirements for, 332–333 (*See also specific states*)

    information, gathering of, 184–185

About the Author

Ann DeLaney began a long association with politics and political involvement as a political science graduate of the State University of New York at Binghamton, where she was student body president. She received her law degree from the Maurer School of Law at Indiana University, where she served on the Board of Visitors. After obtaining her law degree, Ann served as a deputy prosecuting attorney specializing in sex offense and child abuse cases. With her daughter Kathleen she founded the law firm of DeLaney & DeLaney, LLC. Ann was the executive director of the Julian Center, an agency which provided safe shelter, transitional housing, and counseling for women and children fleeing domestic violence. Ann is currently a Standing Trustee in Chapter 13 Bankruptcy for the Southern District of Indiana.

Ann has been politically active as a precinct committeeperson, worker in voter registration drives, delegate to state and national party conventions, and a member of the Democratic National Committee.

Ann was the first women nominated by either party in Indiana as a candidate for Lieutenant Governor. She was legislative director for the first Democratic governor of Indiana in 20 years. Ann served when the House of the Indiana General Assembly was divided 50/50 between Democrats and Republicans and had dual Speakers of the House, a Democratic Speaker one day, a Republican Speaker the next.

Ann has managed statewide political campaigns and was the first woman to serve as Chair of a major political party in Indiana.

Ann continues her involvement in politics as a panelist on *Indiana Week in Review*, an Emmy-nominated weekly political talk show carried on public television and radio in Indiana. She frequently speaks on politics to civic and political groups.

Dedication

I dedicate this book to all those Americans who appreciate the freedoms they enjoy under our democracy. The Americans who believe that participation in our electoral system is what makes our country strong and the envy of the world. Those Americans who inform themselves about the issues and the candidates and vote or go further in supporting our democracy by volunteering in campaigns, contributing, or running for office themselves.

I also dedicate this book to the intelligent, opinionated, interesting, and loving family with whom I have been blessed; my incredible and supportive husband, State Representative Ed DeLaney; our three wonderful children: Kathleen, Jennifer, and Edward Timothy and their spouses and children: Jim, Emma, Kevin and John Strenski; Chris, Miranda and Aidan Reid; Owen, Cormac and Caitlin DeLaney; Cora, Josie, and Elise Lammers and Emily DeLaney.

Author's Acknowledgments

Special thanks to Trevor Foughty for his contribution to understanding social media and the Internet and their impact on political campaigns through his authorship of Chapter 9. Trevor has spent 13 years working on Republican political campaigns and in government offices in the executive and legislative branches at the state and federal level.

Publisher's Acknowledgments

Acquisitions Editor: Lindsay Lefevere
Senior Project Editor: Paul Levesque
Copy Editor: Becky Whitney
Editorial Assistant: Matthew Lowe
Sr. Editorial Assistant: Cherie Case

Production Editor: Magesh Elangovan
Cover Image: © carterdayne/Getty Images